Presented to

Manitowoc
Public Library

as a
gift of the

Theresa A. Holub
Bequest

the new

Samoyed

de Jongh Frères
Neuilly–Paris.

Czar Alexander III and family in 1887 with the prince's family pet, Kamtschatka.

the new

Samoyed

robert h. and dolly ward and mardee ward-fanning

Third Edition

HOWELL
BOOK
HOUSE

Howell Book House
A Simon & Schuster Macmillan Company
1633 Broadway
New York, NY 10019

Macmillan Publishing books may be purchased for business or sales
promotional use. For information please write: Special Markets Department, Macmillan Publishing USA, 1633 Broadway, New York, NY 10019.

Copyright © 1998 by Robert H. and Dolly Ward and
    Mardee Ward-Fanning
Copyright © 1985, 1971 by Howell Book House, Inc.

MACMILLAN is a registered trademark of Macmillan, Inc.

Library of Congress Cataloging-in-Publication Data

Ward, Robert H.
    The new Samoyed / Robert H. and Dolly Ward, and Mardee Ward-
Fanning. — 3rd ed.
        p.   cm.
    Rev. ed. of: The new complete Samoyed. 2nd ed., 1st print. 1985.
    ISBN 0-87605-701-6
    1. Samoyed dog.   I. Ward, Dolly.   II. Ward-Fanning, Mardee.   III.
Ward, Robert H.   New complete Samoyed.   IV. Title.
    SF429.S35W36   1997
    636.7'3—dc21   97-20503
                                                              CIP
ISBN: 0-87605-701-6

Manufactured in the United States of America
10 9 8 7 6 5 4 3 2 1

Book Design: George McKeon
Cover Design: George Berrian

Contents

About the Authors   vii

The Authors' Thoughts—A Preface   x

Pronunciation   xii

Foreword by Anne Rogers Clark   xiii

A "Symphonic" Thank You   xv

Introduction   xvii

1 History Is History   1

2 The Samoyed in Postwar America   36

3 The Samoyed in America: 1976–85   57

4 SCA Specialties: Where the White
   Water Shines Brightest   103

5 Background of the Samoyed Standard   133

6 Official AKC Standard for the Samoyed   140

7 Commentary on the Current Standard   145

8 Judging the Samoyed   154

9 Ideal Samoyed Movement
by Karl Michael Smith (Ice Way Samoyeds)   164

10 Selecting a Samoyed Puppy   170

11 On Raising Puppies by Susan North   180

12 Special Care for Samoyeds   191

13 The Well-Groomed Samoyed
by Mardee Ward-Fanning   206

14 Show Handling and Related Issues
by Mardee Ward-Fanning   212

15 To Be or Not to Be Obedient
by Don and Dell Wells   222

16 The Samoyed Club of America's Working
Samoyed Program by Pam Landers   229

17 The Versatile Samoyed   249

18 Spinning Samoyed Hair by Carol Chittum   258

19 A Short History of the Samoyed
in Canada by Dr. Bob Gaskin   263

20 The Global Samoyed   275

The Author's Thoughts—A Denouement   302

About the Authors

Few authors of dog books can match the expertise, experience and active participation with their breeds that Bob and Dolly Ward bring to their celebrated classic on the Samoyed.

Until retirement Bob was a high school administrator, and Dolly was a teacher. But for more than four decades, together with their family, in both breed and obedience, dogs have been the major interest. They have owned and shown Welsh Corgis, Poodles, Doberman Pinschers and Boxers—Bob even operated as an all-breed handler from 1947 to 1954—but the number one breed for the Wards has always been Samoyeds.

Although Bob had a pet Sammy as a boy, the Wards' serious devotion began with the acquisition of the puppy that became one of the great sires of the breed, Ch. Starchak, CD, 1943–57. Since 1944 they have been prominent in every area of Samoyed sport. In obedience, they finished seven Sammys and two Corgis to CDX degrees. For more than fifteen years, they competed in Samoyed sled dog racing. They supported local and national clubs. Both Bob and Dolly are past presidents of the Samoyed Club of America.

Bob became an AKC-approved judge in 1954, and Dolly in 1960, and they are among the select number of Samoyed specialists also approved to judge other breeds and Groups. Currently Bob judges the Sporting, Hound, Working, Non-Sporting and Herding Groups and Best in Show. Dolly judges the Working, Toy, Non-Sporting and Herding Groups and Best in Show. They have judged at Specialties and all-breed shows throughout the United States and in Canada, Mexico, England, Ireland, Sweden, Australia, New Zealand, Japan, Hong Kong, Taiwan and Bermuda.

As authors in a lighter vein, to reach the kindergarten set with colorful education on dogs and their care, Bob and Dolly wrote a series of coloring books, *Color Me Puppy* and *Color Me Obedient*, illustrated by Mel Fishback-Riley.

The Wards have two daughters, each of whom has been declared Best in Bred-By by their proud if prejudiced parents. As authors of two previous editions of the highly respected Howell book on the Samoyed (1971 and 1985), Bob and Dolly are happy to have daughter Mardee joining in their breeder-author category for this revision.

As grandparents, the Wards are proud of daughter Lindy who has "Bred-bys" of her own, grandchildren, Lance, Megyn and Molly.

Therefore, the Wards say, "we dedicate our three editions of our book on the Samoyed to growing family, both human and canine."

Mardee continued the breeding program with English bloodlines and imports from Denmark, to strengthen the dominant American lines originally developed from White Way's English/Arctic lines with Ch. Siberian Nansen of Farningham of Snowland.

Mardee was highly competitive and campaigned many of the dogs to outstanding records. She began to judge and again excelled. Mardee and Michael Fanning married and added Hoof to the Paw in Montana, raising cattle in addition to the Samoyeds, the Labradors Pie and Quill, and lately Shiba Inus, making Hoof 'n Paw complete.

Lindy was pictured age one with a puppy from the Ward's first litter by Ch. Starchak, CD, out of Ch. Staryvna of Snowland. Lindy also excelled in Junior Showmanship when it was called "Children's Handling." Today, Linda's philosophy about pets and show dogs reflects a wisdom all would do well to note.

Not all people who have purchased pets and/or show dogs participate or even attend dog shows. Some prefer to enjoy their "pedigreed-purebreds" completely as companionable members of the family, sharing whatever is their lifestyle. It may be in an apartment, residential home, or as in Lindy's case on a mini farm just outside the rural city of Paso Robles, California. Lindy Leigh has taught school nearly thirty years (and may be thinking "That's thirty") and raises the Ward's grandchildren exceptionally well (but that's another book). She has also chosen a role of inspirational writing and photography for her unconfined creativity.

The authors (from left) Mardee Ward-Fanning, Robert H. Ward and Dolly Ward at the seventy-fifth Anniversary show of San Joaquin KC. It is most unique for three members of the same family, covering two generations, to serve on the judging panel of the same dog show!

The Authors' Thoughts— A Preface

If it ain't broke don't fix it! This is precisely the premise we are using on updating this book since the previous edition. Some of the material should not be changed, like *history!* Some of the instructive material like Obedience is as true today as when it was first written. Dog structure and gait can be explained no better than how it has already been done. So, if it wasn't broke, we did not try to fix it.

We left some of the old pictures of Samoyeds because when you study them and compare them with Sams of today, you will find that the breed has not changed. We think the breed is in *good shape.* That has been the subject we have discussed in columns in *The Samoyed Quarterly,* published in Colorado by Don Hoflin Enterprises, for many years since it began. It is the *significant other* magazine for Samoyeds besides the Samoyed Club of America, Inc., *Bulletin.*

We have added many exciting features based on activities of Samoyeds and their people in recent years: Herding Instinct, Therapy and Agility—new working titles from the Samoyed Club of America. Sled racing and sledding excursions became more formalized in recent years. Packing and sledding continued along with the constant presence of conformation dog shows that are also the proving ground for breeders and for breeding programs.

Samoyeds in the United Kingdom (UK), Canada, New Zealand, Australia, Columbia, South America and now Spain are also making their marks. We are indebted to the many fanciers who have contributed here to bring you all the latest and best possible work on the Samoyed as we approach the twenty-first century.

Join us. Get yourself a Samoyed *if* you are ready to take care of it properly. Join in the sport of dogs and enjoy.

ON RECORDS

In the dog game, there are advertisements of so many Bests in Show (BIS), Bests in Group, Bests of Breed, Highs in Trial, OTCHs and other achievements on every level. Soon there will be Agility Best Times, and on and on and on we go. One has to evaluate the background of the "Records" to determine how valuable they may be.

Therefore, we see extensive advertising in the dog magazines, monthly, weekly but, not to date, "daily"—that, however, may come with the burgeoning electronic age. Faxes are so much fun for quick, concise communication. We even have a SamFan network for your computer talents—and gossip, unfortunately!

Our point is that we see nothing wrong with records; in fact, they are indeed interesting to read about. We just do not plan to try crediting every record to every Samoyed since the last edition. As we finished *The Complete Samoyed* for Howell Book House with the fabulous record of Ch. Quicksilver's Razz Ma Tazz with fifty-four BIS, we are certain that will stand probably through our lifetimes, but we would not promise that it will not be broken someday. We wish anyone trying to break that record in the near future—even with all the many shows and improvements in breeding and exhibiting—to remember that it will take a marvelous dog and a great deal of money to achieve this. Razz Ma Tazz was professionally handled by Roy Murray, but of equal importance he was accompanied to the shows and groomed by his owners, Chris and Danny Middleton and Eugene and Joyce Curtis. The total care by all concerned is vital and is no small task when driving or flying a dog all over a country the size of the United States, plus keeping the interest and show temperament tops in such a Samoyed.

In this edition, we plan to note some special wins of special dogs, to spotlight some successes but not to present long lists of wins and records. Let's not forget, records are made and records are broken.

Pronunciation

The word *Samoyed* is a transliteration of (i.e., sounds like) the Russian word that is spelled this way (in the Cyrillic alphabet, that is): ñáñëä. The letter *ñ* is always pronounced like our *s*. The letter *a* can be pronounced two ways, depending on whether it is accented. Unaccented it is like the *a* in can or Sam. Accented it is long like the *a* in AWOL, except it would be pronounced not only as a long *a,* but it would be proceeded by a *y* sound—sort of like "yeah-wall." Clearly this means it is unaccented, i.e., the whole syllable (Sam) is unaccented. The Russian *í* is like our *m* only it doesn't actually look like our *m* when written. So the first syllable (*ñáí*) is Sam. The second syllable, another vowel *o* is also *not* accented. Like the *á* vowel if it were accented, it would have to be pronounced with a *y* sound in front of it. Thus, it would come out as samyo for the first two syllables of the word. Clearly, this is not the case. The next line is very important: an unaccented *o* in Russian is pronounced like a short *a.* Quite the revelation, *boshe moi!* (That's more Russian.) So, now for the first two syllables we have sam-a. The last syllable, in transliteration, is written with a *y* in front. From the preceding information, you should already have concluded that this is the accented syllable. The vowel *(e)* is shown preceded by the *y.* Also, the last consonant, *ä* is a hard sound, not a soft sound, which would be transliterated as a *t.* While this letter would indeed be a *d* in Russian, it is only pronounced like a *d* when it is in an accented syllable. Otherwise, it is pronounced "soft"; that is, like a *t.* So, you must shift your pronunciation to emphasize the last syllable: Sam-a-'yed.

In other words, the first syllable, Sam, is not accented. Next, an unaccented *o* in Russian is pronounced like a short *a.* Now we have two syllables Sam-a; the last syllable, yed, is accented—so, it is Sam-a-'yed.

After this complete explanation of pronunciation, you should be glad to say two boys' names, Sammy + Ed, when you're talking about the Samoyed.

Foreword

by Anne Rogers Clark

Meet Anne Rogers Clark. If you have not already met her, it's a pity. She is dogdom's premier person; one to become acquainted with, better yet to know. She will answer your every questions, and, if need be, she will look up an answer for you. We like to call her Annie, just because she's Annie.

We suggest you read the March 1996 *AKC Gazette* 113 No. 3 to fully appreciate Annie Clark's illustrious career. Four pages (both sides, fine print) are hard to condense here. Make that impossible! Annie knows her dogs and the whole dog game and is not afraid to keep on learning.

Annie demands good temperaments in both dogs and people. She is pictured here with one of her Norfolk Terrier, which looks nothing like the Poodles for which she is famous, but to which she is equally devoted. One last quality, of which there are so many, is her sense of humor. I mention it in closing lest I go on too long. So after reading our book, go out and meet Anne Rogers Clark for yourself. You will thank me, as I thank her for writing the foreword to this, our last book.

DOLLY WARD (ALIAS MAMA POLAR BEAR)

*T*he *Complete Samoyed*—an up-to-date book on this well-established, multipurpose breed—is a labor of love produced by authors that are fanciers in the truest sense of the word. All the aspects of breeding, raising, training, exhibiting and judging of this true Nordic canine are covered in depth. In our world of purebred dogs today, the accent is on knowledge for both breeder and judge. Learning to evaluate breeding stock, which is what judging is all about, is made much more logical if the student is made aware of what the breed was developed to do, how far the breed has evolved to this point and in what direction the breed should be encouraged to progress. Often a breed

should be protected, not changed from its original use and form. A book of this caliber, that gives extensive background and history of the breed as well as an in-depth look at all the traits described by the Standard, including temperament and character, is a must in the library of any who have interest in the Samoyed—fancier, breeder or judge.

Ann Rogers Clark.

A "Symphonic" Thank you

In the past two editions of our book on the Samoyed, published by Howell Book House, the first in 1971 and the second in 1985, we thanked many people especially, Ab Sidewater our editor, who took great interest and demanded precision and accuracy. This time we could not have completed this book without the willingness and expertise in the high-tech computing field that was required for this update. The orchids go to Frank and Gini Addamo of Symphony Samoyeds for putting our entire manuscript on disk.

To Seymour Weiss, our editor for this third edition, our heartfelt thanks. Seymour worked diligently with us—answered questions promptly and helped achieve the publishing date "so Dolly could see the book completed." We are especially appreciative for such a knowledgeable editor—grounded significantly in dogs—a judge of the Terrier Group but with a feel for the Arctics. We are all blessed by his generous input. Muchas gracias, Seymour, from all the Wards.

And thanks to the authors of contributions included herein from Samoyed fanciers worldwide and to the many who have cooperated in the request for pictures. We hope that their reproduction here will give you as much pleasure as they give us.

Samoyeds were among the breeds that served the Roald Amundsen Expedition across the South Pole.

Introduction

In the comparatively short span of 105 years, the Samoyed has risen from an almost extinct breed to one of the more popular, currently forty-seventh, AKC registrations.

The tribes of the Samoyed people, from whom the dogs were obtained by early explorers, have been dispersed by the Russians and their mode of living altered by industrialization. It is fortunate for us that the handful of dogs released in the period from 1890 to 1912 were handled so skillfully and that the breed was preserved. With wars and political upheaval, not more than a half dozen were obtained from Russia in the 1920s, and since then the door has been closed.

Because the Samoyed is one of the breeds most nearly akin to the prehistoric or natural canine, it has been one of the easier breeds to duplicate. The erect ears, the smiling face, the buff to white coat, the plumed tail—all come naturally. The disputes that there have been over proper size for a Samoyed are a problem created by humans and not by nature. We would indeed be more successful as breeders if we would trust nature more. As it is, we have been quite fortunate, because Samoyeds have no coat color problem, no docking, no cropping and no trimming. In man's desire to "improve" the breed, he concentrated on the black points—the eye rims, the nose and the lips. Although this contrast of black against white face is very pleasing, records show that the pink or Dudley (pink with black) noses were natural.

Research reveals that the black, black and white, and even brown and white dogs that existed in the sled teams along with the white Bjelkiers were Laika and Ostiak dogs from around Archangel and were of a different ancestry. The Bjelkiers were from 1,000 miles east of Archangel, in the area east of the Yenisei River stretching to the Olenek River, where the Samoyed tribes of the Tungunese and Yakutsks lived. If this difference in the dogs was not so, we Samoyed breeders have found a way to refute the Mendelian theory because there have been no mixed colors in England or America plaguing the registrations for the past 100 years.

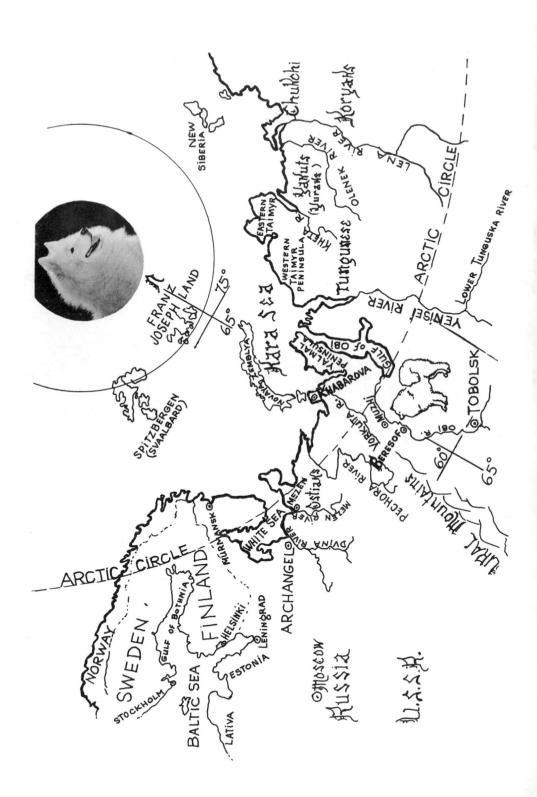

NEW SIBERIA

FRANZ JOSEPH LAND

75°

65°

Chukchi

Koryaks

ARCTIC CIRCLE

LENA RIVER

OLENEK RIVER

Yakuts (Yurats)

KHETA

EASTERN TAIMYR

WESTERN TAIMYR PENINSULA

Tungueses

Lower Tunguska River

YENISEI RIVER

Kara Sea

NOVAYA ZEMBLYA

YAMAL PENINSULA

Gulf of OBI

OBI

WABAROVA

KARA R.

YORKUTA R.

IRTYSH

BERESOF

TOBOLSK

60°

65°

URAL MOUNTAINS

PECHORA RIVER

MEZEN RIVER

Ostians

MEZEN

DVINA RIVER

WHITE SEA

MURMANSK

ARCTIC CIRCLE

NORWAY

SWEDEN

FINLAND

GULF of BOTHNIA

HELSINKI

STOCKHOLM

ESTONIA

LENINGRAD

BALTIC SEA

LATVIA

ARCHANGEL

MOSCOW

Russia

U.S.S.R.

SPITZBERGEN (SVAALBARD)

Chapter 1

History Is History

DISCOVERY OF THE SAMOYED

The white dog with the smiling face, the dog we know as the Samoyed, came to the attention of Western civilization through the noted Norwegian explorer Dr. Fridtjof Nansen.

Dr. Nansen firmly believed that sledging with dogs was the answer to Arctic conquest. He recommended the dogs and the services of his dog broker, Alexander I. Trontheim of Tobolsk, Siberia, to many explorers. This proved most fortunate. Most of the dogs used in their expeditions thus came from the same area and, because the native dogs had not been interbred with outsiders for thousands of years, were of a strongly developed strain. As you shall see later, dogs from these expeditions, brought to England largely through the efforts of Mr. and Mrs. Ernest Kilburn-Scott, became the nucleus for the modern Samoyed.

Tribes of the Siberian Tundras and the Eskimos of North America had early discovered that the safest method for traveling the frozen regions was the sledge, usually drawn by dogs. (Dr. Nansen, in his book *Northern Mists*, quotes the explorer Ibn Batuta [1302–1377]: "Four dogs to sledges going to the 'Land of Darkness'—dogs or guides, a leader who has been there before is worth 1,000 dinars.") But it was in Siberia that this method of locomotion was first applied to polar exploration.

In the seventeenth and eighteenth centuries the Russians made extensive sledge journeys and charted the Siberian coast from the borders of Europe to the Bering Strait. Baron Wrangell wrote of traveling the barren wastes of Siberia with sledge teams and of their use by the "Yassak" men (tax collectors for the czar).

The Russians usually traveled with many dogs and few men. The early English explorers, in contrast, used many men and few dogs. Dr. Nansen's research, and the experience of a trip across Greenland on skis in 1888, convinced him of the wisdom of using dogs in overwhelming ratio to men.

1

Samoyed dogs in upper Lapland in the early 1800s, from an early tintype.

A sled team in a harrowing encounter with a polar bear.

In preparing his expedition toward the North Pole in 1894, Nansen asked his friend Russian explorer Baron Edward von Toll to procure good sledge dogs from Siberia. The Baron had used these on his trip to the Arctic. Baron von Toll engaged Alexander Trontheim to buy thirty dogs. When he heard that Trontheim planned to buy Ostiak dogs, he asked that the dogs be bought instead in eastern Siberia from the Tungunese branch of the Samoyed people, whose draft dogs were better than those of the Ostiaks.

Trontheim headed toward the Petchora district to obtain the dogs. Hearing of a disease raging in that area among the dogs, he turned instead to Berezof, which is located north 64° latitude and east 64.5° longitude, and there bought forty sledge dogs. Trontheim hired a native named Terentieff, who used a herd of 450 reindeer and sledges to convey him, the 40 dogs and 9,600 pounds of food for the dogs to the coast at Khabarova. This, a distance of 400 miles, was the arranged meeting place where Fridtjof Nansen was to pick up the dogs. The trip took three months.

Dr. Nansen's account of his first meeting with the dogs reads:

> Many of them appeared to be well bred animals, longhaired, snow-white, with upstanding ears and pointed muzzles. With their gentle, good-natured-looking faces, they at once ingratiated themselves into the affections. Some of them resembled a fox, and had shorter coats, while others were black or spotted. Evidently they were of different races, and some of them betrayed by their drooping ears, a strong admixture of European blood.

What Nansen saw as a difference in the dogs stemmed from a difference in the people who owned them. There were two types of Samoyed tribes— one nomadic, the other pastoral—and each had their own kind of dog.

The nomadic Samoyed tribes had the all-white Bjelkier dogs that served as hunting and draft dogs for their owners. *Bjelkier* means "white dog that breeds white." In native usage, the term was also applied to the ermine, the white fox and the white bear.

The pastoral tribes had dogs of the Renvall-Hund or Elkhound type. Some were white, some black and white and some brown and white.

The books *Dogs of All Nations* by Count Henry de Blyandt, *The Voyage of the Vega* by Dr. Otto Nordenskiolds and *In Northern Mists* by Fridtjof Nansen, all repeat this classification of the nomads with white hunting dogs and the reindeer-herding tribes with their smaller Renvall-Hund type, which were either solid white or white marked with black or brown and weighed thirty to fifty pounds.

In reports by explorers and expeditions sent by the Smithsonian Institution, the Peabody Fund and the British Zoological Society, accounts have been given of the various dogs in the Siberian area. One account told of white sled dogs hitched four abreast being used to pull barges on the Yenisei River. The Yenisei River is 200 miles east of Berezof where Trontheim procured Nansen's dogs. The Smithsonian Institution Report of 1898 quotes from *Die Tungusen* by Dr. B. Langkavel, who in 1872 said:

> The tent-living Samoyeds use only reindeer as draft animals and have the dogs for herding, but the remainder of the Samoyeds and Yakuts use dogs and indeed each one can pull two to three and one-half pud [a pud is thirty-two pounds].

Another German explorer, in 1892, told of the people in the area of the Sameanda. He declared there were two types of tribes: the dog people who had no reindeer and the reindeer people who had no dogs. The two classes of natives were continually battling because the dogs would kill the reindeer and the reindeer people would then kill the dogs. These dogs were described as pure white and quite gentle, but terrific hunters. Their speed deeply impressed the expedition.

Thus there were tribes of similar peoples with fairly similar dogs, yet there were distinct differences. The question arises, "Did these tribesmen have a breeding program?" Written accounts of the devious means used by the Europeans to obtain the dogs that the natives refused to sell, make it clear that the natives prized their dogs highly. Small wonder, for the natives' total existence depended on their possessing good dogs. They must have felt the same intense personal pride in their strains that breeders exhibit today.

EXPLORERS AND EXPEDITIONS INFLUENCING THE BREED

The great age of polar exploration, from 1870 to 1912, brought all Arctic dogs to notice. However, we shall confine ourselves here to the explorers of note who used the Bjelkier, now known as the Samoyed.

Fridtjof Nansen—Dr. Nansen, a professor in seven chairs or departments at the University of Norway, designed his own ship for his expedition. The Fram was so well-built and excellent in its design that it was used for five expeditions over thirty-five years.

Nansen did considerable research in selecting the dogs for the sledging phase of his expedition. The cataloging of the weights of the twenty-eight dogs chosen for the final journey toward the North Pole, recorded after nearly a year and a half of living and working in the Arctic regions, shows that the nineteen males averaged 58.7 pounds, and the nine bitches averaged 50.5 pounds.

Nansen's theory for sledging was a disastrous one for the dogs. He and partner Frederic Johansen set out with many dogs but planned that as they ran out of food, the weaker dogs would be fed to the stronger ones. The trip over the ice packs eliminated all the dogs but two, their lead dogs Kaifas and Suggen. And even these two had to be sacrificed when they arrived at open water, for the men were cautious about taking them in their kayaks.

After choosing the draft dogs of the Samoyed people for his attempt at the pole, Dr. Nansen recommended them to other explorers. He sent an all-white Samoyed bitch, named Grasso, to the Duc d'Abruzzi as a good example of a sled dog.

Jackson-Harmsworth Expedition—Major Frederick G. Jackson led this English expedition to Franz Josef Land, above the Arctic Circle. Here they met Nansen and Johansen, returning from their eighteen-month journey by

Fridtjof Nansen's drawing of himself, Frederic Johansen and some of their dogs enroute to Franz Josef Land in kayaks lashed together by their sleds.

sledge and kayak, and brought them home. Major Jackson was also very interested in the Samoyed and returned some to England. He presented his best dog, Jacko, to Queen Alexandra. Jacko was all white, by Nimrod out of Jenny. Dr. Kotelitz, a physician with the expedition, brought the bitch Kvik back with him, and she is found in early pedigrees. Eight other dogs brought back by Major Jackson went to Mr. Kilburn-Scott's kennels in 1899.

The Duc d'Abruzzi, or Luigi Amadeo, the distinguished Italian adventurer, aimed for the North Pole and sought the counsel of Fridtjof Nansen. On advice, he ordered 120 dogs from Alexander Trontheim in July 1898. Not many explorers have given detailed comment on their use of dogs, but the Duc left the following:

> Although born in an intensely cold country, they were not insensible to temperatures below a -30° centigrade. When it was very cold they were often seen to raise their paws out of the snow from time to time, and to go about looking for straw or wood to lie upon.

The Duc's account of the harnessing of the dogs is very interesting to sled drivers because he was the first to use the double tandem hitch. He wrote:

> While Trontheim showed us how Nansen had harnessed the dogs abreast by separate traces attached to the sledge [fan hitch], as was done by the Samoyeds and Esquimaux to allow them more liberty in their movements

and to utilize all their strength, it had great disadvantages. The traces became all mixed up and required much continual, tiresome labor. To avoid this inconvenience I decided when at Christiana to follow this method used by the Yakuts of the Lower Lena River who make use of a single long trace, to each side of which the dogs are harnessed by shorter traces attached to the central trace. The dogs showed strength and endurance and I felt more confidence in them after a four-day trip of 70 miles. Rings were fixed on the central trace on a level with the dogs' heads when they were pulling, and to which they were hooked by short chains, which also served to tie them up during the night. Our dog harness, like that made by other explorers, consisted of three or four layers of canvas, two lines of which passed between the animals' forelegs and two along their backs, where they were all united to the trace.

Most interesting is the Duc's description of his best lead dog, an all-white Bjelkier named Messicano.

We are decidedly rivaling not only Nansen, but also Wrangell, who was celebrated for the rapidity of his marches. We are able to accomplish these remarkable stages now, partly because we have only four sledges, and partly on account of the tracks which Messicano, the leading dog, was able to follow again today, even where they had been almost entirely effaced by the wind. It is a small white dog, with thick hair, and very intelligent eyes. It is so called Messicano on account of the abundance of hair which fringes its legs, resembling trousers which widen at the feet. Ever since our departure from Templitz Bay, it has held the first place of the first sledge, because it followed the man at the head of the convoy better than the others. Has followed obediently from the outset, being the most obedient to the word of command. Although not as big as some of his companions he always pulls, and falls upon the dogs of the other sledges which try to pass it. One would say that it feels all the importance of its position, and is proud of it. Messicano gallops like a dwosky horse with its nose always down in the snow. Sometimes it loses the track and then goes more slowly. Messicano shows its anxiety, it whines and runs up and down with its tongue out until it finds the track again. Then he darts off in the right direction, often for long stretches where it is utterly impossible for us to see a trace of our former passage.

One Samoyed male from the Abruzzi Expedition was returned to England. This dog was Houdin. Houdin was shown and used at stud and left a good mark on the breed. Russ, another dog that had been purchased in Tobolsk by Trontheim for this expedition, also eventually made his way to England and appears in early Samoyed pedigrees.

Carsten E. Borchgrevink, a Norwegian who lived in Australia, led an English expedition to the Antarctic, February 17, 1899–February 2, 1900. He had more than 100 Samoyeds with him at the start of the trip. Although he did not write much about the breed, two dogs from his pack

Carsten Borchgrevink and some of his expedition dogs in Antarctica.

Borchgrevink's notes from his expedition state, "Dogs were sheared before crossing the equator on the way to the South Pole."

had tremendous impact on the breed. The greatest was Antarctic Buck, left in the Sidney Zoo after the expedition, and in 1908 imported to England by Mr. and Mrs. Kilburn-Scott. The other dog, Trip, went to the Ernest Shackleton Expedition and was returned to England by Lieutenant Charles

Adams. Borchgrevink handed over twenty-seven of his dogs to Dr. Douglas Mawson in 1911 for another Australian expedition.

Sir Ernest Shackleton, on his 1907–09 Antarctic expedition, had a few teams of dogs from other expeditions that had been left in Australia. He was a strong advocate of the use of ponies for sledge work in the Antarctic, but the problems created by their weight and the need to provide food for them made it necessary to destroy them all. Captain Robert Falcon Scott followed in the pattern of Shackleton and used many men and ponies, with but few dogs, for his expedition in 1911. Why he did not use dogs as a main plan in dashing to the South Pole is not clear. Perhaps he did not care to use them in the customary cannibalistic way of the other explorers, or he may not have trusted them. This is particularly puzzling in that he was a good friend of E. Kilburn-Scott, who did so much to establish the Samoyed in England. In fact, E. Kilburn-Scott gave his friend the dog Olaf, a son of Antarctic Buck, to take on the expedition. Captain Scott did take thirty-three dogs with him to the Antarctic, but planned to rely on twenty ponies and men to pull the sledges. The ponies broke through the snow, sweated and froze, and eventually all became snowblind. The ponies froze because they sweat through their hides, whereas dogs sweat through their tongues and pads of their feet. Someone docked the tails of one team of Scott's dogs, and they died of pneumonia within three weeks because of the lack of the thick, bushy tail, which is a great protection to the dogs while sleeping.

Scott made his dash to the South Pole with six men laboriously pulling the sleds. From his diary, found after his death, it was learned that he did reach the pole, only to find it covered with paw prints of dogs and a note from Roald Amundsen giving him greetings dated a month before.

Roald Amundsen, first to reach the South Pole (planting the Norwegian flag thereon December 14, 1911), was the most successful "dog man" of all the explorers. His accounts of the training and selection of his sledge dogs are outstanding. He acquired ninety-seven dogs for his expedition and after much training used fifty-two of them and four sledges for the dash to the pole. As planned, they returned with the four men, one sledge, and twelve surviving dogs. The round-trip covered 1,860 miles in ninety-nine days, and the first animal over the pole was an all-white Samoyed lead dog. Twenty-seven of Amundsen's dogs were given to Douglas Mawson for an Australian expedition in 1911, and the rest returned as pets of the crew.

The points made by Luigi Amadeo had been proven. He had written,

Dogs are undeniably the most useful animals for man in his expeditions with sledges over the ice of the Polar Sea. They have this advantage, too, that unlike horses or reindeer, they readily eat their fellows. Their weight is small, and they can be easily carried on light boats or ice floes. Their loss represents but a small diminution of motive power in comparison with that which results from the death of a horse or reindeer.

On each of these expeditions, except the ill-fated Scott Expedition, the Samoyed played a major part. Almost all Samoyeds today can be traced to expedition dogs.

Although the utility of the dogs was the main concern, the warmth of their personalities was often noted by the explorers. Samoyed admirers of today will recognize their dogs in such comments as: "and the white dogs crowded around to be petted" (by Fridtjof Nansen); "At night we could tell the white dogs, as they poked us with their noses to get attention" (by James Murray, biologist for Shackleton); and "We found that at night the best way to thaw our sleeping bags was to spread them out, for the white dogs would jump right on them" (by Roald Amundsen). In his book *First on the Antarctic Continent*, C. E. Borchgrevink wrote: "It was curious to watch the marked difference in the habits and manners of the Greenland dogs to that of their brethren from Siberia. The former were much more wild and seldom or never mixed with the other dogs, nor did they attach themselves as much to man as the Siberian dogs did."

While not an explorer in the sense of the polar expeditions, W. B. Vanderlip in 1898 made a two-year trip through Siberia and left a detailed account of travel by dog sled. Frequent references to the Tungoos, Uraks and Koraks show that he covered much of the land where Trontheim collected dogs for the explorers. From the book *In Search of a Siberian Klondike* we quote:

The reader may well ask how the natives can use both dogs and reindeer if the very sight of a deer has such a maddening effect on the dogs. The explanation is simple. The two never go together. There is the dog country and the deer country, and the two do not impinge upon each other. Even among the same tribe there may be a clear division. For instance, there are the Deer Koraks, and the Dog Koraks. In some of the villages of the former, there may occasionally be seen a few low-bred curs which are not used for sledging and have been trained not to worry deer.

Need we ponder further on the background of our beautiful breed? Were our Samoyeds hunters, draft dogs or reindeer herders? No matter, because they all had the common faculty of being the "right hands" of their masters and the means of survival in the cold, bleak land.

One common reference weaves a thread through all the accounts of travel in Siberia—the note of a white dog that breeds white. This dog is always living inside the chooms or combes, the houses, with his master. He is continually referred to as a friendly likable dog, very unlike the wild creatures found in the same environment.

Thus, although the true origin of our breed is lost in antiquity, we do know that the Samoyed came from a general area east of the Urals, near the Arctic Circle, and we do know that the generic dogs that were combined were selected from Bjelkiers, the white animals that breed white. We know, too, that any black spots or markings have been a disqualification in the breed in England for eighty years. Nature must be telling us that fallible humans have allowed the one true dominant strain to come through loud and clear—the white dog that breeds white, or white and biscuit, or biscuit.

BEGINNINGS IN ENGLAND

Of the first dogs of the breed in England, only a few came from western Siberia. Later imports were from the Ural Mountains and the Island of Novaya Zemblya and were likewise limited in number. Most numerous of the original dogs and most influential in the establishment of the breed in England were the dogs from the expeditions, which Alexander Trontheim had originally obtained from the area east of the Yenisei River, stretching to the Olenek. All of these were imported before 1914. A very few were brought to England in the mid-1920s, and since then none.

The first importers and establishers of the breed in England were Mr. and Mrs. Ernest Kilburn-Scott. Mr. Kilburn-Scott was a member of the Royal Zoological Society and in its cause had made a trip to the Archangel in 1889, from which he had brought back a dog. This was the chocolate-brown Sabarka ("the fat one" in Russian). Sabarka was not from the same district in Siberia as Fridtjof Nansen's dogs. He came from at least 900 miles west of the Olenek River. Mr. Kilburn-Scott had sympathetically bought Sabarka to save the young puppy from providing the natives a "feast." He was said to be typical in many good points of the breed such as head, stand-off coat, curled tail and good carriage. Soon after this, Mr. Kilburn-Scott brought in the famous cream-colored bitch, Whitey Pechora. The mating of Sabarka and Whitey Pechora produced a daughter Neva, who went to Lady Sitwell, newly interested in the breed.

Earliest mention of the Samoyed seems to have been in a 1891 advertisement in the English papers placed by Mr. Kilburn-Scott under the Foreign Dogs and Various Classifications. It read:

> Lovely white Russian (Samoyed) sledge dog pups, like small polar bears, most gentle and affectionate. Splendid coats and tails. Very rare. Parents imported.

Samoyeds were first shown at the Leeds show in 1893 in the Foreign Dog class.

Lady Sitwell later imported a snow-white dog named Musti from northern Russia. When Musti was mated with Whitey Pechora in 1901, the white proved dominant, and the litter was the beginning of all-white Samoyeds in England. It included the famous dog Nansen, who swept the shows in 1903, and the great bitch Olgalene. A third dog, Rex Albus, did not affect the breed as much.

The mating of Musti and Neva produced Ch. Olaf Oussa, important behind pedigrees of today.

When the Kilburn-Scotts wanted more stock, they went through Alexander Trontheim, who had obtained Nansen's dogs in 1894. In 1899, while selecting dogs for the Duc d'Abruzzi, Trontheim chose Russ for the Scotts. This dog was bred to Kvik, the bitch brought back by Dr. Kotelitz when he was the physician on the Jackson-Harmsworth Expedition in 1897. This breeding produced Ch. Pearlene, famous for her beautiful head and ears and for her progeny.

Major F. G. Jackson, who brought back many dogs in 1897, had given seven to Kilburn-Scott, and one (the male, Jacko) to Queen Alexandra. Major Jackson and Mr. Kilburn-Scott worked together in the early years and joined in the proposal of a Standard for the Samoyed. (Both judged the breed in England until the mid-1920s).

Jacko, the Queen's dog, was shown in the first class solely for Samoyeds, in 1902. Six dogs were judged by Mr. Kilburn-Scott; Jacko was the winner, defeating among others the Honorable Mrs. McLaren Morrison's Peter the Great, bred by the Scotts. Queen Alexandra had other Samoyeds, notably Sandringham Pearl.

Bred to Nansen, Ch. Pearlene produced Kviklene in 1902, carrying on the whites for her grandmother Kvik of the Jackson-Harmsworth Expedition.

When Antarctic Buck was released from quarantine in 1909, he was bred to Kviklene and Olgalene. Olgalene's mating to Buck produced Kaifas, Kirchie and Bucklene, all whites. When bred to Jacko, Olgalene produced Ivanoff, a fine biscuit specimen.

But it was the all-male litter resulting from the breeding of Kviklene to Antarctic Buck that was to have the profoundest influence on the breed. In that one litter, Kviklene produced Southern Cross, South Pole, Fang, Mezenett and Olaf. This was the same Olaf that Captain Robert Scott took to the South Pole in 1911. And without Southern Cross and South Pole, there would not be many show Samoyeds today.

Antarctic Buck was a dazzling white dog standing twenty-one and a half inches (measured at the shoulder, rather than at the withers), and thirty-five inches long from the tip of his nose to the tip of his tail. He died in 1909, at ten years of age, having contracted distemper after being shown at Redhill, England. From this epidemic, only seven of his famous puppies survived.

Trip, another dog originally from the Borchgrevink Expedition, made his way to England in 1911. He was brought there by Lieutenant Adams of the Shackleton Expedition. Trip appears in some pedigrees but not in as many as Houdin from the Abruzzi Expedition.

Mrs. Helen Harris, whose Snowland Kennels was so prominent on the American scene in the 1930s, once summed up the early Siberian imports: "There are twelve dogs of importance to the pedigrees of American Samoyeds:

Ernest Kilburn-Scott with Prince Zouroff, of the dogs from the litter pictured below.

This 1902 litter by Jack ex Olgalene was bred by Mrs. Kilburn-Scott. Subsequently one of these Samoyeds was presented to Queen Alexandra.

the Kilburn-Scotts' Sabarka, Whitey Pechora, Russ, Houdin and Antarctic Buck; Lady Sitwell's Kvik; Queen Alexandra's Jacko; Trip; Ayesha (brought in in 1910 by Gordon Colman, and sold to Mrs. Cammack); and from Russia in 1925, Pelle of Halfway and Yugor of Halfway, imported by Mrs. Grey-Landsberg."

Mrs. Kilburn-Scott had refused to buy Ayesha because she did not like the "Spitz-like face, a faulty foreface, and slightly prominent round eyes." Mrs. Harris concluded her summation with: "The credit really goes to the bitches for launching this breed, and the most influential bitches were Kvik and Whitey Pechora."

The breed received some wide attention in 1911 as a result of the Glasgow Exposition. As part of the show, a group of Lapplanders were on display with their tents and reindeer. Spectators began asking, "How do you herd your reindeer?" Of course, the Scots used the Collie for their sheep and expected to see some type of work dog. But the Lapplanders had not brought the smaller Renvall-type dogs that they used.

When the director of the exposition discussed this with Mr. Kilburn-Scott, the latter offered some of his Samoyeds to be put on display as reindeer herders with the Lapplanders. Many of the English newspapers photographed the dogs and publicized them as reindeer herders.

Will Hally, a longtime dog columnist, Samoyed breeder and judge, questioned the Lapplanders about the similarity of the white Samoyed to their herding dogs, and they were most emphatic in stating that there was no resemblance. But *reindeer herder* would not be an altogether wrong classification for the Samoyed because they are indeed an all-purpose dog. Basically, the Samoyed was a hunting and family guard but where occasion demanded it became a herd and draft dog for certain tribes. Joe Stetson, writing in *Field & Stream*, once summed it up: "The Samoyed is a three-H Dog . . . Hunting, Herding and Hauling."

At first the Samoyed was shown in the Foreign Dog class in England and labeled Samozia Sledge Dogs. But by 1909, Mr. Kilburn-Scott's choice of name for the breed, the Samoyede, had become the established designation, the Samoyede Club had been founded and a Standard formulated. Subsequently, the second *e* was dropped from the breed name. Beginning in 1912 the Kennel Club ruled that Samoyeds should be classified separately.

The Samoyede Club as originally formed had excluded woman members, so in 1912 the Ladies' Samoyede Association was founded. In this same year, the Samoyed and the Laika were combined for show purposes, but only the dominant white was to survive as a breed and type.

Also in 1912 a breeder came on the scene who was to become one of the legendary figures in the development of the Samoyed. Miss J. V. Thomson-Glover acquired her first Samoyed, Snow Cloud, from the Kilburn-Scotts. Miss Thomson-Glover was a strong influence in guarding breed quality for many years and was particularly influential in maintaining the Samoyed's typical smiling expression. She played an important part in the founding of the Samoyed Association of Great Britain, which absorbed the earlier Samoyede Club and the Ladies Samoyede Association in 1920.

With importation halted by the cessation of the expeditions and the rumblings of World War I, English breeders took over on their own.

Ch. Pearlene (Russ ex Kvick), bred in 1901 and traced back to dogs from the Jackson-Harmsworth Expedition. Pearlene introduced the pure white color, thicker, plush coat, more rounded ear tips, better eye color and nose pigment.

Antarctic Buck, imported to England by the Kilburn-Scotts from the Borchgrevink South Pole expedition.

Nansen, bred in 1901 by Mrs. Kilburn-Scott, lived to age sixteen. He was of Musti-Whitey Pechora breeding—the beginning of the pure white Samoyed in England.

Scotland contributed mightily to the breed when in 1915 Miss E. Marker bred Antarctic Bru (by Southern Cross out of Zembla). She followed with Mustan of Farningham, a great sire.

But the greatest was yet to come. Ch. Kara Sea, by Mustan of Farningham out of Ch. Zahrina (later to become Ch. Zahrina of Norka in the United States), was whelped on February 7, 1924. Kara Sea was bred by

Ch. Antarctic Bru of Farningham (Southern Cross ex Zemla) born in 1915 and bred by Mrs. Kilburn-Scott, was an expedition dog that figured into the pedigrees of many of the earlier show dogs.

The immortal Eng. Ch. Kara Sea.

Eng. Ch. Polar Light of Faringham.

Eng. Ch. Kosca of Kobe, owned by Mrs. Dorothy L. Perry. Agnes Mason commented on this photo: "Good front legs, good stifles, feet, tail. Well-balanced dog. Head well set."

Ch. Starctic Storm (1950–61) by Ch. Starchak's Witan ex Mazzi's Duchess was a successful winner in the mid-1950s.

Mrs. D. Edwards in Scotland. He was shown to a fabulous record that included twenty-one Challenge Certificates.

But even more than for his extensive winning over a long period, Ch. Kara Sea rates attention for his importance in the concentration upon all-white dogs by certain breeders. His first-generation descendants included Eng., Am. Ch. Tiger Boy of Norka; Eng. Ch. Kara Queen of the Arctic; Eng. Ch. Leader of the Arctic; and Am. Ch. Siberian Nansen of Farningham of Snowland. Second generation offspring of note included the English champions White Fang of Kobe, Ice Crystal (also Am. Ch.), Surf, Riga and Greta of the Arctic; Kosca of Kobe; and Am. Ch. Norka's Moguiski.

Another Scottish breeder, Mrs. Simon, bred the winning Polar Light of Farningham (Polar Sea out of Ch. Snowy) in 1923. This dog, owned by Mrs. Kilburn-Scott, was Best of Breed at the Crufts dog show for five years (1925–29), and also contributed greatly as a sire.

Climaxing all of the activity in breeding and showing was the first Samoyed Club show in England in 1923. In the same year, the Samoyed Club of America was formed across the Atlantic.

In closing out the story of these beginning years, we think all Samoyed owners and breeders will find interest in the observations on size, type and consistency over the first forty years of the breed, expressed by Will Hally in this 1934 commentary:

> The first fact is that we have not made the Samoyed bigger. I saw every one of the original importations, and I saw all the dogs which were secured from the polar expeditions. Now that takes me back to the first days of the 1890s, to the very, very beginning of Samoyeds in this country (England), and I say emphatically that Samoyed size has not altered in the very least during all that period.
>
> Then, too, in my travels as a young man, I saw the genuine Spitz in various countries, and no one who really knew the two breeds could possibly say that they were one and the same. The true Samoyed (and I am not writing of the white dogs, and dogs which have not been white, that have been paraded as Samoyeds) is radically and fundamentally different from the Spitz. The Samoyed is a product of the Samoyed people, and this is corroborated by every traveler and explorer who has gone into the matter deeply and intimately.

A statement such as this is very reassuring to contemporary Samoyed breeders, for few owners of other breeds can look at pictures of their breed of 80 to 100 years ago and see in them present-day show winners.

THE SAMOYED IN THE UNITED STATES (1906-44)

From origins steeped in the mystery of the frozen remoteness of north central Siberia, the Samoyed was brought to the attention of Western civilization by a Nobel Prize winner (Fridtjof Nansen) and by a king's cousin (the Duc d'Abruzzi) and was supported in England by their Highnesses, Queen Alexandra and King Edward VII. It was only fitting then that it should be introduced into America by royalty, and this it was through the Princess de Montyglyon.

Mercy d'Argenteau, a Belgian countess and the daughter of a royal favorite of the Court of Napoleon II, was also a hereditary princess of the Holy Roman Empire. The princess was one of the great beauties of her day. Her world was what today would be termed cafe society. Despite her upbringing and contacts with royalty, she met and married Captain John Bonavita, a well-known lion tamer. Captain Bonavita was to be written up more fully in the story of Lillian Russell's life than in the princess's autobiography.

1906-23

Princess de Montyglyon had the first Samoyed registered in the American Kennel Club Stud Book (December 1906). The dog was the Russian champion Moustan of Argenteau, #102896. Moustan was obtained in 1902 in St. Petersburg, Russia, from the Grand Duke Nicholas, brother to the czar.

The reported story of how the princess became the owner of Moustan is a romantic one.

At the time, the princess owned Collies and Chow Chows and exhibited them often throughout Europe. In St. Petersburg, as she was leaving the show grounds for refreshments, she found at her heels one of the string of Samoyeds being shown by the grand duke. In her book she describes the dog as being a big, square-headed, good-tempered beast dragging his chain. The princess took his chain and led him back to the bench. Next day, she paid a visit to the bench to see the dog, and he followed her again. This time the grand duke was there as she returned him and said, "You seem to like Moustan very much." She replied, "I would give anything in the world to have him, but I hear none of this breed can be obtained. I well know that this one is not for sale."

Nicholas replied, "Oh, surely not for sale—but to give anything in the world for him? Is it not a reckless offer? I must think it over." All this with a smile and a drawl so filled with meaning that the princess hastily dropped the subject.

The next few days and nights were filled with parties and court balls. As her departure approached, the grand duke asked the date of her leaving. When the princess arrived at the station, she saw one of the Imperial coaches on the train. She was informed that the grand duke had put his private car at her disposal. In the drawing room, she found a huge basket heaped with roses and orchids. When she began to remove them, there emerged the shaggy white head of the Russian champion Moustan, with a card from the grand duke tied to his collar. "Moustan is not for sale," it read, "no price could buy him, but it will be a favor to him and me if you will graciously accept him."

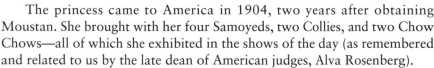

The princess came to America in 1904, two years after obtaining Moustan. She brought with her four Samoyeds, two Collies, and two Chow Chows—all of which she exhibited in the shows of the day (as remembered and related to us by the late dean of American judges, Alva Rosenberg).

Registered in 1906, Moustan of Argenteau holds honor as the first Samoyed in the AKC Stud Book. Moustan has at various times been rumored to be from the Fridtjof Nansen Expedition (1894–97). This would have made him ten to twelve years old when he began siring litters. Some books have attributed him to Antarctic Buck of the Borchgrevink Expedition, but Moustan's own son, Ch. de Witte of Argenteau, was born in 1900—the date of the expedition.

Even without known parentage, Moustan's name appears behind many Samoyeds today. In the 1940s, one veteran remembered his being "a large powerful dog and of sturdier build than many of the breed seen today."

Moustan's son, Ch. de Witte of Argenteau, whose dam Sora of Argenteau was also of unknown ancestry, became the first American champion Samoyed of record in 1907.

Of the four Samoyeds that the princess had brought to America, only Martyska of Argenteau had known parentage. She was by Houdin out of Olgalene. Moustan, Sora and Siberia of Argenteau were all shown as unknown. Siberia became an American champion in 1908.

Another almost unknown dog of the princess's was the dog Etah, given to her in 1913 by a member of the Amundsen Expedition. Etah was one of the Samoyed lead dogs of the expedition. The princess dedicated her autobiography to Etah, and a picture of him at eleven years old is included in it.

The only get by Moustan of note and impact on the breed was Czarevitch, who was out of Martyska. Czarevitch and a grandson of Moustan, Ch. Zuroff, won constantly in the early days but were shown largely against their kennel mates.

Early competition for the Argenteau dogs was provided by the Greenacre Kennels of Mrs. Ada Van Heusen (of the famous Van Heusen shirts). Ada, as Mrs. Elmo E. Lincoln (Mr. Lincoln was film's first Tarzan), had imported the two full sisters Volga and Tamara, along with Soho and Katinka—son and daughter of Southern Cross—in 1912. Tamara became the first bitch of the breed to win an American championship.

The mating of Czarevitch and Tamara produced Zuroff. Czarevitch also sired Ch. Greenacre Kieff and Evalo. Ch. Greenacre Kieff was the grandsire of Chs. Zanoza, Kazan of Yurak and Fang of Yurak.

New owners and exhibitors were appearing on the scene. However, we must bear in mind that they faced problems that the great advances of veterinary medicine have largely erased. Many dog owners of this era, indeed up until the mid-1930s, would not exhibit because of the distemper problem.

In 1908, Miss Elizabeth Hudson obtained her first Samoyeds, Togo and litter sister Alice, from Mrs. King Wainwright of Bryn Mawr,

Pennsylvania. Twenty to thirty years later Miss Hudson was to import two great ones, but we'll talk of them in their time cycles.

Mrs. Sidney Borg and her sister Mrs. Cahn imported Samoyeds from Mrs. Cammack and Mr. Common of England to compete at the shows with the princess and Mrs. Van Heusen.

As could and does happen (even today), with the large kennels importing dogs to improve the breed, an individual bitch brought in as a gift to a schoolgirl by her father had some of the greatest impact on the early dogs. Miss Ruth Nichols was given the bitch Wiemur in 1914, which was registered in 1918. Mated to Czarevitch, Wiemur produced the champions Malschick and Shut Balackeror, as well as the uncrowned Boris. (Shut Balackeror, born on April Fools' Day, was named after the last court jester to the czar.)

As we look back, these early days were discouraging because type and quality were rather ignored. Beauty to the eye of the individual was the sole criterion. A great size discrepancy existed, and a standardized type had not really been set. Few dogs survived in pedigrees. But isn't this true of other breeds as well? Many early dogs have been lost in oblivion after brief show careers, and the breeds have been carried on by just a few.

In all, from 1906 through 1920, exactly forty dogs had been registered with the American Kennel Club. There had been fifteen imports with well-authenticated English pedigrees traced by Catharine Quereaux, plus two imports from China, three from Russia and one from France. The breed had seven champions of record.

The end of World War I was a turning point in breeding in both England and in America. This new era got its start in America with the import of Tobolsk by the Yurak Kennels of Mrs. Frank Romer. Tobolsk (by Fang ex Vilna) was obtained by the redoubtable handler-broker Percy Roberts, who later became a legendary all-breed judge.

Tobolsk was heralded as the greatest Samoyed of all time in America and at the same time was condemned as leggy and ungainly. No matter, for Ch. Tobolsk (#285263) proved to be a magnificent dog and a good sire. He produced the constancy of size needed in the breed and together with later imports Ch. Donerna's Barin and Ch. Yukon-Mit was vital in giving America back the type of dog from which Trontheim had made selections for the expeditions.

Ch. Tobolsk, when mated with Otiska, sired a great line of winners, including Ch. Toby of Yurak II, Nanook II and Nanook of Donerna. (Ch. Toby of Yurak II won until he was twelve years old and, in fact, was Best of Breed at Westminster at that age.) Tobolsk, mated with Sunny Ridge Pavlova, produced Chs. Fang of Yurak and Kazan of Yurak. (Kazan, who had difficulty finishing his championship because he was twenty-six inches tall, was a large, heavy-boned dog, shown from 1922 to 1927.)

Many daughters of Tobolsk were excellent specimens and good producers. They included Queen Marie, Queen Zita, Ch. Patricia Obin and Donerna's Nara and Chs. Valeska, Semstra and Snow Cloud of Yurak.

Ch. Draga, litter sister to Tobolsk and imported at the same time, was bred to Shut Balackeror and Zev of Yurak and produced Ch. Kritelka of Yurak, Boy Yurak and Toby of Yurak. The Frank Romers were active in the breed for twenty-one years until 1937, when their Yurak Kennels was transferred to Eddie Barbeau. The Romers (and Barbeau, too) also were active sledding enthusiasts.

In 1920, Miss Mildred Trevor Sheridan imported Hasova (#292683), a seven-year-old dog from Russia, and Loree (#294040), a bitch from England. They are best remembered as the sire and dam of Lady Olga (#320651), born in 1920. Lady Olga was the dam of Ch. Icy King, who became the sire of such big winners of the 1930s as the litter brothers, Ch. Icy King Jr.; Siberian Icy King Duplicate, CD; and Ch. Prince Kofski. Miss Sheridan, later Mrs. Mildred Sheridan Davis, owned Park-Cliffe Kennels, in operation as of 1984 over sixty years later, but no longer active as of the 1990s.

Two notable kennels were added in 1921. The F. L. Vintons' Obi Kennel continues through the Obi suffix found in today's pedigrees. The other was Mr. and Mrs. Harry Reid's Norka Kennels. In 1929 the Reids were to give great impetus to the breed by importing Ch. Tiger Boy.

In this continuing period of imports, the years 1922 and 1923 brought to the Romers' Yurak Kennels the great bitch Olga of Farningham (by Antarctic Bru, a grandson of Antarctic Buck, out of Olga, a granddaughter of Buck); Trip of Farningham (by Antarctic Bru out of Miss Muffet); and Yurak's Fox Laika—all from Mrs. Kilburn-Scott. To Yurak also came Donerna's Kolya of Farningham and Donerna's Tsilma, a litter sister to Donerna's Barin. To Louis Smirnow came Nico of Farningham, who was on the small side, as were his progeny. Miss Grafton of England sent Polas of Farningham to the W. B. Donahues. Mr. and Mrs. James L. Hubbard of Howardsville, Maryland, imported Olaf of Farningham, another son of Antarctic Bru out of Nish Nish (thus the grandfather was again Mezenett from Antarctic Buck's famous litter).

The second of the three pillars of the American Samoyed was imported at this time by Mr. and Mrs. Alfred Seeley for their Donerna Kennels at the foot of the George Washington Bridge in New York City. He was Ch. Donerna's Barin, a son of Eng. Ch. Kieff out of Ivanofva, bred by Mr. Pitchford of England.

It is interesting to note that Barin was sent to the United States in place of Snow Crest when the American Kennel Club waived the three generations rule for Ch. Tobolsk. Barin, you see, went back to the expedition import Antarctic Buck in just two generations. He was himself an able sled dog and proved a great worker in the sled teams of the Donerna Kennels.

Ch. Donerna's Barin had 120 registered sons and daughters. Therefore, by sheer numbers, he had great influence on the breed, an influence that was especially positive for size and coat. Barin measured twenty-two inches and weighed sixty pounds. Some of his get were larger, but judging from the picture of him in this book at his tenth birthday, he reproduced his size.

Donerna's Kolya was influential because sixty of his progeny soon appeared in the Stud Book, mostly bred in the Midwestern States. Bred to Polas of Farningham, Kolya produced Pollyanna and Princess Illeana. Pollyanna, who died in 1940, was the dam of Ch. Duke of Norka and the great winner Ch. Norka's Lubinlay.

The forty-two Samoyeds registered in 1922 equaled the total registration of the previous fifteen years of American Samoyed history. In this last year before the formation of the parent club there were six large kennels: Donerna, Yurak, Top O' the World, Obi, Park-Cliffe and Wingbrook.

It was a year of turmoil for Samoyed owners, breeders and exhibitors. Some dogs, both registered and unregistered, imported and homebred, were being denied ribbons or were being excused from the rings because of their inferior quality and discrepancies in size and type. Without a Standard and without any uniformity in the classes, further loss of status to the breed occurred. In Cleveland, the show committee had provided for the Samoyeds in the Miscellaneous Class, with the designation of dogs of twenty-five pounds or over. Still in 1922, judge J. Muss-Arnolt had a very nice entry of twelve and placed Nico of Farningham to Winners Dog and Kazan of Yurak as Reserve. Both dogs had been refused ribbons at earlier shows.

1923-44

The Samoyed Club of America was formed February 14, 1923. But even with so auspicious an event, the day was a shocker for Samoyed exhibitors. At the Westminster Kennel Club show of the same day, the judge, J. Willoughby Mitchell of London, England, provided a skyrocket sendoff. He withheld the awards for Reserve Winners in both dogs and bitches. Mr. Mitchell declared they were apparently not true Samoyeds because of their small size and flattish lay-down coats. Three of the animals involved were newly imported from the kennels of Mrs. Kilburn-Scott in England.

Catharine Quereaux later wrote: "Whether this was a back-handed slap at English breeders or indigestion, it assuredly was decidedly in error, and even today we speak of the wrath of the 1923 Westminster!"

Will Hally, veteran Samoyed columnist for the English publication *Our Dogs* wrote:

> That remark of the London judge has created a lot of indignation amongst the Samoyed's supporters in the States, and with reason, I think. While I am not able to speak of all the exhibits at New York, the authenticated

British pedigrees of most of them are the surest proof that Mr. Mitchell is mistaken. I noticed that Mr. Smirnow refers to the New York Winners dog, Billy Boy of Yurak, as a flat-coated dog of good character, and perhaps it is that flat coat which led to Mr. Mitchell's criticism. Such a coat is faulty, but it by no means indicates a Collie influence. The American fanciers, from what I know of the stock they now own, are on the right road, and if they breed to the Standard, they need not worry over what one or two judges say of their exhibits.

Nevertheless, following the judging at the Westminster show, the serious exhibitors and breeders of the Samoyed met in the club rooms of the Madison Square Garden of the day and organized the Samoyed Club of America. The club's stated purposes were to promote the breeding of purebred Samoyeds; to urge adoption of this type on breeders, judges, dog show committees, and so on; and to bring to the notice of the general public the wonderful characteristics and affectionate dispositions of these superlative dogs.

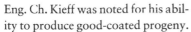
Eng. Ch. Kieff was noted for his ability to produce good-coated progeny.

H. N. Pinkham with the Laika Kennels' team at South Poland, Maine, in 1929. This group of working Sammies included Chs. Donerna's Illinishna, Barin and Laika Natiya.

Styles may change, but Samoyeds stay constant. Miss Katherine Morey, later Mrs. H. N. Pinkham, wears a suit made of Samoyed combings in this 1929 photo. Ten-year-old Ch. Donerna's Barin is shown at Miss Morey's left.

They adopted the English breed Standard, adding the words "black or black spots to disqualify" and a description of disposition. This Standard was adopted as the sole Standard for excellence in breeding and awarding prizes of merit to Samoyeds by the American Kennel Club when it approved the Samoyed Club of America for membership in the AKC on May 15, 1923.

Thus the Samoyed Club of America was formed out of an emotional realization of the concrete need for a parent club to guide and standardize the breed beyond all doubt.

In 1923, there were fewer than 300 Samoyeds in the United States, and at least half of these were in just five kennels. At that time Samoyeds were classified in the Non-Sporting Group with the Collies, Doberman Pinschers, French Bulldogs, Great Danes, Maltese, Old English Sheepdogs, Boston Terriers, German Shepherd Dogs, Saint Bernards, Toy Poodles and Yorkshire Terriers. Registrations in the 1923 Stud Book were the heaviest yet, with seventy-four recorded.

The breed was beginning to move across the United States. Princess Montyglyon had moved to La Jolla, California, and new owners were showing elsewhere in that state.

Publicity for the breed was provided by A. H. Seeley when he wrote a feature article for the *American Kennel Gazette,* February 1925. This article was entitled "Dogs that See the Midnight Sun" and gave a history of the breed and a plea for research to aid in gathering more facts. As he stated, "The breed history was indeed lost in antiquity."

Mr. Seeley was killed in an automobile accident shortly thereafter, and many of his dogs were acquired by Mr. and Mrs. H. N. Pinkham for their Laika Kennels in Ipswich, Massachusetts. Among them was the famous Ch. Donerna's Barin. Mr. Pinkham, like Mr. Seeley was a sledding enthusiast and an avid believer in the working ability of the Samoyed. He wrote three feature articles for the *American Kennel Gazette:* July 1930, "The Dog Nobody Improved"; a series article in November and December 1930, "The Gamest Dogs in the World"; and in February 1932, "The Real Way to Raise Dogs."

Mr. Pinkham kept his dogs in the north woods and gave them immense runs of twenty acres. He retained the desired disposition in his dogs, and they were able to run together. The Laika Kennels' winter home was twenty miles from a traveled road, and all supplies were transported by dog team. These desired traits were brought to California in 1935 when Mrs. Agnes Mason of Sacramento went to the Pinkhams for Dasha of Laika, with the aim of breeding dogs with sledding ability, conformation and good Samoyed dispositions. Both the Pinkhams and Masons bred for show dogs that could work.

The most influential import in 1925 was Yukon Mit, imported by Morgan Wing, first Samoyed Club of America Delegate to the AKC. Mit passed his style and true Samoyed type to his get. His dominance in producing style, Barin's in improving coat and gait and Tobolsk's in establishing size gave American-bred Samoyeds of the type of the original expedition strains.

The mating of Yukon Mit to Barin's daughter, Nona of Donerna, produced the great Ch. Gorka. Gorka was the pet of Mrs. Horace Mann, who was urged to "support" a show with her eight-year-old dog. She walked off with the wins, including Best of Breed and Working Group First at the Trenton KC. Ch. Gorka ideally fulfilled the dual role of pet and show dog. Yukon Mit, mated to another Barin daughter, Nanci, owned by Catharine Quereaux, produced Ch. Mitboi, who belonged to Dr. and Mrs. William Bridges and Tarquin (who sired Ch. Tarquin II), owned by the Very Reverend Monsignor Robert F. Keegan.

The distinguished Yukon Mit and Barin lines were carried on through Tarquin, Ch. Tarquin II, Ch. Prince Igor, and Ch. Dobrynia in the kennels owned by Msgr. Keegan, who showed and bred Samoyeds from 1928 to 1948. Ch. Dobrynia, son of Ch. Norka's Lubiniey, was Best American-bred in the Working Group at the Westminster Kennel Club, 1936. Following the show, the *New York Times* reported, "Upon seeing the Samoyeds for the first time, there is no more beautiful dog in the world."

Msgr. Keegan was featured in the *American Kennel Gazette* in February 1937 in an article by Arthur Frederick Jones, which pictured his dogs, kennels and home in the Adirondack Mountains. Msgr. Keegan was a believer in raising dogs in the natural state and never kept them in heated buildings.

By 1929, the breed had arrived at some semblance of solidarity, and the *American Kennel Gazette* stated, "The growth of the breed has been both conservative and constant, and augurs well for the future. The Samoyed is an established fixture in American dog circles, and becoming more popular in the right direction for the future of the breed."

The first Specialty of the parent Samoyed Club of America was held with the Tuxedo Kennel Club show in September 1929. An early summation of the progress of the breed was given by Louis Smirnow, first club president, before his judging of the Specialty:

The progress of the breed depends largely on careful breeding. Those of us who have seen Samoyeds know we are apt to see some specimens shorter in body than others, and unless a short-bodied Samoyed is bred to a longer-bodied one, the results will be undesirable from the viewpoint of the Standard of the breed.

A careful breeder will try to eliminate the various faults of his dogs by breeding to a dog who is strong in the characteristics that this breeder is endeavoring to correct.

Occasionally we see an excellent dog, big boned, excellent coat, proper size with a small head. Precautions should be taken to breed a dog of this type to one where the head condition will be improved.

The real champions in England and the old champions in this country, such as Tobolsk, Olga of Farningharn and Nico of Farningham, all had fine heads. Unless a champion has a real, true head there cannot be the proper expression, which is a very strong point in the beauty of the Samoyed.

The fact that a breeder may have 20 dogs among which are a half-dozen bitches and three or four studs is no reason why this breeder should not endeavor to breed outside his kennel, if by so doing, the proper characteristics will be had. It seems to me and to some of the old timers that too much stress is being laid on size. I need hardly emphasize the fact that the large dog lacking other features will not do as well in the ring as the smaller dog with good head. One of the largest dogs ever bred in the history of the breed is Snow Crest of English fame. I have seen many photographs and read many discussions of this dog, but he was too long in the muzzle for me; his head has the appearance of a Collie. Yet the owner of this dog, by careful breeding, bred the finest champions of English fame. [*Author's Note:* The breeder referred to was Miss Thomson-Glover.]

This first Specialty had an entry of forty for Mr. Smirnow's judgment. With only forty Samoyeds registered between 1906 and 1920, such a large entry less than a decade later was remarkable. Tiger Boy of Norka, owned by the Reids, only three weeks in America from England and reported by Miss Thompson-Glover as taller than most English dogs, made his debut and was Best of Breed.

People as well as great dogs are needed to weld a breed together. Such a person was Mrs. Catharine S. Quereaux of New York. She took up the breed in 1926 and by 1929 was enthusiastically collecting pedigrees and breed information. As the parent club secretary and publicity director,

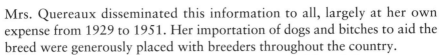

Mrs. Quereaux disseminated this information to all, largely at her own expense from 1929 to 1951. Her importation of dogs and bitches to aid the breed were generously placed with breeders throughout the country.

Mrs. Quereaux wrote a history of the Samoyed breed that was never published in its entirety. Parts of this, titled "Dog of the Ages," appeared in a few magazines and club bulletins, but the complete twenty chapters were still unprinted at her unexpected death in 1952. For many years, her columns in the *American Kennel Gazette* aided owners. With permission of Mrs. Serena A. Bridges, her sister, the authors were given access to Mrs. Quereaux's files when first compiling the early history for this book.

In the late twenties, Miss Elizabeth Hudson, an enthusiast since 1908, visited Russia. She reported, "There were no Samoyed dogs in Moscow or Leningrad, nor could I get any information about the breed. All apparently had disappeared in the Revolution. Undoubtedly, if the breed is preserved in Russia it was in the original habitat, with the Samoyed tribes." She brought back with her from England the influential Ch. Storm Cloud in 1929. Storm Cloud, was by Ch. Sea Foam out of Ch. Vara. He too, was reported taller than most in England and weighed slightly more than sixty pounds. In America, he became the sire of Ch. Tucha, owned by Mrs. Helen Harris.

Later (1939), out of the great bitch Morina of Taimir, he sired Vida of Snowland, the foundation bitch for Mrs. Harris's Snowland Kennels. Ch. Storm Cloud won the second parent club Specialty, held in 1930 at the Morris and Essex show.

Early in the 1930s, Mrs. Helen Harris began her famous Snowland Kennels at Merion, Pennsylvania, by importing Pedlar of the Arctic. She and her daughter were on a trip to Europe, and in a park in London they became acquainted with a Samoyed dog. Her daughter, Faith, simply "had to have

Mrs. Ivy Kiburn-Morris and "Polar Bru" swimming in the waters off Hong Kong in 1940.

Morina of Taimir (1933–48), bred in England by Miss E. Creveld and chosen by Miss Thomson-Glover to be sent to Miss Elizabeth Hudson in the United States. The dam of Vida of Snowland (by Storm Cloud), she had a strong influence on the breed.

one," so Pedlar was obtained. Unfortunately, this puppy contracted distemper, and blindness resulted. That did not prevent Pedlar from enjoying a full and long life until 1942. The stories of the other dogs acting as his "seeing eye" are amazing; he seemed to rule the sighted dogs. Another trip to England followed, and Mrs. Harris purchased Sabarka of Farningham and tried valiantly but unsuccessfully to obtain Kara Sea from Mrs. Edwards. In 1936, Mrs. Harris returned to England for a puppy of Ch. Kara Sea. This is the event that put so much of the bloodline of Ch. Kara Sea into America. Mrs. Harris requested a litter by Kara Sea and Pinky of Farningham. Due to the age of Kara Sea, thirteen years at the time, it required some discussion. She agreed to take the entire litter home to America. The entire litter

A group of notable champions at Snowland Kennels: Ch. Siberian Nansen of Farningham of Snowland (a Kara Sea son) and Chs. Nim, Nalda, Nadya and Norna, all of Snowland. Nim, Nadya and Norna were from the famous *N* litter by Nansen out of Vida of Snowland.

consisted of two, Siberian Nansen of Farningham of Snowland and his litter sister, Martyska of Farningham. Both were brought to America, but the bitch died at an early age. Nansen proved to be a great stud dog. He sired many champions, even at the age of eleven years. Thus, we find Ch. Kara Sea on the paper of modern pedigrees spanning twenty-four years. Included in his later progeny were Ch. Pinsk of Snowland, owned by the Ralph Oateys, and Ch. Staryvna of Snowland, owned by the authors. These dogs were showing as late as the 1950s. This is truly a remarkable time span in dog bloodlines.

PEDIGREE STUDY—CH. STARYVNA OF SNOWLAND

This is an explanation of the following pedigree. After importing several dogs from England, among them her foundation bitch, Vida of Snowland, Helen Harris chose a breeding she wanted. This was Ch. Kara Sea, (then thirteen years) out of Pinky of Farningham, because she could not obtain Ch. Kara Sea from Mrs. Edwards. In 1936, she brought home the entire litter as agreed. They were the dog Ch. Siberian Nansen of Farningham of Snowland and his sister Martyska of Farningham. This put her Snowland stock only four generations from the expedition dogs in Pennsylvania through the dominance of Ch. Siberian Nansen of Farningham who luckily was a great stud.

Behind Antarctic Buck there was no record. Behind Kviklene was Nansen and Pearlene to the expedition dogs, Musti and Whitey Pechora, and Russ and Kvik. Behind Houdin and Ayesha there were no records.

Antarctic Bru (pictured) was by Southern Cross out of Zemla who were expedition dogs. The dog Sam was given to W. Lavallin Puxley (whose book on the breed appeared in London in 1934).

Snowland Kennels' Vida was sired by Ch. Storm Cloud out of Morina of Taimir (pictured), providing an excellent combination of these English bloodlines for America.

Our super pedigree sleuth and recorder, Jim Osborn, has composed an in-depth report with respect to foundation stock for the breed. For instance, it quantifies the relationship of Samoyed X to say Antarctic Buck or whoever. Jim Osborn says, "The Samoyed breed is most similar among the stock in the UK, America, Canada, Australia, and New Zealand." Jim estimates "about 25 to 30 total dogs may be called foundation stock and those are the earliest imports. Beyond that we have no record."

Jim went on to say, "There is little, if any, true recording in Russia as culturally they have a far different attitude towards purebred dogs than we do." Jim asks the provocative question, "Can you tell the early American-bred dog (say before the fifties) that had the most influence on the Samoyed breed?"

In 1947 Ch. Starvyna of Snowland, a Ch. Kara Sea granddaughter, became the first bitch to win the SCA National Specialty. Starvyna was acquired by the Wards from Helen Harris.

Ch. Siberian Nansen of Farningham of Snowland

- Ch. Kara Sea
  - Moustan of Farningham
    - Southern Cross
      - Antarctic Buck
      - Kviklene
    - Hecla
      - Houdin
      - Pearlene
  - Ch Zahrina
    - Ch. Zahra
      - South Pole
      - Ch. Voltchitsa
    - Frona
      - Snowcloud
      - Ayesha
- Pinky of Farningham
  - Ch. Polar Light of Farningham
    - Polar Sea
      - Danmoos
      - Sasha
    - Ch. Snowy
      - Antarctic Bru
      - Antarctic Olga
  - No No Nanette
    - Ch. Siberian Keeno
      - Sam
      - Keena
    - Sheeba
      - Antarctic Bru
      - Muffit
        - Zero of the Arctic

Ch. Nalda of Snowland

    Ch. Sprint of the Arctic

        Ch. Snow Chief of the Arctic

            Ch. Tchita

        Ch. Silver Glow

            Ch. Leader of the Arctic

            Ch. Ice Crystal of the Arctic

    Ch. Siberian Nansen of Farningham of Snowland

        Ch. Kara Sea

        Pinky of Farningham

            Ch. Nadya of Snowland

            Ch. Storm Cloud

    Vida of Snowland

        Morina Taimir

        Dol of Snowland

        Mustan of Farningham

Ch. Norna of Snowland

    Ch. Siberian Nansen of Farningham of Snowland

        Ch. Kara Sea

            Ch. Zahrina

        Ch. Polar Light of Farningham

    Pinky of Farningham

        No No Nanette

            Ch. Sea Foam

    Vida of Snowland

        Ch. Storm Cloud

            Ch. Vara

        Morina of Taimir

            Siberian Shannon

            Desreena

Earlier, Mrs. Harris had purchased Vida of Snowland (Ch. Storm Cloud out of Morina of Taimir), Tucha of Snowland, Ch. Sprint of the Arctic and Ch. Moscow of Farningham of Snowland. When she bred Nansen to Vida, she had her remarkable N litter—Chs. Nim, Nadya, Norna, Nianya and Nikita. There is scarcely a Group-winning or Best in Show Samoyed that does not have one of these as an ancestor. These great examples of the breed were successfully shown by J. Nate Levine, the famous handler of Working Dogs.

The pride of Mrs. Harris's kennels, Ch. Nadya, in turn, became the dam of Ch. Novik of Snowland, owned by the Ruicks. Ch. Nianya of Snowland, owned by the Masons, became the dam of Chs. Chum, Cleo and Soldier Frosty of Rimini and was behind many, many other famous Pacific Coast champions.

Mrs. Harris once wrote to us of meeting a French painter named Jacques Suzanne while at Lake Placid, New York. He seemed to know the Samoyed breed well and said he had painted the dogs and horses of the late czar. He had traveled to Siberia and had something to say on the size of the Samoyed dog. He related that the majority of the native dogs were not as large or so beautiful as those resulting from the good grooming and feeding provided by our society. He believed that in their native habitat they were stunted by the infrequent feedings, because they varied in size, whereas the Samoyeds owned by the czar were all beautiful, big specimens. He presented Mrs. Harris with a picture of three puppies that came from the kennels of the czar.

Headlines in Boston on May 21, 1930, read "Famous Champion is Host to Byrd Dogs on Birthday." Ch. Donerna's Barin observed his tenth birthday surrounded by seven sons and four daughters and friends. Barin was pictured with Dinney and Torgnac, who served with Admiral Byrd's South Pole expedition.

Mrs. J. C. McDowell of La Crescenta, California, founded the Khiva Kennels in 1928 and for the next decade was active on the show scene. She imported Ch. Snow Frost of the Arctic, who in 1935—at seven years of age— became the first Samoyed on the Pacific Coast to win the Working Group. But it was Mrs. Agnes Mason with her skill in selecting bloodlines and organizing that gave the big push to Samoyed popularity there from the late 1930s through the 1950s.

Mrs. Mason, as a girl in Alaska, was very familiar with dogs because her father had sled teams. Renewing her work with dogs, in 1935 she purchased a Samoyed for her daughter, Aljean, from M. D. Robison of Oakland, California. He became Ch. Czar Nicholas Lebanov. His dam went back to Ch. Snow Frost of the Arctic and his sire was by Nico of Farningham. Mrs. Mason gathered breeding stock from many states and from England. Her English imports, Silver Spark of the Arctic (litter brother to Chs. Sport and Sprint of the Arctic) and Ch. White Way of Kobe, were imported in 1938. These added the bloodlines of Arctic and Kobe (through English Chs. Snow Chief of the

Arctic and White Fang of Kobe) to West Coast pedigrees. Further, she combined her West Coast and English bloodlines with an infusion of the Snowland Kennels of Pennsylvania by obtaining Ch. Nianya of Snowland. With the addition of Dasha of Laika from the Pinkhams, she had the best in American bloodlines.

Mrs. Mason and her daughter, Aljean Mason Larson, owned and finished fourteen champions and bred twenty-two champions. Many more would have finished except for her preoccupation with other activities and strong interest in sled work and sled races. She wanted to prove that show dogs had stamina and endurance and that sled dogs are not vicious. She succeeded at both.

Worldwide publicity came to the breed when the Masons' sled team of champion Samoyeds performed at the World's Fair on Treasure Island in San Francisco. Their daily performances encouraged much picture taking and exposure to the public. Further publicity occurred when the picture of Ch. Sprint of the Arctic, Ch. Moscow of Farningham of Snowland and Ch. Siberian Nansen appeared on the cover of *Western Kennel World*, which began a tradition of the Samoyed as the "Christmas Dog" on the cover each December.

The get of Ch. Tiger Boy of Norka were proving themselves in the East, because at Westminster in 1937 Winners Dog and Best of Breed was the four-and-a-half-year-old Norka's Viking (by Tiger Boy ex Norka's Dutochka). This dog was of the same large type as Ch. Norka's Moguiski, who won the 1938 parent club Specialty under the breeder-judge Msgr. R. F. Keegan, at the Morris and Essex show.

Contributions to the breed by Miss Juliet Goodrich were many and valuable. She not only imported, bred and showed, but also was a pioneer the field of study of hip dysplasia in the mid-1930s. Her Snow Shoe Hill Kennels was situated on 5,000 acres of beautiful woodland, complete with lakes, in Land O' Lakes, Wisconsin. Here the dogs Jack Frost of Snow Shoe Hill, her first, and Keena (by Ch. Kandalaska Yena of Marne) had runs of several acres each if they so desired.

When the new field of Obedience entered the dog shows in 1937, the first obedience-titled champion Samoyed, Ch. Alstasia's Rukavitza, CD, was owned by the well-known breeder-judge, Mrs. Anastasia MacBain of Ohio. Mrs. MacBain was a pioneer member and founder of the Inter-State Samoyed Club. Rukavitza won the 1941 parent club Specialty show at the Morris and Essex Kennel Club. He was shown forty-two times and won thirty-three Bests of Breed with thirteen Group placings.

The Inter-State Samoyed Club held the first separate Specialty show for the breed in 1938 on the Friday before the Western Reserve KC show. Ch. Jack Frost of Sacramento was Best of Breed.

Dogs very close in type to those from the American Snowland Kennels were developed by Mrs. Ruth Bates Young. She bred her Olga Pogi of Obi to

Natalie Rogers' import Ch. Sport of the Arctic, a brother to both Sprint and Spark of the Arctic. One of the puppies from this litter, Snow Chief, became the sire of the Poiriers' Int. Ch. Kola Snow Cloud of Loralee.

The year 1940 was a banner one for Samoyeds because they placed seventeen times in the Working Group. Three won Companion Dog degrees: the MacBains' Ch. Rukavitza, the Kroepils' Ch. Icy King Duplicate and the Burnettes' Polar Sea. The Western Reserve KC show, in Cleveland, Ohio, had an entry of fifty-six Samoyeds with eight champions. Mr. Harold Danks of Wisconsin had his sled team on exhibition at the show and gave children rides in the Cleveland auditorium.

With 1941 came the war years. Breeding and showing were curtailed, but some activity occurred. The pioneers—the Romers, the Reids, the Pinkhams, the Seeleys, Mercy Argenteau and the Van Heusens—were gone, but by this time the breed was reaching out to all parts of the country.

The Samoyed Club of the Pacific Coast held a Specialty in 1941 in conjunction with the Oakland Kennel Club. Best of Breed with an entry of forty-one was Agnes and Aljean Mason's Ch. Petrof Lebanof.

Bloodlines were beginning to reach back and forth across the land. Mrs. Perrin Wintz of Indiana bought a bitch from Mrs. McDowell, a double granddaughter of Ch. Snow Frost of the Arctic. She believed that bitches should be closer to the size of the males and owned the imported Ch. Kandalaska, who was twenty-two and a half inches tall, weighed sixty-eight pounds and carried a four-inch coat.

Wartime travel moved some other dogs around, a widening that greatly aided the breed. Captain and Mrs. Ashley were the breeders of a litter sired by Nikita of Snowland out of Ch. Nova Sonia of Kobe, which placed Ch. Echo of Kobe of Breezewood in Indiana. Then, while the Ashleys were stationed in Washington State, they bred Nikita with Niarvik of Inara, owned by Mrs. Edna McKinnon. This produced the males Sooltan and Am., Can. Ch. Snohomish of Oceanside, who began introducing new bloodlines in the Seattle area. Lewis and Claire Bajus in Milwaukee had the influential Ch. Yeinsei's Czar Nicholas II in their kennels. Their nephew, Joe Scott, brought Queen Senga of Lewclaire to the West Coast.

One of the outstanding sires of the breed appeared in 1943 and marked the introduction of the authors, Bob and Dolly Ward, to serious participation in the Samoyed fancy. The great sire was Ch. Starchak, CD (Ch. Herdsman's Chattigan ex Ch. Silver Star of White Way), bred by the Masons' White Way Kennels. "Chatter," as Starchak was affectionately called, was an outstanding winner of thirty-two Bests of Breed. He sired sixteen champions, was grandsire of over forty champions and won the parent club Stud Dog Trophy in 1956.

Chatter's mating with Ch. Starvyna of Snowland (personally selected for the Wards by Mrs. Helen Harris, and Best of Breed winner at the 1947 SCA Specialty) was to have an especially strong influence on the breed. Out of the

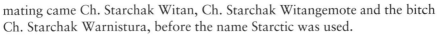

mating came Ch. Starchak Witan, Ch. Starchak Witangemote and the bitch Ch. Starchak Warnistura, before the name Starctic was used.

Witan sired, among others, Ch. Starctic Storm, who became implanted in hundreds of pedigrees through his son Ch. Kazan of Kentwood, and his grandsons, top-winning and producing Ch. Karshan and Ch. Sayan of Woodland.

Ch. Starchak's Warnistura, called Sissy, went to Mrs. Mason and produced Ch. White Way's Silver Streak, a multiple Group winner.

Ch. Starchak's Witangemote and Ch. Princess Startinda, a daughter of Ch. Starchak ex Princess Tina of Tonia, went to Mr. and Mrs. Kenneth Bristol of Thousand Oaks, California, and were the start of their Startinda Kennels. Witangemote sired a dozen champions; his mating with Startinda resulted in three champions in one litter: Talnik, Sarana and Chrinda. In 1956, Ch. Startinda's Talnik, handled by Lloyd Bristol, was second only to Ch. Yurok of Whitecliff as the top winning Samoyed on the West Coast. While very active in shows, the Startinda Samoyeds became best known in sled dog racing. For many years the Bristols entered two full teams of five to seven dogs in many races from Donners' Pass, California, to Williams, Arizona.

Another influential Starchak son was Ch. Rainier, which was bred by Miss Elizabeth Wyman and owned and trained by the authors. Ch. Rainier was the second Samoyed to win a Working Group on the Pacific Coast. His progeny included Int. Ch. MacGregor of Glenstrac, winner of four championships in Europe and the CACIB award.

Mrs. Pamela Rhanor had her Petsamo bloodlines carried on extensively when she sent Snow King of Petsamo to Mrs. Betty Arneson in Seattle in 1944. That same year, Tynda of Petsamo went to Mrs. Margaret Tucker and was the start of the famous Encino Kennels when she was bred to Ch. Starchak, CD to produce Ch. Kun To of Encino.

In the years 1939–43, an annual average of only about 195 all-breed and 150 Specialty shows were held. Today, there are more than 1,400 all-breed shows each year. In this connection, a point should be made that many fail to account for when discussing great winners. Before 1950, for a dog to win twenty or thirty Bests of Breed, it had to be a flyer and shown extensively. For example, Eng. Ch. Kara Sea had twenty-two Challenge Certificates and was a hallmark of the breed. Am. Ch. Donerna's Barin, a pillar in America, had only approximately nine Bests of Breed in the 1920s. Ch. Alstasia's Rukavitza, UD earned thirty-three BBs in the late 1930s and early 1940s. Ch. Starchak CD obtained thirty-two BBs in the late 1940s. One must learn to judge any dog's record by the competition and the availability of shows at the time.

chapter 2

The Samoyed in Postwar America

1945-1975

Following the end of World War II, Samoyed enthusiasts had a new parent club structure to aid in protecting the breed. The club had expanded from an Eastern group into a national organization with three areas or divisions to promote more local activity and interest.

In 1946, Dr. William Ivens of Pennsylvania, who had been showing and breeding Samoyeds since 1937, imported Ch. Martingate Snowland Taz from England. On his arrival in America, Taz made a permanent impression on the breed on the East Coast.

Ch. Martingate Snowland Taz was selected personally for Dr. Ivens by Miss Thomson-Glover, through the efforts of Miss Ruth Stillman, who had been visiting in England. Imported at the age of two years, Taz enjoyed a glorious show career in his new home from 1946 to 1950, garnering fifty Bests of Breed in fifty-four outings, including four in succession (1946–49) at Westminster, three Group Firsts and nineteen other Group placements. In 1951, at age seven, Taz was purchased from Dr. Ivens by Mrs. Elma Miller of Elkenglo Kennels.

Taz brought much substance and heavier heads to many American bloodlines. He was in strong demand as a stud, siring twenty-eight champions, and was the grandsire of twenty-nine other champions. His mating with Mrs. Bernice E. Ashdown's Eng., Am. Ch. Princess Silvertips of Kobe produced a litter of five champions that included two Best in Show winners—Ch. Silver Spray of Wychwood and Ch. Silvertips Scion of Wychwood.

The 1947 Glendale (California) KC show had a special significance because it was agreed to test the AKC rule permitting the entry of champions in the Open class.

Ch. Martingate Snowland Taz, originally owned by Dr. William Ivens and later by Elma Miller, was an important sire and winner during the 1950s.

The Pacific Coast Division hosted the parent club SCA National Specialty with the Pasadena KC in June 1947 and the author's Ch. Staryvna of Snowland, by Ch. Siberian Nansen of Farningham of Snowland, a Ch. Kara Sea son, topped the entry of forty-seven, the beginning of multiple Best of Breed awards for bitches. It was a tremendous loss to the breed that Staryvna died so young from distemper—eighteen months after her litter by Starchak.

Not all dogs receive a Good Conduct Medal, but Soldier Frosty of Rimini (Ch. Petrof Lebanov ex Ch. Nianya of Snowland) was awarded his with the Victory Medal. Frosty was presented the medal in a ceremony at Camp Stoneman, California. During World War II, he was number P-254 in the K-9 Sled Dog Corps. He served in Attu, Iceland, and in Greenland as a lead dog to take supplies to marooned fliers. He left a mark as the sire of Ch. Omak, and thus the grandsire of the outstanding Ch. Yurok of Whitecliff.

1950-65

In the wake of the breed's first Best in Show in 1949, the Samoyed rose to great eminence in inter-breed competition in the 1950s. Spearheading this rise were the dogs of the Wychwood Kennel, owned by Mrs. Bernice B. Ashdown and trained and shown by Charles L. Rollins.

Although Mrs. Ashdown owned Samoyeds as far back as 1930, it was not until about ten years later, when she acquired Rimsky of Norka, that she became seriously interested in breeding and showing. Obedience Trials were then still in their infancy, and Wychwood became one of the pioneers and missionaries for that phase of the sport. Rimsky became the first champion UDT Samoyed.

With the importation of Eng. Ch. Princess Silvertips of Kobe in November 1949, the wins tally by Wychwood went into high gear. Instrumental in securing Silvertips for import to the United States was the eminent English breeder-judge, Miss J. V. Thomson-Glover, who considered her "probably the finest Samoyed in Great Britain today." Princess Silvertips had been undefeated in England with nine Challenge Certificates to her credit. She was embarked on her American show career in 1950, at just a few months short of her sixth birthday. After completing her championship, she was temporarily retired to rear what was to be a historic litter by Ch. Martingate Snowland Taz and then was returned to the ring in 1951 to begin her show career in earnest. Her American record included forty-eight Bests of Breed in forty-nine shows (the one defeat being to her daughter, Ch. Silvertips Saba of Wychwood), thirty-three Group placements, including fourteen Firsts and two Bests in Show. The first Best in Show, won at seven years of age, made her only the second in the breed to have gone BIS. Her second was won at nine years of age. Her winning is all the more remarkable when it is realized that her career was interrupted four times for the bearing of litters.

Ch. Silver Spray of Wychwood, one of the five champions born of the mating of Silvertips with Taz, established what was then a record for the breed with wins of five all-breed Bests in Show and a Best American-Bred in Show. Spray made his championship in just thirty-four days, finishing at but nine months of age. Undefeated in the breed after completing his title, he was Best Samoyed at Westminster four years in succession, matching the achievement of his great sire. He twice placed in the Group at Westminster.

In December 1956, Wychwood brought over another star. This was the young English Ch. Americ of Kobe. Americ's introduction to the American show rings in 1957 was most sensational. At his first show, he went from the Open class to Best in Show. This was followed by four successive Working Group Firsts, thus completing his championship undefeated by a Working Dog of any breed. In all, Americ was shown in the United States thirty-three times, was undefeated in the breed and scored twenty-nine Group placements, including nineteen Firsts and four Bests in Show.

The contribution of Wychwood in bringing the Samoyed to favorable all-breed attention was tremendous. Except for 1956, a Wychwood Samoyed was Best in Show in every year from 1951 to 1959, and in 1953 it was the only kennel of any breed in America to win Best in Show with three separate dogs. Much of this winning was done in a period of outstanding Working Group competition that included such all-time greats of their breeds as the Doberman Pinscher Ch. Rancho Dobe's Storm and the Boxer Ch. Bang Away of Sirrah Crest. In 1952, when Spray placed third in the Group at Westminster, Storm was first (and on to Best in Show), and Bang Away was second.

The 1950s were to see the establishment of another all-time great show record for the breed. In 1948, Mrs. Jean Blank of Fremont, California, began her career with Cheechako and Chumikan, completing their championships in 1949. She raised a few litters, and with Percy and Lena Matheron she co-owned Ch. Yurok of Whitecliff.

Rocky, as Yurok was known, was by Ch. Omak out of Kara Babkrah of White Frost. Handled exclusively by Mrs. Blank, Yurok was an outstanding dog and stayed in remarkable coat, which permitted continual campaigning.

Ch. Silver Spray of Wychwood.

Charles L. Rollins, Wychwood kennel manager, sends Ch. Rimsky of Norka, the breed's first UDT dog, in a broad jump composed of kennel mates Bettina, CD, Ch. Marina, CDX, and Ch. Ballerina, all of Wychwood.

In the five-year period from 1956 to 1960, he acquired 136 Bests of Breed, 98 Group placements, including 26 Firsts, and 5 all breed Bests in Show. Yurok's most monumental win was of Best in Show at Harbor Cities Kennel Club show in 1959, when judge Percy Roberts placed him tops in the entry of 2,500 dogs. It was Percy Roberts who, as a dog broker, had been instrumental in the pivotal importation of Tobolsk in 1920.

A combination of new breeders and owners, the lifting of prior limitations from the war years, and the holding of only three parent club Specialties since 1943 started a rebirth of Samoyed activity. Entries skyrocketed in southern California, which hosted the largest benched Specialty ever held for the Samoyed Club of America with an entry of 110 individual dogs at the Harbor Cities Kennel Club in 1950. After the show, the judge, Christian Knudsen, half jokingly said he hoped he would never see another white "fuzzy wuzzy" dog. The Best of Breed, Shirley Hill's Cinderella dog, Ch. Verla's Prince Comet, was placed fourth in the Working Group. Agnes and Aljean Mason's brace was second in the Working Brace at this 2,500 dog entry in the Long Beach Civic Auditorium. This twelfth Samoyed Club of America Specialty was a resounding success in both numbers and geography, drawing dogs from many parts of the country, plus England and Canada. Samoyed owners enjoyed a nationwide togetherness, seeing dogs and meeting owners from faraway places and talking with the 114 persons at the preshow banquet. This number was greater than the total ownership of twenty years before.

An unusual exhibition marked the thirteenth Specialty show of the parent club held at Bay Meadows Racetrack in California in 1952. Following the judging, twenty-five Samoyeds were taken off the bench to give a demonstration of sled work and races. Five teams competed in a short race with drivers: Tom Witcher with Ch. Vojak, UD, at lead; Bob Ward with Ch. Starchak, CD; Lloyd Van Sickle with Rex of White Way; Charles Burr with Ch. Nick of White Way; and Ken Bristol with Ch. Starchak's Witangemote. Each team consisted of five dogs. Later, an exhibition of a twenty-five-dog hookup was given with a Ford convertible as ballast. A specially selected team of fifteen was chosen for a demonstration for television and motion picture cameras. This team, led by Rex of White Way, including eight show champions, coursed the mile track, executing right and left turns and complete about turns.

Joining the list of proud owners of Samoyeds in this period were Major General Roderick Allen and his wife Maydelle. Their bitch, White Frosting, completed her championship at the 1953 Westminster show, and their Ch. Narguess of Top Acres was Best of Opposite Sex, ably handled by Len Brumby, Jr. The general also imported the English bitch Ch. Janet Jan Mayen.

Ch. Narguess of Top Acres came from a notable litter sired by Ch. Martingate Snowland Taz out of Ch. Sparkle Plenty of Arbee. This famous litter consisted of five sisters, named by the late Shah of Iran, who at that time was the house guest of Major General Allen, then stationed at Fort Knox, Kentucky. The shah said they should be named for lovely white flowers: Narguess or White Narcissus; Pratika or White Rose; Hadesse or White Myrtle; Yasmin or Jasmin; Sosanna or White Lily.

Narguess, Pratika and Hadesse became champions. Yasmin of Top Acres was taken to Japan. Ch. Narguess of Top Acres also went to Japan and whelped one litter there. Yasmin was returned to the States, where she whelped one litter sired by Ch. Bunky of Lucky Dee (Dawes).

In the mid-1950s, the Robert Bowles' Ch. Noatak of Silver Moon and Ch. Silver Moon won the Stud Dog Trophy and the Brood Bitch Trophy three years in a row. They are behind the Best in Show winners Ch. Sam O'Khan's Chingis Khan, Ch. Sam O'Khan's Tian Shan, Ch. Karasea's Silver Nikki, Ch. Karasea's Silver Kim and Ch. Maur-Mik's Kim. John and Lila Weir's breeding program with their "Happy," Ch. Tod-Acres Fang and Ch. Kobe's Nan-Nuk of Encino produced the influential Best in Show winner Ch. Joli Knika and his grandson Ch. Star Nika Altai of Silver Moon, a Best in Show winner in 1967.

The 1956 parent club Specialty, held at the Mason Dixon KC show, brought to light a winning dog that dominated Samoyed circles for the next four years. Judge Marie Meyer awarded Best of Breed to Ch. Nordly's Sammy, owned by Mr. and Mrs. John Doyle of Doylestown, Pennsylvania. Butch, as he was known, was sired by Mrs. Ashborn Ulfeng's Am., Can. Ch. Tazson out of Bluecrest Karenia and was a grandson of Ch. Martingate Snowland Taz. Ch. Nordly's Sammy won four parent club Specialties in succession in four sections of the nation.

Ch. Nordly's Sammy, owned by Mr. And Mrs. John Doyle, was four times BB at the SCA Specialty (1956–59).

A new era marking the end of the old system, by which the parent club had always held a Specialty show in conjunction with an all-breed show, began in 1964. Samoyed owner Richard Breckenridge was selected to be show secretary, assisted by Lloyd Bristol of the first SCA independent Specialty. They operated without a professional show superintendent. Show chairman was Robert Ward. The show was held on the beautifully landscaped grounds of the Mira Mar Hotel at Montecito, Santa Barbara, California. Albert E. Van Court judged the ninety-two entries, including twenty-one champions present. He chose the beautiful open bitch, Shondra of Drayalene, owned by Joe and Mable Dyer of Idaho, as Best of Breed.

The authors were proud to assist in the engineering of this breakthrough for separate Specialties for the Samoyed Club of America. Such an event had not taken place in the forty-one-year history of the club. The advantage of having the Specialty separate from an all-breed show is that it allows for the spotlighting of the breeding efforts and special events within the breed, such as Best Puppy and Best Bred by Exhibitor. A futurity or puppy sweepstakes is best when held with an individual Specialty show. Later, Agility, Herding and Weight Pulling were added to the events schedule. Best of all, a Samoyed is always Best in Show!

In 1965, Sharon Eggiman (later Hurst) began in Samoyeds. Her goal was to have "stars," so her kennel name was destined to be Orion—a star constellation. As so often happens, her first dog was a pet—lovable, but not a show dog as she learned when she attended a Sacramento KC dog show. By 1967, she found an ad for the James Samoyeds in Madera, and she was on her way. She "learned" to show her own dogs with the help of Wayne Nelson and Ray Brinlee, both successful professional handlers who were teaching handling classes in southern California at the time. Many years went by as well with one ex-husband who did not care for dogs. In 1976 she met Jim Hurst, and in two years he built them a fabulous home on forty acres in the Auburn foothills, where they raised horses, Angus cattle and, of course, Samoyeds.

Sharon went to Marilyn Gitelson for her next Sam, Sansaska's Mishka II of Orion. The Hursts toured the shows in their progressively larger, more magnificent motor homes.

Since they loved Samoyeds, the Hursts (like Johnny Appleseed) shared their love with many, some who wanted only pets and some whom they helped show their dogs. The Orion impact still lives through the wins of its "puppy people."

It was about 1988 when Sharon and Jim first saw the soon-to-be-champion, Polar Mist Law Breaker II, and they contracted to purchase a puppy out of Lynette Hansen's next repeat breeding. They later took "Bud Light" home, and he was a *De Lite*. Several years later Bud had a most impressive show career, including several all-breed Bests in Show.

When Bud was three, the Hursts campaigned him in earnest. He finished seventh in 1990 and went on to defeat 1,792 dogs of all breeds at Santa Cruz in August 1991. That was his year—Top winning Samoyed in the United States, all systems, and Top Stud. The Hursts were *SQ*'s (*Samoyed Quarterly*) Top Breeders in 1989 and again in 1993.

Tom Weems and Robin Gowen organized the support needed to have a statue commissioned for the Hursts from a photograph of their Am., Can., Mex., Int. Ch. Orion's Bud Light of Polar Mist, by a waterfall. The statue is spectacular and will be treasured by the Hursts forever.

1966-75

By 1965, interest had grown to such strength that there were three parent club Specialties in 1965, two in 1966 and three again in 1967, whereas there had been only ten in the first twenty-five years of the SCA.

In 1965, the American Kennel Club enthusiastically suggested a new constitution and a revised organizational setup of the SCA, deleting the division structure, to allow more local activity. It was felt that information and education on the breed could be more effectively provided at the local level.

Accordingly, the members reorganized into a structure that retained the parent SCA as a member club of the AKC, with the provision that many independent local clubs—each with their own exclusive territory—could be formed and could hold AKC-licensed matches and, eventually, full-fledged Specialty shows.

Under the Division structure, everyone had belonged to the parent club. Now, under the new structure, local club members did not automatically become members of the SCA.

The first president under the new structure, in February 1969, was author Robert Ward. There were four vice presidents: Tom Tuttle, Clifford Collins, Donald Hodges and Anne Snee. Nancy Alexander was secretary, Lila Weir was treasurer and Peggy Borcherding was publicity director. Mrs. Margaret Tucker was named honorary president.

The first years of the change were turbulent ones. Some groups tried to hold on to the past and to the power they had enjoyed as SCA Divisions. Unfortunately, the growth did not develop as the AKC had expected.

Started in 1955 by John and Anne Butler, the San Diego club has included many active fanciers among its members throughout the years, and it continues to hold annual Specialties.

Beginning in the late 1960s and developing even more so in the 1970s and 1980s, we again have kennels owning five to twenty dogs. Perhaps a reason for this trend was the enactment of restrictive anti-dog laws of many large metropolitan areas, moving dog owners out to where larger kennels were not only more feasible, but also legally permitted.

Joanne Marineau's (Antares) first brood bitch was Larissa of Taymylyr, acquired from Tom and Margi Tuttle. The Tuttles also bred her mother, Ch. Holly of Taymylyr, and a son, Ch. Ivan Belaya of Taymylyr, CD, from their Ch. Trina of Taymylyr, sired by Ch. Kazan of Kentwood, and thus in a direct line to Ch. Starctic Storm.

In 1973, the Marineaus bred Larissa to Ch. Midnight Sun Kimba, owned by Kathy Horton and Art Mondale. From this breeding, they kept Antares Tatiana and sold her sister, Great Sitkin's Midnight Magic, to Dick and Chris Higley for their breeding program.

The Samoyed Club of Los Angeles was the remnant of the former Pacific Coast Division of the Samoyed Club of America (the other remnant was the Nor-Cal Samoyed Club licensed in 1982). It was organized into an independent club in 1966, when the AKC required the SCA to eliminate its four divisions. The first SCLA independent Specialty was held with the California Associated Specialty Clubs at Inglewood Racetrack in September 1968, and there has been an annual SCLA Specialty ever since.

A spectacular national SCA Specialty was held in September 1969 at Thousand Oaks, California. The show was acclaimed by many to be a model for separately held Specialties. A splendid entry of ninety-four (including fourteen champions) competed under breeder-judge Joyce Cain. Best of Breed, scoring his fourth Specialty win and tying Ch. Nordly's Sammy's record, was Bob and Evelyn Kites' Ch. Sayan of Woodland, handled by Jim Manley.

A major highlight of the show was the first publication, by the parent club, of a catalog that incorporated the breed history; the official Illustrated Standard; drawings, including the authors' "Fault Finders," pictures of great Samoyeds of past and present representing bloodlines from coast to coast; and a directory of all local clubs. This catalog is universally considered a collector's dream.

In 1969, the SAC published an *Illustrated Standard of the Breed*, prepared by Mrs. Gertrude Adams and her committee after more than twenty years of discussion. This work was dedicated to Mrs. Agnes Mason, White Way Samoyeds, who first promoted the "illustrating" idea in 1948—a true forerunner of the AKC policies during the 1990s.

The SCLA Specialty was approved to offer Obedience Trial classes, and this privilege was transferred to the Samoyed Club of America when the SCA National Rotating Specialty was held in the East, West, Midwest and Northwest. An added region to provide for the South took effect in 1985.

The SCLA was the first club to initiate the Tournament event. It was this club that gave the parent club the idea of holding the Futurity, designed to encourage better breeding. The breeder nominates a planned litter and then (before the litter reaches age four months) selects the most promising puppies to be shown at the next SCA Specialty, wherever it may be in the United States. Winners are judged by a special judge—usually a breeder—in the competition at the "National," and money prizes go to the puppy owners (who do not necessarily have to be the breeders themselves).

The SCLA Specialty always includes a Sweepstakes event, which, again, is usually judged by a breeder approved by the parent club and the AKC specifically for the event. It is open to puppies from six to eighteen months in age, and winners receive trophies, rosettes and prize money divided per the rules of the day. Its purpose is also to encourage better breeding. What could be more delightful than a ring full of puppies, competing according to their ages? Usual classes for both dogs and bitches are six to nine months, nine to twelve months, twelve to eighteen months, a final Best and Best of Opposite Sex in Sweepstakes. These same exhibits are also entered in the regular classes of the same Specialty show.

SCLA activities, as with most independent Specialty Samoyed clubs, include meetings with suitable programs, social events, practice matches and BOB matches with obedience. Now Agility, Therapy, Herding and Temperament Testing and CGC (Canine Good Citizenship) are included.

One of the most productive achievements during Jim Osborn's presidency was the making of a film to educate fanciers about the breed. Cameramen were Jim and Ken Berry, the commentator was Carol Chittum and assisting in a myriad of tasks were Marian Osborn and Marie Berry. Six Samoyeds (three males, three bitches) were judged for the camera by AKC judges Howard Dullnig, Lowell Davis and Robert Ward, who then commented on "why" they had placed the dogs 1-2-3. The film was shown at the seminar held in Denver for the SCA National Specialty in 1984.

In the 1960s, the partnership Kondako was formed. It included Connie (Kon) and Dave (Da) Richardson and Company (Ko) and was located in Maryland. One of their first bitches was Ona Negra's Silver Bunny who was bred to Ch. Silveracres Nachalnik in 1968. The litter produced Ch. Kondako's Dancing Bear (Ruff), who became the titular head of Kondako. You will find him in pedigrees from coast to coast. Kondako bred excellent stock and were formidable competitors in the West as they had been in the East.

Between 1966 and 1980, Kondako produced seventeen homebred champions through five generations and were breeding participants in creating some fifty-three or so champions, before parting "Kompany" agreeably and putting the whole United States between them.

Dr. Mary Ellen and Joe Torrez started their Statussam Kennels with Tasha of Snowflower (from Carmen Way) and bred her to Ch. Kondako's Rising Sun to give them the two males they kept—Ch. King Kody of Kondako and Ch. Statussam's Troublemaker—and their bitch, Ch. Statussam's Lollipop. The well-known professional handler Cheryl Cates handled their dogs. Mrs. Torrez died of cancer in 1996 and was greatly mourned by the fancy.

Sansaska Samoyeds came into being when Derek and Marilyn Gitelson acquired their first show dog in 1972. She became Ch. Norgemar O'Khan's

Milka, a Specialty Winners Bitch, multiple breed winner and dam of two champions. Since then, Sansaska has bred and owned more than fifty titlists. Notable among them are Ch. Sansaska's Treasure Chest, UD, HIC, CGC, Top Obedience Samoyed for five years; Ch. Sansaska's Mark of Evenstar, BISS at the SCLA 1984 Specialty, three-time Specialty Stud Dog winner and multiple Group placer; Ch. Sansaska's Omarsun of Orion, BIS, BISS and a Top Ten Samoyed; Ch. Sansaska's Mishka II of Orion, Top Brood Bitch; and Ch. Sansaska's Shakti, Best Veteran SCLA 1996, Award of Merit SCLA 1996 and multiple BB winner. The most recent stars at Sansaska were Ch. Sansaska's Wildflower and Sansaska's Black Tie Optional, SCLA 1996 Best Puppy in Specialty; and the youngest is Wildflower's daughter, Evening at the Pops.

The 1970 parent Specialty SCA National was hosted by the Washington State Samoyed Club and established a then record-high of 150 entries (122 actual dogs). Judge Joseph Faigel selected Ch. Darius Karlak Cheetal, handled by owner Dan Morgan, as Best of Breed (BISS).

Some Regional Club Activity

The Samoyed Club of Washington State, Inc., was founded as the Northwest Division in 1952 by the Collinses, the Gleasons and the Beals. The Stefaniks joined in 1959, and in 1964 Joyce and Joe Johnson were typed on the roster. The club was licensed to give independent Specialties in 1968. On August 16, 1969, SCWS held its first Specialty (with the Olympic KC); the forty-seven entries were judged by Kurt Mueller, and Best of Breed was Ch. Lulhaven's Nunatat, owned by Clyde Lulhaven and Sonny White. The club hosted the annual rotating SCA Specialty in 1956, 1965, 1970, 1974, 1978, 1982 and 1996, affectionately dubbed the "Northwest Expedition."

By the 1970s it had become apparent to Samoyed breeders in the Northwest that hereditary eye disease in the form of Progressive Retinal Atrophy (PRA) was a problem threatening the breed. "Vision for the Future" was the theme of the Forty-third National Specialty, which the SCWS hosted in 1974. SCWS also sponsored an in-depth Eye Research Project under the direction of Paul V. Dice III, VMD, MS. Rosemary Jones and the late Ethel Stefanik were co-chairs. The results of the research were published in the September 1979 SCA Bulletin. SCWS remains a supporting member of the Canine Eye Research Foundation, Inc. (CERF).

Northern California Samoyed Fanciers began as a social group in 1962. To encourage interest in the breed, NCSF conducted matches and clinics for nine years and in 1973 hosted the SCA Specialty, held at San Leandro, California.

In 1981 this active group became a licensed Specialty club and held its first show on March 21, 1981. Dr. Malcolm Phelps judged and awarded the top prize to the Merrill Evans' Ch. Di Murdock of Seelah.

The Northern California Samoyed Fanciers produced the *Prologue to the Samoyed,* which contained many helpful articles on grooming, breeding and general care of the Samoyed.

A club is fortunate when it has a "steady" member in its ranks so that no matter who comes and goes, the club goes on. Such a person is La Vera Morgan (Darius) in Northern California. Her late husband, Dan, was memorialized as a breeder judge. Others who are currently assisting the NCSF are Joan and Paula Luna, the Walt Kauzlarichs, Evelyn Coloma, the Gitlesons, Ed Altamarino, Kathryn Molineaux, Wilna Coulter and Bonnie Giffin.

The amazing story of a problem they encountered was related to us by Harold:

> We had a breeding problem for many years at this location. Lots of years we sold from three to ten puppies all year. Our puppies became champions but we did not have many puppies to sell. We finally cleared up the breeding problem by hauling all drinking water for the dogs all the way from Denver. Our well water is so pure that it has no trace minerals. You do not produce animals without trace minerals. Today we have large healthy litters. Same breeding stock, just different water.

The dog who was to become the shining star at Silveracres was Ch. Nachalnik of Drayalene (whelped September 16, 1961). "Chief," who was acquired at the age of nine months from Helene Spathold, a breeder-judge, became the top Samoyed sire in the history of the breed with forty-five champion offspring—a total that stood as the all-time record in the breed until 1984. Ch. Ice Way's Ice Breaker literally broke the ice with 142 champions! The McLaughlins also obtained Ch. Cnejinka from Helene Spathold, before her suicide, and she and Nachalnik formed the foundation stock from which they linebred and inbred to develop the Silveracre line.

Jane and Alan Stevenson began with their interest in Samoyeds in 1966 with Samovar of the Igloo, who won the first SCLA Specialty in 1968 and completed his CDX as well. Inspired with success, they purchased their foundation bitch from Skip and Nancy Alexander, Snoline's Joli Shashan. From that breeding they kept Troika who, when bred to Ch. Kondako's Sun Dancer, produced Jack Feinberg's Ch. Northwind's Running Bear.

Running Bear carried the winning banner in the east and in World Shows with Jack Feinberg. During this time the Stevensons concentrated on raising their family. For fifteen years the dogs held a secondary position until they bought a Samoyed from Hoof 'n Paw in 1988. By 1990 they made him Ch. Hoof 'n Paw's Knight Drifter who was in the top five Sams for four years, winning two BISS and an all-breed BIS, and handled by owner Alan Stevenson usually wearing a red jacket! Drifter became the sire of Oakbrook's Panning For Gold (Digger). Digger won the Grand Futurity at the 1995 SCA National in Austin, Texas, under breeder-judge Connie Konopisos.

Father and son—Am., Int. Ch. Hoof 'n Paw's Knight Drifter, at 1992 National with the future Ch. Oakbrooks Panning for Gold, "Digger" at eleven weeks, owned by Jane and Alan Stevenson.

Pat Morehouse has been a supporter of the breed for twenty years. One of her early champions was Ch. Icelandic Princess Zoe, sired by Ch. Kazan of Kentwood. In 1967 she acquired a male puppy from Mrs. Fitzpatrick, from a repeat breeding of Ch. Noatak of Silver Moon ex Ch. Sam O'Khan's Tsari of Khan. The puppy became Ch. Sam O'Khan's Kubla Khan, and Kubla Khan became the name of Mrs. Morehouse's kennel.

The Aladdin Samoyeds, owned by Joe and Joyce Johnson from Washington State, have contributed importantly to the breed in the Northwest. Ch. Aladdin's Dominator consistently placed in the Top Ten of current winning Samoyeds and in September 1984 was BB at the Washington State Specialty.

The first champion for Polar Mist Samoyeds, owned by Lynette Hansen, was Ch. McKenzies Polar Mist Nikke, in 1965. She was a granddaughter of Ch. Rokandi of Drayalene. This produced Am., Can. Ch. Pepsi Kola of Polar Mist, who became the dam of the Best in Show winner, Ch. Polar Mist Dr. Pepper.

Lynette decided that since she lived in such a remote area, her dogs needed to have greater exposure. So after Polar Mist's Dr. Pepper scored WD at the 1979 SCA National, she formed a partnership with John and Kathleen Ronald. John Ronald then went on to handle Dr. Pepper to wins in the 1980s that have made him the top owner-handled Samoyed winner to date. Am., Can.,

Bah. Ch. Polar Mist's Dr. Pepper's record included 13 all-breed Bests in Show, 8 Bests in Specialty and 144 Group placements, all owner-handled. In 1984, he won the Canadian National Specialty under Thelma Brown. All this was during the period when the Working and Herding breeds were all classified in the Working Group. Lynette Hansen added "Blue" to her name as well as her dogs' win record when she married her veterinarian, Dr. Roger Blue. Lynette Hansen-Blue has bred 103 Polar Mist champions, mostly American champions, with some achieving Canadian, Mexican and International titles. Polar Mist is also the breeder of five Best in Show winners, a Top producing stud and three Top brood bitches. One, Am., Can. Ch. Polar Mist Ain't She Foxy, who we believe still holds the record for the most American champions produced—fifteen plus two Canadian champions.

There have been some exports to Europe and Japan to be incorporated into breeding programs in those countries.

Lynette considers herself a "structure nut" with a goal to breed for sound structure with superior movement, reach and drive and with clean fronts and rears. She aims for a Samoyed that is also pleasing to the eye and is a good example of the breed Standard. Over the years she has sought the best dogs to incorporate into her breeding program that could strengthen those qualities.

An influential stud has been Am., Can., Bah. Ch. Polar Mist Dr. Pepper (thirteen BIS), which she bred, sire of thirty-five champions and a couple of Best in Show winners. Both Dr. Pepper and Breaker are behind the 1994 and 1995 SCA National Specialty Winners Bitches, as well as Ch. Wolf River's Drumlin. Drumlin contributed good things to the Polar Mist line, and the latest stud dog that Lynette discovered as a young champion was Ch. Winterfrost's Gyrfalcon, which has sired some winners that produce pretty heads.

Lynette Hansen-Blue has also been active in the obedience ring, having bred a couple of High in Trial winners, a *Dog World* award winner and one dog with a Tracking title. Her plans are to continue with her breeding program. At this writing she has been granted approval as an AKC judge.

Jack Price and, as he calls them, his "backyard dogs" live at Bubbling Oaks and for the most part in the house, according to wife Amelia. The Prices firmly believe that their dogs must be trained and socialized to be a success in life and in the show ring.

Star of the kennel has been Am., Can. Ch. Bubbles LaRue of Oakwood. Bubbles won the 1975 Potomac Valley Specialty over an entry of 205. In 1978, handled by Joy Brewster, she was Best of Breed at Westminster and went on to second in the Group, a rare feat for a Samoyed bitch. She won the SCA award for Top Winning Bitch that year.

Don Hodges, the Samoyed Club of America's past delegate to the American Kennel Club, with his wife Dot, began Kipperic Samoyeds in 1968.

Ch. Los Laika's Belaya Traicer (Snow Ridge Ruble of Tamarack ex Ch. Belaya Anja Padrushka) was a noted winner and producer. He was the Great-Great Grandsire of Ch. Quicksilver's Razz Ma Tazz. *Joan Ludwig*

In 1970, the Hodges obtained two females. One, by Ch. Saroma's Polar Prince and bred by Charles and Evelyn James, became Ch. Kipperic D'Lite of Frost River. The other, bred by Mel and Miriam Laskey, became Am., Can. Ch. Kipperic Kandu of Suruka Orr, CD. Kandi was by Ch. Nachalnik of Drayalene ex Ch. Kuei of Suruka Orr, CD.

Kandi was BB at the 1973 National under Phil Marsh. Later she won two BIS and was Top Winning Samoyed for 1974. She was BB at Westminster in 1975 and became top producing Samoyed in the 1979 *Kennel Review* system.

The next standard-bearer for the Hodges was the BIS-winning Am., Can. Ch. Nordic's Wynter Sunniglo, co-owned with breeder Gail Mathews and her parents, Leroy and Betty Anderson. Sunniglo was BB at the 1978 National in Portland under Derek Rayne and then went on to BIS at the Vancouver, Washington, show that same weekend.

The third Kipperic all-breed BIS and Specialty winner, Ch. Kipperic Heritage Heroine (Phoebe), made the headlines in 1988 and was BOS at the National the same year. She won the SCA Award for Top winning Bitch in the United States in 1989 and three other Specialties during her career. Her sire, Ch. Kipperic Jaksun, sired the 1987 National BISS and BIS, Ch. Windsong's Classic Composer (Bach), and Ch. Kipperic Sparksun, a Westminster and Specialty winner. Sparksun, in turn, sired another all-breed BIS winner, Ch. Kipperic Flashback, owned by Patricia Nino Roca in Columbia who showed him to titles and wins in several countries.

The Hodges' most recent Specialty winner, Ch. Kipperic Sunny Peterson topped all comers at the 1993 Greater Milwaukee Samoyed Fanciers event. Sunny is now owned by Joyce Eiler in the state of Washington.

Altogether, the Hodges have owned or bred fifty-nine Champions and seventeen Group placers, six of whom have won Specialties or all-breed Bests, or both, in show.

Am., Can. Ch. Nordic Wynter Sunniglo (Tsuilikagta's Wynterwynd ex Ch. Nordic's Ketsie Tu) BB at the 1978 SCA National Specialty under judge Derek Rayne, handler Don Hodges. Duvella Kusler, SCA president, presents the trophy. An all-breed BIS winner, Sunni was bred by Dick and Gail Mathews and co-owned by Mrs. Mathews with the LeRoy Andersons and Don Hodges.

In 1972, on their way to Westminster, the authors attended the famous Crufts Dog Show in the old Olympia Building, London, England. There we spotted a young dog being shown by his owner, Gerald Mitchell, that was a "dead ringer" for our Ch. Starchak of thirty years before. Even his pedigree approximated Starchak's; that is, one-half Snowland, one-quarter Arctic and one-quarter old Kobe. Of course he was not for sale.

Returning to the United States, we counted all of the Challenge Certificates that had been awarded to Samoyeds from 1950 to 1970 and realized that 83 percent had been awarded to ancestors in his pedigree. While such statistics do not guarantee champions, it does increase the chances. (Challenge Certificates are not easily acquired. All champions are shown in the Open Dog class, and not all shows are accredited for CCs.)

We returned six weeks later to judge at the Golden Jubilee of the Irish Kennel Club (on St. Patrick's Day!) and afterward went to Chesterfield, England, determined to talk the Mitchells out of their young dog, Kiskas Karaholme Cherokee, "Painter." This time we succeeded, and Painter was exported a few months later at age eighteen months. Sired by Cavalier of Crensa ex Lisa of Crownie, Painter had been bred by Mr. and Mrs. Tom Stamp. His sire, Cavalier, was not shown much but was a litter brother of

Ch. Kiska's Karaholme Cherokee, owned by Robert and Dolly Ward, was imported from Gerald and Kathy Mitchell in England. "Painter" became an important stud force in the American gene pool and was SCA Top Stud Dog in 1980.

Ch. Grenadier of Crensa, whose tally of forty-three Challenge Certificates stood as an all-time record for the breed in England until the 1990s when Jim Dougal's Scottish Samoyed, Ch. Hurkurs Jingles, broke the old record.

Painter's bloodlines were dominant through three sons, Ch. Ice Way's Ice Crush, Ch. Ice Way's Ice Breaker, and Am., Mex. Ch. The Hoof 'n Paw White Knight. All three became Best in Show and major Specialty winners.

A Painter daughter, Ch. Starctic Aukeo, was Best of Opposite Sex at the SCA National Specialty in 1978 in an entry of more than 300 under Derek Rayne. Aukeo is the "cover girl" on the second edition of our book.

Painter sired his last litter at the age of twelve and a half years, as did his father and uncle in England. He passed on in his sleep at the age of fourteen years, never sick a day in his life!

Ice Way began in the spring of 1969 with the purchase of a Samoyed puppy that became the foundation bitch, Ch. Powered Puff of the Pacific, for Bobbie Smith. Puff's dam was by Ch. Barceia's Shondi of Drayalene and was out of a Ch. Rokanki of Drayalene daughter. Puff was a very beautiful bitch with excellent coat quality, good structure and outstanding show-manship. With her style and ring presence she could dominate a large class of dogs.

Ice Way's Ice Cube exemplified the qualities admired and maintained at Ice Way. With good length of neck, good length of upper arm and a shoulder layback that approximates 45 degrees, Cubie established herself as one of the outstanding movers in the history of her breed. Fortunately, Cubie not only possessed outstanding qualities, but also was a bitch that produced outstanding qualities. Bred to Ch. Kiskas Karaholme Cherokee, Cubie, herself a California Working Group winner, produced the BIS litter brothers Ch. Ice Way's Ice Crush and Ch. Ice Way's Ice Breaker.

Breaker's attributes were many. At 23½ inches, he was well-balanced and moved with a powerful, reaching stride. He proved himself in the show ring;

Ch. Ice Way's Ice Crush (Ch. Kiska's Karaholme Cherokee ex Ice Way's Ice Cube), owned by Ann Bark and bred by Michael and Bobbie Smith. An owner-handled multiple BIS winner, he is shown in the BB presentation at the 1981 SCA National Specialty under Mrs. Peter Guntermann. Here he defeated a field of 370 competitors, including 75 champions, handled by Michael Zollo.

as a sire, he expressed himself in a consistency of outstanding characteristics befitting a good, masculine stud dog. It was through Breaker and Cubie that Ice Way produced good length of neck, exceptional front reach and powerful driving rears, all packaged in elegant dogs of great beauty.

The authors regret being unable to locate Ice Way now because its efforts enhanced the breed for so long.

In the early years with the late Ann Hamlin, we often saw Jeff Bennett with his Ice Cris Samoyeds; then there was a pause. It seems he sought to clear a skin problem on one of his Samoyed puppies. It took him into the field of nutrition and dog food. Although he has since sold the company, you may be familiar with the name Nature's Recipe. Jeff's activities are many, including racing cars and community politics, which led to his becoming Mayor of Corona, California. But concentrating on the dogs, you may also remember some of Jeff and Nan Eisley Bennett's biggest winners in several Variety Groups.

The Samoyed standard-bearer among these, shown by Jimmy Moses, was the "Dancer" bitch, #1 Bitch in 1995; and Robert Chaffin, the new handler "kid on the block," showed "Pop" who was #2 male in 1995.

Ch. Hoof 'n Paws Drifting Snow (Danish Ch. Sir Jonah of Banff ex Hoof 'n Paw Has Klout), owned and bred by Mardee Ward Fanning. "Smurf" is shown here completing her championship under judge Irene Bivin, handled by Mardee.

Am., Can. Ch. Tasha of Sacha's Knight, was the top winning Samoyed bitch in the United States 1980–82. Linebred to Ch. Kiska's Karaholme Cherokee, "Teka" is shown here in a win under judge Hayden Martin, handled by owner Mardee Ward Fanning.

Am., Mex. Ch. Crizta's Lil Drummer Boy was a multiple BISS and BIS winner handled by Terry Taylor-Galley, owned by Jeff Bennett and shown here with Elizabeth Lockman.

In the past, Jeff's favorite was Am., Mex. Ch. Crizta's Lil Drummer Boy who was a multiple BISS and BIS winner. Perhaps his all-time favorite was Drummer, shown mostly by his friend Terry Taylor-Galley and occasionally by another friend Liz Lockman. Drummer was called a super mover, self-confident and the most mischievous—a beautiful Samoyed. A daughter of Drummer called Marshmallow now lives in the Bennett home with daughters, Jocelyn and Jillian.

THE SCA OFFICIAL BULLETIN

If there is any doubt about the power of the written word, one need only look at the influence of the SCA Bulletin, the official organ of the club. Most of the membership of 1,500 Samoyed enthusiasts join specifically to receive the bulletin, having little interest in the business of running the club. This work is accomplished by the board, which publishes the minutes in the bulletin. Lila Weir initiated the pictorial bulletin from formerly "mimeographed copy only" when Bob and Dolly did it after Catherine Quereaux and Ardith Chamberlain.

Peggy M. Borcherding served the SCA Bulletin for a full eighteen years, and what a job she did. Today the bulletin stands among the ever-decreasing number of national club publications that are still totally subsidized by club members, put together by volunteer nonprofessionals, and is still able to gain recognition as a top-quality publication. In 1966 the SCA Bulletin was in the finals for Best National Club Publication held by the Dog Writers Association of America. In 1996 the bulletin was again in the finals.

The first issue of the SCA Bulletin to appear with Peggy's name on it as editor was March 1966. Linda Lashley followed Peggy as bulletin editor, and presently SCA has Jill Smoot who began in 1986.

In 1976, the *Samoyed Quarterly* magazine began publication, providing additional coverage for the breed. However, the bulletin remains the official voice. Managing editor and publisher of the quarterly is Don Hoflin. Barbara Cole, Dave Richardson, Cynthia Kerstiens and the authors contribute columns. It is based in Wheat Ridge, Colorado. The magazine continues to present the breed fancy with columns of information and articles by some of the leaders of the breed, and it includes "Letters to the Editor," always available as a forum for more controversial topics. Oftentimes, a different set of advertisers choose the *SQ* because it has become popular.

Other pen exercises spout spasmodically from the independent clubs. This might be a small newsletter, usually without pictures or advertisers, designed to inform the Samoyed fancy of matches and shows that are planned, announcing successful wins of their members or noting medical problems or articles of strong local interest.

chapter 3

The Samoyed in America: 1976–85

The beginning of this period saw a strong upsurge in registrations, trailing off slightly and reaching a plateau of healthy moderation. At the same time, show ring activity maintained an upward trend nationwide, and the Samoyed made its presence strongly felt in Working Group competitions throughout this ten-year period. In this chapter, we review the events, the people and the dogs that helped further burnish the already bright image of the breed.

Ch. Ice Way's Ice Crush (Crush), by English import Ch. Kiska's Karaholme Cherokee (Painter) out of Ch. Ice Way's Ice Cube, was owned by Ann Bark of Boxford, Massachusetts, and was Best of Breed at the 1980 SCA Specialty over an entry of 370, including 79 champions (the Best of Breed class alone took more than four hours to judge). He scored seven All-Breed Bests in Show and many Group firsts before his untimely death in December 1983.

Ann was also involved with the first New England Samoyed Club of record recognized in 1985 and now known as the Minuteman Samoyed Club.

Winterfrost Samoyeds was established in 1967 in Eastern Canada by Louise O'Connell. Louise based her initial breedings on Kondako Samoyeds and produced several Canadian and American champions from this bloodline during the 1970s and 1980s. She has been a member of SCA since 1968.

In the late 1980s Louise collaborated on a breeding that combined Kondako bloodlines with Ch. White Satin's Kodiak Kub on the dam's (Ch. Casablanca's Dash of Panach) side and Ch. Wolf River's Drumlin as sire. The breeding produced three get, including Ch. Winterfrost's Moonlighting and Ch. White Magic's Grand Illusion. Maddy's first breeding to Ch. Wolf River's Eagle in 1989 produced Ch. Winterfrost's Gyrfalcon. A winner of twelve Specialties—a record—and multiple Group winner, Gyr has sired numerous champions to date, producing five daughters who have won Best in

Ch. Winterfrost's Gyrfalcon, owned and handled by Louise O'Connell, is a Group winner and has won twelve BISS—the all-time record as this book goes to press.

Am., Mex. Ch. Hoof 'n Paw White Knight (Ch. Kiska's Karaholme Cherokee ex Ice Way's Angel), owned by Mardee Ward and Lindi Ward and bred by Mardee. Shown here with handler Marna Pearson, "Knavioux" was a BIS and BISS winner and was among the breed's top campaigners throughout his long Specials career. *Joan Ludwig*

Reference List of Repetitive Terms and Titles

AKC	American Kennel Club	KC	Kennel Club (for the UK)
AM	Award of Merit	OTCH	Obedience Trial Champion
BB	Best of Breed	SKC	States Kennel Club
BIS	Best in Show (All breeds)	TD	Tracking Dog
BISS	Best in Specialty Show	TDI	Therapy Dog International
BOS	Best of Opposite Sex	TT	Temperament Tested
BW	Best of Winners	UD	Utility Dog
CD	Companion Dog	U-CD	United Kennel Club CD
CDX	Companion Dog Excellent	UDT	Utility Dog Tracking
CGC	Canine Good Citizen	UK	United Kingdom
CKC	Canadian Kennel Club	WB	Winners Bitch
HIC or HC	Herding Instinct Certified	WD	Winners Dog

Sweepstakes at regional Specialties. His contribution to the breed has been evident throughout the Samoyed ring.

Hoof 'n Paw Samoyeds (HNP) was established in 1970 as a continuation of the ideals and principles established over the past fifty years by Mardee Ward-Fanning's parents, Robert and Dolly Ward. The kennel name, Hoof 'n Paw, was derived from Mardee's interest in dogs and Morgan horses and currently with Charolais cattle with her husband, Michael, on their ranch in Wilsall, Montana. The goal continues to be to perpetuate the Samoyed as a dual-purpose dog for work and for show. Mardee is also an AKC-approved judge of Working breeds, Norwegian Elkhounds and Australian Shepherds.

Although Mardee, like other breeders, strives for the Standard and dual-purpose dogs, she insists on solid temperaments and outgoing, animated personalities that are, indeed, part of the Samoyed breed type. She likes to do her own handling but in the past has called on Pam Shea or Marna Pearson. Currently, Robert Chaffin is her handler.

At the time of the second edition, the newest star on the horizon at Hoof 'n Paw was Ch. Desert Knight O'Candida, son of HNP's foundation sire Am., Mex. Ch. The Hoof 'n Paw White Knight. Patrick, so named after Patricia Craige-Trotter of Vin-Melca Norwegian Elkhound fame, was picked from a litter bred by the Seiberts. Between 1983 and 1986 Patrick went on to become a multiple Specialty and Group winner like his sire and half sister, Am.,

Ch. Asgard's Lora from Shadow Mtn., owned by Ruth Mary Heckeroth. A "Painter" daughter out of Ch. Starbright Dream Weaver, she was bred three times to three different studs and produced champions from each for a total of eight champion offspring. *Missy Yuhl*

Can. Ch. Tasha of Sacha's Knight, who had nineteen Group firsts; yet he never annexed a BIS.

The year 1985 was significant at Hoof 'n Paw because three puppies were born that contributed greatly to its success. They were Am., Can. Ch. Hoof 'n Paw's Ramblin' Rose, known as Rosey; Am., Can. Ch. Hoof 'n Paw's Knight Rider, known as Kitt; and Kitt's sister, Ch. Hoof 'n Paw's In the Buff, known as Buffy, owned by Genia Cox.

Rosey was a product of a half-brother–sister breeding (Patrick out of Knight Cloud), both co-owned by Terry and Michelle Mumford of Corona, California. Rosey completed her championship with five majors and became a Specialty and Group winner.

Kitt and Buffy were the result of the breeding of a White Knight granddaughter, Ch. Hoof 'n Paw's Drifting Snow, CDX, TT (Smurf), to a Painter grandson, Ch. Andromeda Tugger of Crush. Buffy was the SCA Grand Futurity winner in 1986 and BB at Westminster in 1987. Kitt finished quickly, but his worth has been proven as a stud dog. He sired six Group winners in the United States and Canada with several BIS sons.

Most notable of these sons are Am., Can. Ch. Hoof 'n Paw's Knight Shadow (Shaddie), owned by Jeff Bennett, Sylvia Thomas and Mardee Ward-Fanning; Am., Int. Ch. Hoof 'n Paw's Knight Drifter, owned by Alan and Jane Stevenson; and Ch. Kamelot's Klassic Knight, owned by Jennifer Brown.

The strength of Hoof 'n Paw continued to grow with each generation, excelling in conformation; sledding and weight pulling ability; Obedience; Therapy work; and the newest arena, Agility. Hoof 'n Paw has never relied on any one stud dog or brood bitch to achieve its "look" or success. From each successive breeding come dogs in a "more complete" package—the goal for perfection keeps each breeder going.

Kitt, bred to Ruth Mary Heckeroth's Painter daughter, Ch. Asgards Lora from Shadow Mtn., produced Shaddie, Drifter and their sister, Am., Can. Ch. Hoof 'n Paw's Ivory Knight. Ivory has six champion offspring and several with WSX working titles. Ivory was the #2 Brood Bitch for 1994. Shaddie sired Am., Can. Ch. Hoof 'n Paw's Wild Rose Knight, known as Pop, and Ch. Hoof 'n Paw's MidKnight Maxx.

Maxx's dam, Czar Agape "Misty" Polar Bear was an interesting blend of English and American lines (Moonlighter, Kondako and Novaskaya). Maxx is described as a one-of-a-kind dog, possessing a presence and fluid motion in gaiting not often encountered. Maxx was twice Best Puppy at Specialties, including the 1991 National, finishing at eleven months with three five-point majors and BBs. Owned by Steve, Cheryl and Jason Loper, he was honored with Top Stud Dog honors in 1994 and won the Bronze Medal from the IWPA (International Weight Pull Association) in the under sixty-pound class, earning his WSX title in his first season as a weight puller. He is presently working on his Agility title with the very capable Jason Loper.

Am., Can. Ch. Hoof 'n Paw's Wild Rose Knight (Pop) was shown in the classes by breeder-owner Mardee Ward-Fanning; Pop finished on his first birthday with 4 majors. Beginning his "Specials" campaign at 2½ years, Pop was "retired" from active campaigning with a record of 6 BISS, 6 Group firsts, 110 BB, 42 Group placements, and 2 Westminster Awards of Merit. Pop was shown by Robert M. Chaffin for owners Jeff and Nan Eisley-Bennett and the authors. Pop has significantly proven his worth as a stud dog with ten champions at this writing, including the 1993 SCA Grand Futurity Winner, Ch. HNP Here Comes the Knight (Frankie) out of Ch. Hoof 'n Paw's Prairie Dawg (Varmi).

Now Hoof 'n Paw's newest and youngest campaign effort, Ch. Hoof 'n Paw's A Rose Is a Rose, known as Ana, is the repeat breeding of Pop and the only female in either of the two litters! Ana was three years old at the time this edition was being written. Her achievements are listed under her photo in the White Water Samoyeds (pages 87–102).

Hoof 'n Paw has bred fewer than thirty litters in twenty-six years of breeding Sams for family companions and showing. The quality of its champions is more important than its numbers. Particular pride is taken in having two father-daughter pairs in the top ten in the same year (Knavioux and Teka, Patrick and Rosey) and most recently a brother-sister team (Pop and Ana) achieving the same goal. Noteworthy is the fact that HNP can guarantee excellent Samoyed temperament. The latest litter by Ch. Hoof 'n Paw's Knight Rider (Kitt) at age eleven was bred by Gini Addamo out of her Ch. Wolf River's Surreptitious (Tish) who produced five beautiful puppies. One called Rita is in Arkansas at Kamelot with Jennifer Brown.

In the late 1970s Teena Scherer Schulz joined the Samoyed scene and obtained Hoof 'n Paw's NDN Rain Dance (Violet) (Ch. The Hoof 'n Paw White Knight ex Starctic SnowBasin Sioux, CD). For Violet's first mate she

Ch. Hoof 'n Paw Knight Rider (Ch. Andromeda Tugger of Crush ex Ch. Hoof 'n Paw's Drifting Snow, CDX, TT) is the sire of sixteen champions. *Carl Lindemaier*

Ch. Sansaska's Mark of Evening Star (Sansaska's Sherman T ex Sansaska's Czarina Mouschka), a BISS winner, owned by Derek and Marilyn Gitelson. *Bergman*

chose Ch. Ice Way's Ice Breaker. Teena, an advocate of style, movement and substance, selected one male puppy and successfully won a Specialty Match and then his first points at eight months.

Mrs. Schulz's next dog was Ch. Ice Way's Flash Cube, one of the famous "Super Seven" litter, the brother-sister breeding by the Mike Smiths that had produced four champions. Ch. Flash Cube was Best of Breed at the 1983 Samoyed Club of Los Angeles under judge Howard Dullnig in an entry of more than one hundred Samoyeds and was sire of two puppies exported to Japan under Teena's kennel name of Crizta.

Steve Gallien's first champion was Pharaoh Nights Over Egypt in 1981. He was WD at the 1986 SCLA Specialty. Steve's next show dog was Ch. Crizta's Light Foot, bred by Teena Schulz, Ch. Ice Way's Flash Cube ex Crizta's Chariot of Fire. Light Foot won WD in an SCLA supported entry at the Rio Hondo KC in 1988.

His third show bitch, Ch. Crizta's Capri of Bakari, (Ch. Kondako's Show Biz ex Ch. Crizta Sugar Wolfe) bred by Teena Schulz, was acquired in 1987. Capri won Best in Sweepstakes at the 1988 SCA Specialty and at the 1989 SCLA Specialty. She has produced two champions, Crizta's One Step Beyond, owned by Carole Cheesman, and Bakari's Capra Lite of Nityen, owned by Tom and Lisa Polk.

Samoyeds of Seelah Kennels, owned by Major General (Ret.) Merrill B. Evans and his wife, Rowena, of Prole, Iowa, was officially started in late 1971 with two puppy bitches. Their bloodlines emphasized both the Kobe (Tucker) and White Way (Mason) heritage.

The first planned breeding of Bo Peep was to Ch. Oakwood Farm's Kari J'Go Diko. This combined the lines of Silvermoon, Drayalene, Kobe and White Way. From this December 1974 litter, they selected a male puppy, Di Murdock of Seelah. Rowena handled him as a puppy, and then in September 1977, he was placed with professional handler Jerry Kesting and was off to glory.

Murdock finished in 1978. He became the top-winning Samoyed in the United States on the SCA system for 1979 and 1980, compiling a

Ch. Ice Way's Flash Cube (Ch. Ice Way's Ice Breaker ex Ice Way's Cherokee Sun O'Somar), owned by Teena Deatherage and bred by Mike and Bobbie Smith. He is shown here winning BB in an SCLA supported entry at the Orange Empire Dog Club, 1984, under Arlene Davis. Flash Cube was a noted winner and a sire of quality.

Ch. Di Murdock of Seelah (Am., Can. Ch. Oakwood Farms Kari ex Ch. Snowfire's Bo Peep), owned and bred by Dr. Merrill and Rowena Evans. He was the SCA top winning Samoyed in 1979 and 1980, the Top Stud Dog for 1982 and a BIS and BISS winner.

coast-to-coast record of 216 BB, 100 Group placements including 16 firsts, 2 BIS, and 2 BISS. He was also the Top Stud Dog (SCA) for 1982.

The Moonlighter Kennels, in Waldo, Wisconsin, were owned by Wayne and Jeanne Nonhof. All the "Moonlighter" Samoyeds trace at least once to the foundation bitch, Moonlighter's Altai Star Mist (linebred on Joli).

Misty's most famous son was probably Ch. Moonlighter's Hallmark, a multiple Group winner. Besides his illustrious show career, Ike did the breed proud in weight-pulling contests, with his record pull being 1,400 pounds. Ike was the result of a linebreeding, sired by the BIS winning Am., Can. Ch. Saroma's Polar Prince. Also from that breeding was Ch. Moonlighter's Celestial Hipy, Am., Can., CD, owned by Anne Copeland in Chicago. Ike produced a number of champions, most notably Ch. Karalot's Kit 'N Kaboodle, (dam of the BIS winner, Am., Can., Bda. Ch. Karalot's Jak Frost 'O Westwind).

Misty has principally carried on through her daughter, Ch. Moonlighter's Ice 'N Spice—a second-generation Top Producing Brood Bitch by Ch. Kondako's Sun Dancer. Spice is the dam of ten champions.

The BIS and five-time BISS winning Am., Can. Ch. Moonlighter's Ima Bark Star TT, Can. ROM, died at age fifteen of natural causes. With about sixty champion offspring, Bark had an influence on the breed for soundness, type and smiling attitude. Three generations later, his smiling face can still be seen. His death marked the end of an era at Moonlighter, but a new one was already opening.

New blood to complement the remaining dogs was added in the form of Ch. Sambushed Spoonful O' Sugar bred by Elizabeth Metz. This bitch was good enough to beat the boys for BB and was BOS at the San Jose, California, SCA National in 1986. She earned SCA Awards of Merit in 1987 and 1989 and won the Brood Bitch class at the 1989 National. Spoonie was mated to Ch. West Free's Double Oh Seven, whose pedigree shows Bark Star, his littermate Am., Can. Ch. Moonlighter's Ima Better Bet, TT, and the multi-Group winning Ch. Moonlighter's Hallmark up close.

This combination produced six champions, the most notable among them Ch. Moonlighter's Grandstander. Stanley, as he was called, showed early promise in winning Group placements from the classes and went on to win multiple Groups and four Specialties with Wayne's handling.

Wayne, who loved to help the newcomer to the sport, was diagnosed with cancer in 1993, and the breed lost a true fancier in 1994 when he died.

With Wayne Nonhof's death, the focus of Moonlighter changed. Dog shows weren't as much fun anymore for Jeanne, but the desire to breed good dogs continued. By this time Jeanne had been approved to judge a number of Working breeds, which made it more difficult to exhibit extensively. However, she managed to get to some Specialties and added two more BISS when Stanley was seven and also won the Stud Dog Class at the 1995 National. Stanley showed he had talents beyond the conformation ring and stud paddock. In the SCA weight pulls, Stanley had a top pull of 2,410 pounds!

Jeanne Nonhof continues to be active on the SCA's board of governors, after having served two terms as president and writing the breed column in the *AKC Gazette*.

The latest generation of Moonlighters includes the Group winning Ch. Moonlighter's Smilin Eyes, the Specialty winning Ch. Moonlighter's Glad All Over, the Award of Merit winning Ch. Moonlighter's Ima Grand Kid, Ch. Moonlighters' Icestar Natasha, the Group placing biscuit beauty Moonlighter's Ima Almond Joy and Ch. Moonlighter's Jump for Joy.

Adding to the strong upsurge of the Samoyed in Wisconsin (which surely helped swell the entry at the 1981 SCA Specialty to about 450) has been the contribution of Bob and Wanda Krauss of Poynette, Wisconsin. Bob and Wanda had a Samoyed for four years before they became totally involved in all phases of the dog sport. They acquired Ch. Prairiewind's Shanna, CD, as a young adult from Phyllis Hellems of Kansas. Shanna is an inbred daughter of Ch. Nachalnik of Drayalene. Because the Krausses own horses, their breeding program has been strongly influenced by the need for soundness and

Ch. Moonlighter's Grandstander (Ch. Westfree's Double Oh Seven ex Ch. Sambushed Spoonful O' Sugar), owned, bred and handled by Wayne and Jeanne Nonhof. "Stanley" has won five Specialties and has a weight pull record of 2,410 pounds.

Ch. Moonlighter's Ima Grand Kid (Ch. Moonlighter's Grandstander ex Sno Kiddin's Silent Running), owned by Jeanne Nonhof, had two SCA Awards of Merit when this book went to press. At six months she was Best in Sweepstakes at the Chicagoland Specialty.

good movement in a working animal. In particular, they believe that fronts are the weakest part of the Samoyed breed today; therefore, they have placed strong emphasis on producing a line of dogs with sound fronts.

Shanna was first bred to Ch. Kondako's Sun Dancer. This produced two champions, Ch. K-Way's Garmouche, CD, and Ch. K-Way's Gay Gazelle, CD. The Krausses felt that these dogs were sound and stylish with good coats and type but did not have their dam's reach and side gait. To obtain this, they bred to Ch. Ivan Belaya of Taymylyr, CD, a descendant of Ch. Starchak, CD, and Ch. Shondi of Drayalene.

It should be noted that K-Way dogs have Obedience titles. Bob and Wanda train and show their dogs in Obedience as well as conformation and have also raced a team competitively in Wisconsin for three years. They feel that a truly balanced Samoyed not only moves well but also has a title at both ends and can work well in harness. Their success is proof that the Samoyed is, indeed, the versatile dog that the Standard requires.

Elizabeth (Liz) Hooyman Lockman had the Blue Sky Samoyeds. Her breeding of Ch. Blue Sky's Pound Cake to Ch. Ice Way's Ice Breaker produced Ch. Blue Sky's Breaking Away, Ch. Blue Sky's Piece of Cake, Ch. Blue Sky's Bedazzled and Ch. Blue Sky's Simply Smashing, owned by Joan Luna.

Using her well-established, successful lines to their fullest potential, Mrs. Lockman bred Ch. Blue Sky's Smiling At Me to his aunt Ch. Sulu's Fascinating Rhythm. That is how Barbara Arnaud got her lovely Ch. Sulu's Mindy on My Mind. Mindy won the 1984 SCA Specialty Brood Bitch award.

Mrs. Lockman became a Samoyed breeder-judge in 1984. After resigning from showing and judging, she became the editor and publisher of the widely known all-breed magazine *Canine Chronicle*. Shortly before this edition of *The New Samoyed* went to press, she sold *Canine Chronicle*.

The Samoyed Club of Houston was formed in 1974 and held its first organized meeting that October. A nucleus of about twelve members formed the club, and within a year the membership grew to twenty-six. The roster has varied since that time, but members of the original nucleus still active include Archie and Anne Peil, Danny and Chris Middleton and Don and Barbara Winslow.

By 1975, keeping pace with the increase in breed registrations was giving the SCA growing pains. The roster contained 787 names, and the SCA membership and mailing lists became computerized. Even the club bulletin had grown to eighty-four pages. Gini Addamo currently has the job of data coordinator and membership chairman and maintains the roster, which now contains approximately 1,500 names.

The concept of a Futurity had been accepted by the SCA's board of directors, and Dave Richardson was elected Futurity secretary. As is the usual practice, puppies are nominated before birth. At birth, they are further nominated with another fee. Fees keep the nomination in effect during the growing period, and then the individual awards are made at the judging of the National Specialty in which the nominated puppy becomes of eligible age for competition.

After a decade, the Futurity was turned over to Karen McFarlane (Frostyacres), who adores puppies and did a superb job of keeping the records.

An Award of Merit was instituted. It was to be presented to the Best of Breed and Best of Breed runners-up at the National Specialty, as is the practice of some other breed clubs—notably the German Shepherd Dog Club of America. The German Shepherd Club names as "Select" #1 down to a specified number or a limitation based upon 10 to 20 percent of the champions entered. This enables a champion to be in the top 10 or 20 percent of 50 to 100 champions, which is quite an honor. The Samoyed system chooses both dogs and bitches.

Tarahill Kennels, Inc., owned by Cheryl Wagner, began its winning career about 1972. While Nancy Sheehan Martin handled for Tarahill originally, Cheryl herself enjoyed handling some of her "class dogs" at Specialties. We recall especially her excitement over winning BB at the 1985 Westminster show under J. D. Jones with her beautifully headed Ch. Tarahill's Casey Can Do; Jack and Amelia Price's bitch, Ch. Me Too of Bubbling Oaks, handled by Joy Brewster, was Best Opposite.

Professional handler Nancy Sheehan-Martin went on to handle Casey to a successful Specials career. In her hands, he became America's #1 Samoyed in 1985 and again in 1986.

In later years, Chris Long became Tarahill's kennel manager. At first, Tarahill was in the Chicago area but later moved to Georgia. This operation took on the look of an earlier time when large kennels were the norm throughout the dog game.

Cheryl Wagner's Ch. Tarahill's Everybody Duck was the #1 Samoyed in 1992 and 1993. He retired as the second top-winning Samoyed of all time with fourteen BIS. Called Buddy, he was both an American and Bermudian champion.

Tarahill produced about thirty-five champions from only one or two litters a year. Other multiple BIS and Group winning Sams were Buddy's grandfather, Ch. Tarahill's Casey Can Do, Ch. Tarahill's Lucky Duckling and Tarahill's All Ducked Out. Tarahill became less active in Samoyeds about 1994 and is now concentrating on horses.

Audrey Lycan, Winterway Samoyeds, in Huntsville, Alabama, owned a one-of-a-kind bitch in Ch. Kim's Ladybug (May 1967–June 1977). Ladybug whelped thirty-nine puppies of which thirty-two lived. Ten became champions and were certified with OFA. She was bred to four different males, two linebred partners and two outcrosses, and produced champions and Obedience titlists. Audrey bred Am., Can. Ch. Winterway's Omega, PT, HCT, owned by Francis and Louis Thompson. Later she also bred Am., Can. Ch. Winterway's Jeopardy, an AM winner at the 1991 National. In more recent years she has been concentrating on judging. Her comments on her assignment at the 1996 National appear in chapter 4.

North Starr Samoyeds, owned by Dr. Robert J. and Pat Hritzo, of Hubbard, Ohio, is an outstanding kennel of record-establishing dogs. Long-term fanciers, the Hritzos have bred and shown dogs since 1964. In addition to forty-eight Samoyed champions, they have finished two Papillons, a Pointer, an American Foxhound, and a Greyhound to their championships.

In March 1985, Dr. Hritzo, a surgeon, was elected to the board of directors of the American Kennel Club. In the nineties, Dr. Hritzo was elected treasurer of the AKC.

The Hritzos' homebred Am., Can. Ch. North Starr's King's Ransom, whelped in 1969, was for a time the all-time top winning Samoyed, handled first by daughter Kathy, who had an outstanding career in Junior Showmanship, and later by Tom Glassford.

Jack and Amelia Feinbergs' lovely home-bred bitch, Ch. Northwind's Black Magic (Ch. Scandia's Kejaare ex Northwind's Ladybug), became a champion in eleven shows and was an AM winner at the 1979 SCA Specialty.

Ch. Northwind's Running Bear (Ch. Kondako's Sun Dancer ex Troika V), bred by Alan and Jane Stevenson of Moorpark, California, was a big winner. Bear was the #1 Samoyed in America, all systems, for 1981 and #1 on the Phillips System for 1980. His career winnings included four all-breed BIS and sixty-four Group placements.

The Whitecliff line originated with Percy and Lena Matheron and Jean Blank who handled the memorable winner Ch. Yurok of Whitecliff. After Jean had shown Yurok to his fabulous record, she retired from breeding and showing and asked the late Don and Wilna Coulter to carry on the Whitecliff name.

Two sons of Ch. Yurok, Ch. Sho-off's Czar of Whitecliff and Ch. Sho-off's Dorok of Whitecliff, a Best in Show winner, were probably the most prolific of Yurok's offspring. Some of the get are Am., Mex. Ch. Midnight Sun Kimba; Ch. Pushka Czar of Snowcliff, Best in Show winner; Ch. Czar Dorak of Whitecliff; and Ch. Yeti of Whitecliff.

An all-time favorite of Wilna Coulter's was the bitch Ch. White Star IV. Star did not begin her show career until age seven. Within a year she was a champion, with several BBs. She was co-owned with Karl and Joy Geletich of Shalimar Kennels. A natural showman, Star was BB or BOS almost every time shown. At age ten she won a Group third under judge Robert Ward. At age twelve she took the AM and first in Veterans at the SCA Specialty by judge Derek Rayne. The following year, 1979, at the SCA Specialty hosted by the Greater Metropolitan Atlanta Samoyed Club in Georgia, Star won an AM and was first in the Veteran Bitch Class at age thirteen. Wilna Coulter has always been active in Samoyed rescue.

Michael and Dianne Hoffecker of Huntington Beach, California, purchased a bitch puppy in 1976, bred by Gail Stitt Oesterriech and sired by Czar's Kobe-Wah of Whitecliff ex Sunshine of Midnight Sun. As usual, a big win at a puppy match drew them into the dog show life. This was followed by a Best of Breed win at a Samoyed Club of Los Angeles Specialty B match in an entry of sixty-two, judged by the well-known breeder-judge from Australia, Mrs. Yvonne Sydenham-Clark. The puppy became Ch. Shawndi of Midnight Sun. At Shawndi's first outing, she was BB and fourth in the Working Group. Shawndi was BB at the August 1980 SCA Specialty in San Diego, California, under Virginia Lynne of Canada.

Ch. Frostyacres Borne Blonde (Frostyacres Double Image ex Frostyacres Hot Salsa), owned by Karen McFarlane. An owner-handled multiple Group winner, "Blondie" is shown here winning BISS at the 1996 Samoyed Club of Los Angeles Specialty under judge Mardee Ward-Fanning. Ms. McFarlane is shown handling; Marie Witherspoon presents the Ch. Sayan of Woodland Memorial Trophy; and at the extreme right is SCLA president, Terry Bednarczyk. Blondie repeated her BLISS in 1997 under judge Joan Zuver. *Bergman*

Ch. Li'L Paws Sun of Torch, owned by Diane Dotson and bred by John and Kathy Regan, was BIS at Cen-Tex KC under judge Dudley McMillin. "Sonny" is handled by Roy and Shirlee Murray. *Wayne Cott*

The Hoffeckers philosophical comment was: "Isn't it funny that the dog wins the breed and the awards and has the puppies, and *we* take the credit."

Dave and Marguerite Seiberts' began showing in 1978. They obtained a puppy from Lorraine Newville of Sherica Samoyeds by Ch. Ice Way's Ice Breaker ex Ch. Sherica's Lucky Seven Charm, CD. This "pick-of-litter" put them on the winning path. Ch. Sherica's Ethereal Candida won her first points at thirteen months and finished with wins at large Specialty shows.

Their latest Special is Ch. Candida's The Sun Rider, who sired the BIS winner Ch. Li'l Paw's Sun of Torch, handled by Roy Murray and owned by Diane Dotson, and Ch. Li'l Paws Keawe, owned by Cliff and Heather Gomes.

Jim and Elfie Shea of Elfenbein Samoyeds, Blaine, Minnesota, purchased their first Samoyed in 1978 and have been in love with the breed ever since. Under the Elfenbein kennel name ("ivory" in German), they have produced forty-nine puppies in nine litters. Twenty are American champions, three are CDs, one is a CDX and six are Therapy Dogs. Two of their breeding have novice Agility titles, and one has an open Agility title. They have also been successful at shows and trials in Canada. From the beginning, Jim and Elfie have been very active in the Samoyed Association of Minneapolis-St. Paul and are SCA members.

One of the many highlights of their showing was taking a Group first from the classes with Elfenbein Roman Candle (Roman). The #1 and #2 Agility Samoyeds for 1994 were Elfenbein Mercedes Euphoria, CDX, Can., UKC CD, CGC, TDI, NA (Rory) and Ch. Elfenbein LaSalle Coup, CD, Can., UKC CD, CGC, TDI, WDS, OA, USDAA, AD (Keila). Who says Sammies aren't smart! The Sheas are very proud of Rory and Keila and their owners, Lynn and Earl Kyle and Rose Ann and Chuck Baune.

In the early 1980s, Frances Powers bred Ch. Whitecliff's Loga Kovsh' Karu, CD to Ann Bark's male, Ch. Ice Way's Ice Crush, the 1981 SCA BISS and all-breed BIS winner. The Norris's foundation bitch, Ch. Crush's Kalim of Whitecliff, BISS, co-owned by Ann Bark, came from this breeding. Flying Cloud Samoyeds began with Kalim's first litter, but not until her last litter did the Norrises find the puppy bitch they wanted to continue their breeding program. She became Ch. Flying Cloud's Song of the Sea (Chantey), also co-owned by Ann Bark. Her sire, Ch. Seawind's Mister Mister (Joshua) owned by Jack Jermyn and Ann Bark, was WD, BW and AM recipient at the 1988 SCA National Specialty in California.

A tradition of National Specialty winners began with Crush and was continued by his grandson Joshua. So it was not a surprise when Chantey went WB, Best Puppy and received an AM recipient at the 1989 SCA National, at the age of eight months, under Joe Gregory. The following December, Kalim and Chantey, at the prestigious Eastern Dog Club Show in Boston, became the first Samoyeds to win Best in Show in Brace, and they did this again in 1990. Kalim retired from the show ring after winning the National, but Chantey went to PVSC in the spring of 1990 and won Puppy

Sweepstakes under Audrey Lycan. She finished her championship later that year with a BB from the classes and a Group IV. Chantey is now retired from the show ring, but she has several champion offspring the Norrises hope will carry on the tradition.

The Norrises have been strong supporters of the breed since they met their first Samoyeds at the Cooks in 1977. They have been active members of the Minuteman Samoyed Club since 1978, and Bud is on the board of governors of the Samoyed Club of America. Bud was the chairman of the 1987 SCA National Specialty.

Gail and Terry Campbell have enjoyed the campaign of this decade. Although not achieving "the record 55 BIS" of Ch. Quicksilver's Razz Ma Tazz, Ch. Tega Joe Knows, TT, was "that winningest Sam" (mostly owner-handled) since he started in 1991 when Mary Morstad found him for Best in Futurity at the SCA National in Denver.

Whew! That takes a lot of flying around, planning accommodations and nourishing meals, keeping the dog and you well, grooming under all types of conditions, renting cars, being at the right place at the right time, getting some rest sometime, deciding which show you are going to after entering several perhaps, figuring your chances under different judges, and so on, and so forth.

Ch. Tega's Joe Knows, TT, was bred by the Campbells with Bonnie Giffin's stud Ch. Bykhal's American Dream out of Ch. Tega's Emerald City Rose. Whelped November 1, 1990, he finished his championship at twelve months!

We are struck by the similarity of expression between Joe Knows and the great stud in the UK, Ch. Hurkur's Jingles, owned by James Dougal, Scotland.

Ch. Tega's Joe Knows' record through January 31, 1996, is captioned under his picture in the White Water Samoyeds on pages 87–102. Joe was #1 Samoyed 1994 and 1995—All Systems.

Janice Hovelmann developed the successful Sanorka Kennels in New York. She is rightly proud of her achievements. Exerting influence especially is her Ch. Sanorka's Moonlight Gambler, sired by Ch. Risuko's Mister Moonlight out of Ch. Sanorka's Maid'en Northwind, born in 1988. She describes him as a big dog standing twenty-four inches tall with large bone and a gorgeous stand-off coat. He never really took to the show ring, but he tolerated it long enough to win Best in Sweepstakes at the 1989 Potomac Valley Specialty and a Group 2 at South Shore KC in Massachusetts, 1990.

Gabby, as he is called, was Top Stud in 1991 in both the ratings of the SCA and the *SQ* (*Samoyed Quarterly*) and again in 1994.

Gabby must be doing something right having produced twenty-seven champions, five of whom have placed in Groups, and one girl with an obedience title. Some of his progeny have outdone his show record, such as Ch. Ren J's Go Go Dancer, BISS at the Minuteman Specialty 1992, SCA Top Winning Bitch for 1993 and 1994, #2 Samoyed 1994 for *SQ* ratings and

Canine Chronicle. In 1995, Dancer was campaigned seriously with Jimmy Moses and was #2 Samoyed for the year.

Gabby sired Janet Cherne's and Kent and Diane Stutzman's Ch. Cloudnine's Penny's From H'VN, the Best Puppy in Show at the 1994 National, and Am., Can. Ch. Sanorka's Moonlite Trip T'Ren J (Travis), who boasts Multiple Groups. Travis was BW at Canada's National in 1994 under Dolly Ward. He had an Award of Merit at the SCA 1995 National under Michelle Billings.

Ch. Sanorka's Moonlite Trip T'Ren J following in his father's footsteps, sired the 6–9 Intersex PD in Futurity in the Texas National. Behind every outstanding winner is also the dam. Renee and Jim Miller of Ren-J Kennels in Illinois have been "creating beauties" for many years. Most recently their brood bitch Sno-Questor's Callico O'Ren-J (Callie) has produced well. Behind Callie is the sire Ch. Millcreek's Stacked Deck (Griffin)and the dam Ch. Mithril's Bethil O'Luin (Trojan).

Often, when a successful niche is found where the combination of a certain dog and certain bitch works well, that breeding is repeated with the hope of the same good results. So it was in the case of Ren-J and Sanorka: Ch. Sanorka's Moonlight Gambler was a niche with Callie. They produced Ch. Ren-J's Kachina Dancer, Ch. Ren-J's Spirit of a Warrior, and Ch. Ren-J's Moonshot of Sanorka out of three litters—by Gabby from New York and Callie in Illinois.

Moonstar began in 1988 with a birthday present from Braxton (B.J.) Moses to his wife Sakura. Their first puppy (Tsiulikagta) came from Donna Pagel-Yocom, and although only intended as a pet, he also became Can. Ch. Tsiulikagtas Illamar. A second Samoyed came from Pat Cummins of Sancha Samoyeds from British Columbia, Sanch'a Iliana.

Moonstar had one litter that produced their first home-bred champion, Can. Ch. Moonstar's Arukas (Sakura spelled backwards!) and Can. Ch. Moonstar's Swiftwynd.

Seeking to improve on the structure and movement of their dogs, Moonstar's direction changed when B. J. made arrangements to get a puppy bitch from a line known for strong fronts and good movement. Hence, the arrival of Ch. Hoof 'n Paw's Midknight Maxxine (Maxxine), Moonstar's foundation bitch.

Maxxine, owned by B. J. Moses and Mardee Ward-Fanning has thus far shown herself equal to the challenge of producing quality.

Moonstar's Hollywood Knight (Seger) is from the first breeding of Pop and Maxxine. Moonstar's Cold Smoke HNP (Smokey) is a litter brother to Seger. At two years old (as of this writing), these two dogs were creating considerable ringside interest.

Texas fanciers Tom and Toni Maurer did a lot of work helping Joan Auld make plans for the 1995 National in Austin. They have been Sam fanciers for some time and have recently "hitched up" with Krauss's K-Way of

Wisconsin to improve their stock. Their K-Way's Star Dancer of TNT is a Best in Specialty and Multi-Group winner. He was in the top fifteen for 1992 and 1993 and in the top ten in 1994, after finishing his championship at fourteen months! Now that's a K-Way's Omen of Destiny son for you, and Omen was one of the most influential studs in this past decade.

Cascade Samoyeds started with Cheri Hollenback and a former co-worker, Darlene Miller. Cheri lives at the foot of Mt. Rainier, and Darlene lives at the foot of Mt. Hood, thus, the kennel name of "Cascade." Darlene is no longer active in the Fancy but still has Kodi's dam, Trailblazer Denali's Destiny. Cheri's plans are to continue breeding under the Cascade name, albeit on a limited basis. All of Cheri's dogs are well-loved house pets first, show dogs second. Cheri has been active with her Sammys in a variety of activities. Kodi, "Kodiak," is a good example, in that at this writing he is well over halfway toward the goal of his working title, earning points through herding, weight pulling, pack hiking and therapy. He is an accomplished obedience performer, too, although his Sammy sense of humor and creativity has been known to frequently pop up in the obedience ring! He also has experience as a Hobie Cat sailor (complete with his own life preserver), possum hunter (has left one on the deck as a "gift") and salmon fisherman (caught one out of a river).

In 1984 Sandra Dukes, Lafayette, Indiana, kept a male from her first litter who was to become a banner for Sandy and the breed. Called Bear, he was registered Ch. Image's the Barrister. Bear was the SCA National BW from the 9–12-month puppy class. Sandy thought this was easy, at this point. Used as the reason for "vacations to great places," Sandy and Bear competed in Specialties from coast to coast and border to border, gathering numerous BBs and AMs, including four National Awards of Merit. At eleven years of age he was the National's Veteran's Sweepstakes winner!

Although Bear was used sparingly at stud, mostly when Sandy was ready for a new puppy, Ch. Image's the Barrister has several champion sons and daughters.

Sandra Dukes began service to the SCA when she was asked by President John Ronald to serve as the ADOA representative. So she served several terms on the SCA's board of governors, was president in 1991 and served as the club's legal advisor for several years. Her Sam is not named the Barrister for nothing! Sandy and Bear have graced our Nationals and Special events for many years, always in the spirit of great competition and good fellowship, and there is no higher compliment to one who is gallant in both wins and losses. Bear did not lose much even though he has not yet won the coveted BISS at the SCA National. But there is time—Bear was *only* twelve years old in 1997!

Mystiwind Samoyeds, of Portland, Oregon, began in 1988. Joe and Joy Ritter have finished upwards of eighteen Samoyeds of their own and for other people. Since 1991, they have bred, trained, shown and finished five Samoyeds to their American, Canadian and International championships, as well as others that they have purchased. Joe and Joy's emphasis is on type, temperament and soundness.

Their lines go back originally to Ch. Ice Way's Ice Breaker through the Summerhill Kennels in British Columbia. There is also a strong Windy Ridge background.

Most notable of their dogs, is Am., Can., Int. Ch. Mystiwind's Arctic Dancer, CGC, TDI, HCT. He is currently four years old and a multiple Group winner and placer in the United States and Canada, as well as being a first-rate Working Dog.

Following in Dancer's footsteps is his son, Am., Can., Int. Ch. Mystiwind's Arctic Prince, co-bred by Mike and Karen Rochat (Stormcloud). Prince, at less than two years old, is a multiple Group placer as well as a multiple Best in Sweepstakes winner. He lives with the Ritters and represents the future of Mystiwind's Samoyeds.

The Ritters keep only a few Samoyeds at a time, believing that to truly enjoy these furry white clowns, they need to be part of the family and raised as house dogs. Joe and Joy currently have six Samoyeds and one Norwegian Elkhound.

Saratoga Samoyeds with Heidi and Don Nieman of Colorado was started in 1987. The foundation bitch was from Katie LeCour, now Katie Carter, of the Elmfield kennel, Ch. Elmfield Saratoga Sage. Toga's second litter was sired by Ch. Wolf River's Drumlin, with four champions from that breeding: Ch. Saratoga's Speed of Sound; Ch. Saratoga's Lost Aviatrix, CD; Ch. Saratogas Sonic Boom, WSX; and Ch. Saratogas Mr. Mishka.

Ch. Saratoga's Speed of Sound (Mach), was the 1991 SCA National Best in Sweepstakes. In 1994 and 1995 Mach received an AM at Westminster, was tied with his sire for Top Producing Stud Dog and was a multiple Group winner. Ch. Saratoga's Lost Aviatrix, CD (Amelia), was Best of Opposite in Sweepstakes at the 1991 SCA National. In 1993 she was bred to Ch. Hoof 'n Paw's Knight Rider, producing Ch. Saratoga's Summer Knight Storm, also a Group placer.

Ch. Saratoga's Sonic Boom was a 1993 SCA National Award of Merit Winner. Elmfield's Moon River Mirage, one of the last of the Elmfield line, is owned by Katie Carter and Heidi Neiman.

The Nieman's daughter, also named Heidi (Scooter), shows both in Junior showmanship and Conformation winning with the pros!

Hobby Horse Kennels, owned by Jeffrey A. Skinner and Dr. Shauna Brummet, began in 1983 and has since completed twenty championship titles (fourteen U.S. and six Canadian) and eight obedience titles (five U.S. and three Canadian).

Hobby Horse Kennels had eight other dogs nearing their titles at the time of this writing. Shauna Brummet is active in molecular biology research and works informally for the AKC as a consultant on canine genetic research. Shauna and Jeff strive to produce a moderate dog of beauty and soundness, both of mind and body. To further their participation in dogs, both were working on obtaining AKC judging approval at this writing. These fanciers are also very active on the all-breed club front in northeastern Ohio.

Am., Mex., Int. Ch. Sunburst's Torch of Liberty is the Special pride and joy of Larry and Lia Bensen of Starlite Samoyeds. Torch was by Ch. Sansaska's Mark of Evenstar out of Crizta's Tonda of Haviai.

Torch finished his championship very quickly winning BB or BOS from the classes over top Specials on numerous occasions. His first time in the ring as Special was at the Samoyed Club of Los Angeles Specialty in 1989. Torch was awarded Best in Specialty over an entry of 117 Samoyeds. That was the beginning of an illustrious show career for both Torch and the Bensons. Torch quickly became ranked among the top five Samoyeds in the country. He was shown at mostly local shows, winning well over 100 BBs, many Working Group firsts; numerous other Group placements; several BISSs, and Specialty AMs; and an all breed BIS. Torch was the SCA #2 top winning dog for both 1990 and 1991.

As a sire, Torch won the SCA's Top Producing Stud Dog award for 1992 and was named the *Samoyed Quarterly's* Top Producing Stud Dog award for 1992 and 1993. The Bensons bred their Ice Way linebred bitch, Starlite's Cassiopeia, to Torch and kept pick bitch out of that breeding. That puppy became Ch. Starlite's Bear Necessity (Vanessa). She finished her championship as a puppy winning BOS over Specials enroute to her championship. Vanessa was later linebred to Ch. Twilight's High N' Mighty, producing three Specialty winning daughters out of that breeding. One of those bitches, Ch. Starlite's Bear Essential (Whitney), owned by Janet Chu and co-owned by the Bensons, finished her championship from the puppy classes winning BOS over Specials. Whitney has several BBs, Specialty BOS wins, Specialty AMs and Specialty Sweepstakes to her credit.

The Bensons co-own another bitch Special with Sheri Hudson. That bitch, Ch. Starlite's Northern Exposure (Kiska) is out of their Ch. Torch bred to Ch. Samkita's Taiga of Weisland. Kiska is a multiple BB winner and Group placer. She finished her championship by winning BW at the Samoyed Club of Central Arizona's first Specialty in 1993.

Ch. Danica's D'ble Dutch Chocolate BISS, bred, owned and handled by Dr. John and Judy Kovitch, was the only puppy in the litter by Ch. Wolf River's Drumlin ex Ch. Danica's Russian Foxfire.

Dutch entered the ring for the first time at eleven months of age winning BW for a three-point major. The following weekend he won Best in Sweepstakes at the Pittsburgh Specialty. He finished quickly with several BBs from the classes. Although Specialed on a limited basis, his wins include multiple Group placements as well as a Best in Specialty at the Pittsburgh Samoyed Club in 1990.

Dutch is now pursuing his WS with activities, including Therapy Dog certification and pack hiking.

Dutch is the sire of several outstanding young dogs. His daughter Ch. Foxfire's Rosebud finished in five shows with back-to-back five-point majors, including a PVSC Specialty win. Her brother, Ch. Foxfire's Tailspin, is a sound, fluid-moving dog who finished easily. He has also qualified for Therapy Dog certification. Proving that Samoyeds can be multidimensional, Sylvan's Flying Free is excelling in Obedience, Herding and skijoring, as well as the conformation ring with WD at the Denver Specialty. Amo's Midnight Sun started his career with a BOS in Sweeps at PVSC, Fall 1994, a major his next time out and one week later went BW for a five point major at PVSC, Fall 1995. He is working toward his WS, has passed his herding instinct test and started pack hiking. Summit's Miss Muffit has attained her WSX competitive sled racing. She was the winner of the Denver Samoyed Tournament, 1993, chosen by three judges as the best example of the breed. Her owner received a trip to the National for this honor.

JoAnne Marineau shares her thoughts on the Samoyed:

What is it about these beautiful animals that so captivates the true Samoyed lover and effects our psyches and our lives. Besides the obvious attributes such as breath-taking beauty, great intelligence, their canny knowledge of when they are entertaining us and obvious delight in doing so, I think it goes much deeper.

I have studied wolves all my life and find them to be among the most fascinating, misunderstood, and mistreated creatures on our planet. When I had eleven adult Sams and was very active in the breed, I had no runs, and the dogs lived in and out of the house as they pleased, and had one acre of fenced land to run and play on and dig body sized caves on! I spent many hours watching them under all different conditions, and I believe they are about as close to wolves as any domestic animal.

When you look deeply into your Samoyed's eyes, are you not deeply stirred by some far off echo of more primitive times when man lived on this planet and treated our fellow creatures more as equals (or superiors!) rather than trying to dominate Nature? I think that the Indians have much to teach us about this trait.

It is my opinion that if a person really wants to understand all the wonderful traits of our Sams, wolf studies are in order. I used to love my "pack chorus" every night at midnight. It made chills run up my spine and brought to me mental pictures of Arctic wolves calling to each other in the night. Anyone who owns a Samoyed, and really knows their friend, will have stirring tales of their Sam's uncanny knowledge and sense of when to be calm and when to be "on guard." One of my sweetest males presented an absolutely frightening posture when he felt that I was in danger. Otherwise, he was a big lap dog!

I haven't been at ringside regularly for eight years now, so I really don't know if the breed is retaining its true temperament. I certainly hope so. It's up to the breeders of today and tomorrow to be ultra-responsible so that we do not lose this precious gift. In this ever more stress-filled world, I believe people's pets are all the more important to their mental health.

Debbie Madsen obtained Ch. Polar Mist Code Breaker at four months of age from Lynette Hansen of Polar Mist Samoyeds. Debbie observes,

Obie is my first show dog and also my first Samoyed! Obie is always owner-handled and we have done all of our learning together, and I often say that he doesn't win because of me he wins in spite of me!

With a couple of local fun matches under our belts, we entered our first circuit of AKC point shows in May of 1989 in Laramie, Wyoming. Obie was then 10 months old. On the second day, Obie went BB over seven Specials. Our judge was Mr. Robert Forsyth. Four years later, on the same Colorado/Wyoming circuit, Mr. Forsyth again awarded Obie BB and a Group 1 at the Terry-All KC show enroute to BIS under judge William Fetner.

It has been a wonderful seven years with Obie, our other Sams, and all the "Sammy-people" we have formed friendships with along the way. I certainly don't need to expound to you the virtues of our magnificent breed, but I can tell you that I could never imagine another day for the rest of my life without a Samoyed in it!

d'Keta Samoyeds is owned by Christie Smith. She acquired her first Samoyed, Can. Ch. Kamelot's Danish Shadow v. HNP, WSX, CGC, HIC, from Mardee Ward-Fanning and Jennifer Brown (Kamelot) in 1989. Christie's goal has been to acquire and produce a truly beautiful Samoyed. This is what initially attracts people to the breed—the gorgeous head, coat and tempera-ment. d'Keta prefers a larger male, masculine and confident, and the bitches should be feminine, pretty and confident. d'Keta's first champion was a bitch, Am., Can. Ch. Hoof 'n Paw's Midknight d'Keta, called Carmen. Can. Ch. Kamelot's Danish Shadow sired three litters that produced Am., Can. Ch. d'Keta Kai O Silverthaw and Am., Can. Ch. Kira O Silverthaw, bred by Linda Scallion.

Christie and Celinda Knott co-bred Am., Can. Ch. Kira O Silverthaw to Ch. Sanorka's Moonlight Gambler. Christie and Mardee Ward-Fanning co-bred Can. Ch. Kamelot's Danish Shadow to Am., Can. Ch. Hoof 'n Paw's Ivory Knight and Ch. Hoof 'n Paw's Midknight Maxx, WSX, and Tundra Winds Maroon Belle, WSX. All three males have excellent size, bone and masculinity. The bitches are feminine and pretty. [*Authors' note:* That is the way the sex should be!] Five of them completed championships.

The story of Ch. Windy Ridge Wild Card (Annie), owned by Carol Hjort and John Studebaker, is a success story in every way. Annie came into Carol's life like a comet, unexpectedly and unplanned, at the 1992 National Specialty in Mars, Pennsylvania. John Studebaker walked in the door with this beautiful seven-week-old puppy bitch in his arms, and after looking at her pedigree, Carol decided that if this little bitch could move, she was going home with her! John and Carol drew up a co-ownership contract on the back of a place mat that afternoon in the coffee shop—and the rest is history!

Annie was named after John's wife, JoAnne, and she soon became Windy Ridge Wild Card since we felt that "lady luck" had brought her our way.

She completed her championship quickly in December 1994 with back-to-back majors and then retired to the kennel until spring 1995, when it was decided to try her out as a Special. Her third time out as a Special she won her first BB and then went all the way to Best in Show, defeating some of the top show dogs in the country—owner handled all the way. What a thrilling day it was!

Ch. Windy Ridge Wild Card completed four months of showing in 1995, with the following record: #1 owner-handled bitch (ranked #7 nationally); All-Breed Best in Show winner; Group placer (never less than a Group II!); Specialty BOS winner; and ranked in the top ten.

Ron and Jolene Stolba live in Bozeman, Montana, about a mile from the foothills of the Hyalite mountain range. They describe their "Spike" as the howler of all time, thus they have started their Sammy kennel as the Hyalite Howlers. Spike was bred to BIS winner Am., Can. Ch. Snowghosts Go Better with Coke and produced two females. Since they could not decide which to keep, the Stolbas kept both. They are Am., Can. Ch. Hyalites' Classical Jazz and Am., Can. Ch. Hyalite's Little Bit of Coke.

On a repeat breeding they got Ch. Hyalites' Havin A Hissy Fit and Hyalites' Sheza Howler. The Stolbas newest endeavor has been "tracking" with Jazzmine and Tiffany, which is exciting but exhausting and time-consuming. There are only two TDX Samoyeds, and they were passed at eleven and thirteen years of age. The training and testing are rigorous.

Am., Can. Ch. Hyalite Classical Jazz, TD, finished her Canadian championship at seven months in two weekends. This included two Group 4s and two Best Puppy in Shows. At barely eight months, at the Specialty in Washington, she was WB, BOW, Best Bred-by and Best Brace with her sister Tiff. With sixteen Specials, she received one of the AMs. At the 1993 SCA National, she won Best in Sweeps in an entry of 112 puppies. In brace competition, Jazz and Tiff in twelve outings have won Best Brace in Show eight times!

In 1994 the Samoyed Fancy lost Ivy Kilburn-Scott, daughter of the founders of this breed. She was ninety years of age. In May 1994 Thomas Mayfield was killed in his prime in a tragic motorcycle accident. Later in the year John Coloma died of a heart attack while he was being awarded Best of Breed in the Samoyed ring. The Samoyed Fancy lost some important supporters in these people, and the 1995 Los Angeles Specialty was held in their memory.

Angela Frye saw her first Samoyed at the Singapore Kennel Club in 1984. From that time, she read all she could about Samoyeds. Finally in 1989 she took serious steps to acquire a bitch.

Ch. Seamist Strikes Again (Keilah) was bred by Archie and Anne Peil and Kay Hallberg. Angela had seen Ch. Wolf River's Seamist Cascade at the 1993 SCA Santa Rosa National and met Anne and Archie there. Their intention, if they were to breed Cassie, was to combine breed type with movement, which was exactly what Angela was looking for. Right after the Wisconsin National, in 1994, the Peils bred Cassie to Can., Am. Ch. Vanderbilt's Secretariat, TT. Angela wanted a bitch, and as it turned out, Keilah was the only bitch in Cassie's litter!

Keilah started by taking Best Puppy at the San Diego Specialty in May of 1995 and ironically finished at the same show a year later when she was eighteen months old! The following day, at Cabrillo Kennel Club, she won BOB in her first show as a Special! From all indications, the authors would consider her a "White Water candidate"—a star of the future.

SAMOYEDS IN HAWAII

Our fiftieth state, Hawaii, which has had purebred dog fanciers for more than five decades, has added the Samoyed in respectable numbers in the past ten years, even though not managing to develop a Specialty club for the breed.

We include those breeders here as they are separated by problems no other Samoyed breeder faces. They not only have 2,500 miles of water between them and the nearest mainland fancier, but also a four-month state-imposed quarantine on the importation of animals. Although the quarantine kennels do not prevent the socialization of dogs, it does make it difficult. It is possible for the owners to visit and train their new imports each day, but it takes considerable time and effort.

Another facet to the selection and importation of dogs is the fact that animals from New Zealand, Australia, England or any other quarantine country are admitted without the four months at the Hawaii State kennels.

Shiroi Samoyeds, Clifford and Amy Sakata, began in 1976 with Ch. Orion's Tara of Kubla Khan from Mrs. Pat Morehouse of California. Tara won her championship in four consecutive shows. This is an unusual feat since there are only four shows a year on the Island of Oahu where they live.

Years later, Clifford and Amy Sakata report that Ch. Shiroi Dancing Icicle (Icy) came very close to being their perfect Sammy. She is a natural showgirl, even at the venerable age of twelve. She is only 19½ inches at the withers, structurally sound, with a very nice, strong gait.

At the start of her show career, Icy won many BBs. At that time, the Working Group was not split into two Groups, so competition was very tough.

Hoping to get another Icy, the Cliffords did a repeat breeding but to their disappointment got only four males, one of which sired Ch. Shiroi Silver

Challenger (Pudge). Pudge is described as a beautiful English-type male with average movement. He became a champion at an early age, but because of a dislike for the show ring, was never campaigned. The Sakatas entered him in an instinct-testing trial instructed by Terry Parrish, and he was doing very well until a "bully billy goat head-butted him." After that he didn't think it was very much fun. The Sakatas are very happy with White Magic's Myth of Shiroi (Magic) because, as they had guessed, Magic has the qualities consistent with Drumlin's get. Clifford and Amy are hoping that breeding Pudge's daughter, Shiroi's Magical Whisper (Kizzy), to Magic will produce another Icy.

Touche' Raincountry Aleutian (Novaskaya Moonlite Magic ex Samantha Sue Snowball) was imported to Hawaii in the summer of 1990 from Betty Moody's Novaskaya Kennels in Virginia. Lyn and Joe Medeiros acquired this dog after some personal downturns with his original Hawaiian owner. These wise enthusiasts availed themselves of the experienced guidance of Harvey Yamashita, Aleutian was retrained, reconditioned and groomed from a one-year-old rascal to become a champion and a credit to his breed. Handled by Harvey, he has been a multiple Group winner, Top Samoyed in Hawaii and #6 Working Dog Group in Hawaii for 1995!

SAMOYEDS IN ALASKA

The K-Way, Kondako, Moonlighter, Nepachee, Polar Mist, Wolf River and Whitecliff lines are among those that have played an important part in Samoyeds in Alaska.

Millard and the late Margie Primmer were major factors in the development of the Fancy with their Whitecliff-based Laska Samoyeds. Their Ch. Laska's Czar of Whitecliff, CD, was a multiple Group placer and an influential stud reflected in many of today's pedigrees.

Orkdomain (Annella Cooper) started in 1968 with Ch. Tawni Tami of Ala-Cryss. Keeping good bitches and shipping "outside" to appropriate studs helped to expand the Alaskan gene pool. Annella showed Am., Can. Ch. Misty Way's Orkdomain Toika, Am., Can. CD (bred by Peggy McCarthy), to a Canadian BIS winner and son of an AM winner at the 1983 SCA Specialty after winning the Veteran Bitch class. Toika tied for top producing dam in 1981 by virtue of her three champion offspring that year, one of which was Ch. Orkdomain's Jacki Lantern, CD, RWB, at the 1978 National Specialty from the Puppy class. Ch. Orkdomain No Shimano, a Toika granddaughter (Ch. Ice Way's Ice Breaker ex Orkdomain's Squeakie Toi), enjoyed a show career that included multiple Group wins and produced six champion offspring.

Ch. Subarktika's Kodiak Karluk was purchased by Annella from Carol Haas and had previously proven herself by winning a Group second from the classes under judge D. Ward. Annella finished her championship by

Ch. Touche's Raincountry Aleutian, owned by Lyn and Joe Medeiros and bred by Pat Gibo and Francis Kauhane. Shown by Harvey Yamashita, he was #6 Working dog in Hawaii in 1995. *Carl Lindemaier*

Ch. Cerebus Away We Go (Ch. Orkdomains X Marks The Spot ex Ch. K-Way's Strike The Pose), owned by William and Tina Oswald (breeder) and Dorie Engstrom. *Bishop*

Ch. Orkdomain's X Marks The Spot (Ch. K-Way's Marksman's Fantasy ex Ch. Orkdomain No Shimano), owned by William and Tina Oswald and bred by Annella Cooper.

winning a Group first. "Karly" was the first in three generations of Group winners. Two years later her son Ch. Orkdomain's Captivator won the Group, and in the spring of 1996, granddaughter Orkdomain's Antica Ricetta finished her championship (pending confirmation) with a Group second from the classes over four Specials. Karly is also the dam of Orkdomain's all-champion litter of four by Ch. Seamist's Spellbinder.

Carol Haas (Subarktika) of Fairbanks produced Ch. Subarktika's Kodiak Karluk (Ch. Wolf River's Drumlin ex Ch. Polar Mist's Salcha Queen, CD). Carol has finished or produced five champions and has been active with recreational sledding and skijoring. She is presently exhibiting Ch. Orkdomain Subarktika Charley, a Karly grandson by Ch. Krystall's Treasure of Gold out of Orkdomain's Glacier Bay.

Gayl Jokiel (NorthFace) of Anchorage has done limited breeding but has been a major contributor to the Fancy since 1973. Ch. NorthFace Baree was a grandson of Gayl's first champion, Ch. Kondako's NorthFace Oriana, and of Ch. Kondako's Busybody, who spent her retirement with Gayl. She bred her Drumlin daughter, Wolf River's Amarok, to Bizzy's son, Ch. Kondako's Show Biz, and the resulting litter of three males all became champions. Of that litter, Ch. NorthFace Alexander, owned by Dr. Jim Anderson (Hyboraia), has won several BBs and Group placements from the Veterans class. Ch. Wolf River's Dacotah was purchased as a puppy from Kay Hallberg and is a daughter of Ch. Wolf River's Falcon ex BIS/BISS Ch. Wolf River's Terra. "Cody" won a Group second. Gayl also co-owns Ch. Wolf River Arkko of Hyboraea, who lives with and is shown by Jim Anderson. For years Gayl had a working Samoyed team and found the sled dog instinct still very much in existence. She was elected to five terms on the SCA's board of governors.

Tina and Bill Oswald (Cerebus) purchased the puppy to become Ch. Orkdomain's X Marks The Spot, by Ch. K-Way's Marksman's Fantasy ex Ch. Orkdomain No Shimano, from Annella Cooper. "Machee" is a multiple Group winner and placer. They then contacted Bob and Wanda Krauss for a foundation bitch, acquiring Ch. K-Way's Strike The Pose (Kelly,) as an eight-week-old puppy out of Ch. K-Way's Marksman's Fantasy ex Group winning Ch. K-Way's Rainbow Connection. Their first litter out of Kelly was sired by Ch. Orkdomain's X Marks The Spot and produced their Ch. Cerebus Away We Go (Joni.) The Oswalds have high hopes for Joni as a show dog and brood bitch. The Oswalds also purchased a puppy in 1995 from Janice Hovelmann. They hope the combination of K-Way and Sanorka will produce their next generation of champions.

Cindy and Michael McCarron (Prime Time) of Anchorage finished Ch. Orkdomain's Kaanapali Breeze, by Ch. K-Way's Marksman's Fantasy ex Ch. Orkdomain No Shimano. They purchased Ch. Orkdomain's I'm Not Second (Ch. Nepachee's Excaliber ex Ch. Orkdomain No Shimano), a multiple Group placer and an AM winner at the 1989 SCA Specialty. Under their ownership, "Sunny" garnered Best Veteran at the 1995 SCA Specialty. They then leased Kelly from the Oswalds to breed to their Ch. Orkdomain's Prime Time (Cable). They also have a bitch from Gail and Terry Campbell (Tega).

Linda Rockstad (Shasam) of Wasilla is working with Lynette Blue with Polar Mist bloodlines. Linda has bred her foundation bitch Ch. Polar Mist's Rose of Shasam to Ch. Orion's Bud Light of Polar Mist, which produced two champion progeny. Rose bred to Ch. Polar Mist's Mover N-A Shaker produced a third champion, Ch. Shasam's Movin N-A Cruisin.

Mona Brucher (Woodland) from Chugiak shows her Group-placing Ch. Orkdomain's Maximum Ice, by Nepacahee's Excaliber ex Orkdomain No Shimano. Her retired champion, Ch. Orkdomain's Kiana, has already produced one champion, Ch. Orkdomain's Northern Gale, and two other major-pointed daughters: Orkdomain's Annie of Woodland, owned by Mona, and Woodland's Alabaster lady, owned by April Johns.

Barbara Weinig of Anchorage owned Ch. Whitecliff's Ragnar Bjorn, which became one of the top winning Samoyeds in America. She now has a son of Ch. Whitecliff's Saruka Karu and Ch. Whitecliff's Raisin' Kaina Karu called Whitecliff's Karu Isbjorneinar. Barbara has contributed greatly to the breed, generously devoting time to education and training, and demonstrating grooming skills.

Michael and Judy Bundy of Homer have entered the Fancy with their young, major-pointed Orkdomain's Sholokov Shemya (Orkdomain's Snow King of Adak ex Ch. Orkdoommain's C'est la Vie). Michael has a strong competitive racing background and will surely focus on the Samoyed's working abilities.

As with the Samoyed Fancy in Hawaii, Alaskan friends of the breed are faced with a number of daunting challenges not a factor for mainlanders. That they are so successful in holding the breed's banner so high is a great tribute to their love of the Samoyed and their tenacious loyalty to its best, long-term interests.

THE MAKINGS OF GREATNESS

In the 1980s, Ch. Quicksilver's Razz Ma Tazz completely rewrote the record book, and his record still stands. In December 1984, Tazz's record (at only three years of age!) included fifty-four all-breed Bests in Show under fifty-one different judges. His record with handler Roy Murray remains undefeated at this writing (fall 1997) color:

202 Group placements (141 firsts)

232 Bests of Breed

Best of Breed at the 1983 and 1984 SCA Specialties

#1 Working Dog (all systems) 1983 and 1984 (#1 Samoyed, of course)

#2 Dog all breeds for 1983; #3 Dog all breeds for 1984

Quaker Oats Award for the Working Group: 1983 and 1984

Ch. Quicksilver's Razz Ma Tazz—Tazz, as he was popularly known—was whelped August 5, 1981. He was by Ch. Kolinka Quilted Bear (Hoss) ex Ch. Quicksilver's Lucky Starr and was bred by Danny and Chris Middleton, Quicksilver Samoyeds, Houston, Texas. The Middletons co-owned Tazz with the owners of his sire, Eugene and Joyce Curtis.

In January 1983, the owners added the professional handler Roy Murray, and Tazz went on to his history-making record—always accompanied by one or more of his owners, who groomed him and supported him.

To become a truly great winner and campaigner, a dog of any breed must have, in addition to more than 90 percent conformation to the breed Standard in his physical attributes, the following:

- The ability to show in all climates, on all surfaces, in all types of show ring setups and despite all noises and distractions

- The desire to show with animation; never shy; never too aggressive
- The ability to eat, drink and maintain all normal functions while engaging in extensive, long-term travel; impeccable ring presence

These requisites are not spelled out in any breed Standard, but Ch. Quicksilver's Razz Ma Tazz possessed these qualities as his glittering record attests.

Another advantage that Tazz had was partnership of dedicated owners and the attentions of an expert handler. Tazz's owners were so supportive with patience, time and money that after six months of campaigning they formed a roofing company in Houston, Texas, with three partners: Danny Middleton, Eugene Curtis and Razz Ma Tazz. This effort to raise money became very successful when a hurricane moved through Houston, Texas, in the autumn of 1983. A major dog food company's television advertising campaign with the Middletons and their dogs aided in the very costly endeavor of travel, entries and handling; thus one could even say that Tazz supported his own cause.

WHITE WATER DOGS
AND BITCHES—
THE PAST FIFTY YEARS

On the following pages are the chosen White Water Dogs and Bitches for the past fifty years. They are in no particular order as each is BEST just as is each person's own Samoyed. We begin with 1985, going backward as well as forward.

We suggest you also study the AKC Video on the Samoyed because the photos here do not show important details such as gaiting, attitude, intelligence or personality; plus that indefinable quality of a truly remarkable Sam-a-'yed. Unfortunately, there is nothing that takes the place of a live performance!

As a thought-provoking project, *you* rank these WW Greats!

Great Dogs Are Like White Water

The history and progress of a breed can be seen as a river.
Then its great dogs are like white water:
They rise, momentarily and brilliant in the sun
To hang there suspended in the mind's eye,
Long after darkness has fallen
And they have rejoined the river on its way to the sea.
Though they make up but a tiny portion of the breed,
They nevertheless contribute significantly
To our total experience of that breed.
They are the dogs who not only win often and/or produce well,
But they are the dogs who capture the imagination
Of judges and fanciers alike,
Who become fixed in our minds when we think of the river.

—(Reprinted from the *Siberian Quarterly*,
with special permission.)

Ch. Quicksilver's Razz Ma Tazz, owned by Danny and Chris Middleton (his breed-ers) and Eugene and Joyce Curtis, was whelped on August 5, 1981, and became the top winning Samoyed of all time. At the end of 1984, Tazz's record included 54 all-breed BIS; 232 BBs; and 202 Group placements, including 141 firsts. Tazz won BB at the 1983 and 1984 SCA Specialties and the Quaker Oats Award for Top Working dog. He was handled by Roy Murray throughout his illustrious show career. He is shown in one of his Bests under author Dolly Ward.

Ch. Moonlighter's Ima Spark O' Bark, owned by Randy and Kathy Lensen and bred by Sharon Kremsreiter, was BISS SCA 1985. One of seven champions by Am., Can. Ch. Moonlighter's Ima Bark Star ex Ch. Samkists Classy Chassis, "Sparkle" won the National quite handily as a Veteran! Sparkle is a littermate to Karen McFarlane's Ch. Frostyacres I've Been Samkist (Cricket). Sparkle was always the showgirl; Cricket was the producer.

Can., Am. Ch. Orenopac's Chaena, owned by Dr. and Mrs. Robert Gaskin was Top Dog in Canada for three years. He is the sire of twenty-six champions and grandsire of twenty-eight champions. *Alex Smith*

Eng. Ch. Zamoyski Lucky Star of Ostyak (Eng. Ch. Hurkur Jingles ex Eng. Ch. Fairvilla Silver Jewel), owned by Mrs. Carol Fox and bred by Mr. and Mrs. Hamilton. With fifty-two C.C.s, this dog holds the win record for Samoyeds in all of Great Britain. *Dalton*

Ch. Tega's Joe Knows, TT, owned and bred by Terry and Gail Campbell, was #1 Samoyed all systems for 1994 and 1995. Owner-handler Gail Campbell campaigned him to the rank of #10 Working Dog, 1994, and in the Top 20 Working Dogs in 1995. His record included 184 BBs and 120 Group placements, including 30 firsts, 4 BIS, 5 BISS and BISS at the SCA National Specialty 1994 under judge Edd Bivin (pictured), all after finishing his championship at just twelve months. *Mikron Photo*

Growing up together—Am., Can. Ch. North Starr King's Ransom was the top SCA Award winner from 1974 to 1977 with a record that included ten American and one Canadian BIS. He sired thirty AKC champions, including four BIS winners. Kathy was Top Junior Handler at the Westminster KC's 100th Anniversary show. Kathy's subsequent handling triumphs include showing three Samoyeds from one litter to BIS wins. Now Mrs. Kathy Heimann, she enjoys being a wife and mother of two children. She returned to the dog scene to handle all the exhibits for the AKC video on Samoyeds.

Am., Can., Bah. Ch. Polar Mist Dr. Pepper (Ch. Belaya's Sergeant Pepper ex Ch. Pepsi Kola of Polar Mist), owned by John and Kathy Ronald and breeder Lynette Hansen, is the top winning owner-handled Samoyed in history. Dr. Pepper's record includes 13 BIS, 8 BISS and more than 140 Group placements. He is shown here going BIS at Minnesota River Valley KC, 1984, under judge Robert Ward. The handler is John Ronald. *Olson*

Am., Can. Ch. Hoof 'n Paws Wild Rose Knight achieved the rank of #2 Samoyed for 1995 for number of Samoyeds defeated (including five career Specialty wins). "Pop" was campaigned by his breeder, Mardee Ward-Fanning in 1994 and by Robert Chaffin in 1995 for owners Jeff and Nan Eisley-Bennett. *Callea*

Ch. Ice Way's Ice Breaker (Ch. Kiska's Karaholme Cherokee ex Ch. Ice Way's Ice Cube), owned by Bobbie Smith, was a BIS and BISS winner and SCA Top Stud Dog for four consecutive years with a remarkable total of 142 champions. *Missy Yuhl*

Ch. Kiska's Karaholme Cherokee, a celebrated English dog with an American Indian name. The #1 SCA Stud Dog for 1980, he had two champion sons, Breaker and Crush, who sired 142 and 51 champions, respectively. His devoted owners Robert and Dolly Ward called him "Painter."

Ch. Ice Way's Ice Cube (Am., Mex. Ch. Snowline's Joli Shashan, CDX, CACIB ex Ch. Powered Puff of the Pacific), owned by Mike and Bobbie Smith, was both a noteworthy winner and an important producer. She is shown here winning the Working Group at the Del Monte KC under judge Howard Dullnig. *Bergman*

Ch. Yurok of Whitecliff (1955–70), owned and handled by Jean Blank and the Percy Matherons to a fabulous record in his day.

Am., Can. Ch. Moonlighter's Ima Bark Star, owned and bred by Moonlighter Samoyeds—a great producer.

Ch. Wolf River's Terra (Ch. Wolf River's Star ex Ch. Wolf River's Prairie) established a record as an outstanding show bitch, working/racing bitch and dam of champions. Terra is the oldest Samoyed to win the National, taking BB at nine and a half years under Dolly Ward in 1992 and BOS at ten and a half years under Mary Morstad in 1993. She was Best or BOS in every SCA Veteran Sweepstakes in which she was entered. Due to her racing sled dog career, Terra was never campaigned but still finished among the top five Samoyeds in America, ranking nationally in the Group more than once. An all-breed BIS winner, Terra was always owner-breeder handled by Kay Hallberg.

Am., Can. Ch. Polar Mist Ain't She Foxy, owned by Lynette Hansen Blue, was the SCA Top Brood Bitch for 1981.

Ch. Wolf River's Drumlin (Ch. Sassillie's Merlyn of Vicrian ex Wintercrest's River Wolf II, CD), bred, owned and shown by Kay Hallberg, finished his championship by taking BOB from the classes at the SC of San Diego Specialty. Drumlin had an outstanding show career, in addition to being one of the breed's all-time top stud dogs. He excelled as a working and racing sled dog. Drumlin was the only male in an all-champion litter of five. *Joan Smith*

Ch. Sitkin's Simply Scrumptious (Ch. Blue Sky's Simply Smashing ex Ch. Sitkin's Stardust Melody), bred by Christine and Dick Higley and shown by owner-handler Joan Luna for co-owners Connie, Paula and Laura Luna. "Scarlett," a show bitch supreme, won 2 BIS, 7 BISS and 126 BBs. *Steven Ross*

Ch. Kazahk's Lucky Duck (Ch. Nordika's Polar Barron, CD ex Ch. Kazahk's Ms Plain Jane) owned by Flo and Saul Waldman, was an eight-and-a-half-year-old veteran when he was BISS at the Potomac Valley SC. *John Ashbey*

Ch. Starchak, CD ("Chatter"), a noted winner of the 1940s and the sire of sixteen champions, was bred by White Way Kennels and owned by Robert and Dolly Ward. The fancy agrees a beautiful headpiece!

Ch. Kondako's Sun Dancer (Ch. Kondako's Dancing Bear ex Ch. Kondako's Koko Lossal), owned by Dave and Connie Richardson, sired twenty-one champions and won two Specialties and a Tournament.

Ch. Rainier (1947–59), a "Chatter" son bred by Elizabeth Wyman and owned by the Wards. "Raini's" Group first at the 1949 Sun Maid KC of Fresno event was the first for a Samoyed in sixteen years and a significant "ice breaker" for the breed on the Pacific Coast.

Ch. Nachalnik of Drayalene (Ch. Rockandi of Drayaelene ex Drayalene's Clarisse), owned by Harold and Doris McLaughlin, was the sire of forty-five champions. This tally made him the breed's top sire until 1984.

Ch. Kondako's Dancing Bear, 1968–80 (Ch. Nachalnik of Drayalene ex Ch. Oni-Agra's Silver Bunny), bred and owned by Dave and Connie Richardson, sired twenty-seven champions and had SCA Top Producer Awards for 1972 and 1975.

Ch. Frostyacres Golly Ms. Molly, owned and bred by Robert and Karen McFarlane, is a two-time BIS winner. *Downey*

Ch. Ren J's Go Go Dancer, owned by Jeff and Nan Eisley-Bennett and Janet Hovelmann, was both a four-time BIS and a BISS winner. *Booth*

Ch. Sulu's Fire 'n Ice, owned by Bill and Bernadette Rambow and Julie Hoehn and bred by Barbara Del Santo, was campaigned for three years. During this period she amassed 141 BBs, 32 Group firsts, 63 other placements, one BISS and four all-breed BIS. She was handled by Nancy Sheehan Martin. *Petrulis*

Ch. K-Way's Omen of Destiny, CD (Ch. Sassillie's Merlyn of Vicrian ex K-Way's Mint Julep of Vicrian), owned by Bob and Wanda Krauss, was a most influential stud. He was the grandsire of Ch. Quicksilver's Razz Ma Tazz and other important Samoyeds.

Ch. Hoof 'n Paw's A Rose Is a Rose, owned by Jeff and Nan Bennett, Mardee Ward-Fanning and Dolly Ward. "Ana" is one of the breed's standouts during the latter half of the 1990s. A multiple BIS and BISS winner, she was the #1 Samoyed in the United States all systems in 1996 and again in 1997 and was BB at the Westminster KC in 1997. In mid-1997 Ana added a World Championship and CACIB and established an all-breed BIS record for Samoyed bitches with six Bests. *Allen Photography*

chapter 4

SCA Specialties: Where the White Water Shines Brightest

1986-96

The 1986 SCA National (the 55th)

The Northern California Samoyed Fanciers club put on the 1986 National, using the theme "Putting on the Ritz." Robert H. Ward judged dogs and intersex. The late Dan Morgan judged bitches, Regular and Non-Regular classes, and put up Pemstar's Fantasia owned by John Donner. It was held in the glamorous ballroom of the Red Lion Inn and Convention Center, San Jose, California, on September 26–28.

Martha Beal judged the Futurity, putting up Nancy Golden's Krystal's Treasure of Gold to Best Puppy. Reserve from 9–12 Intersex was Connie, Joan and Paula Luna's, Azteca's Waterford Krystle; Best 12–15 Bitch was Hoof 'n Paw's In the Buff, co-owned by Genia Cox, besting her litter brother who was Best 12–15 Dog, Hoof 'n Paw's Knight Rider, and Best 12–15 Bitch, the Luna's Ch. Sitkin's Simply Scrumptious, bred by the Higleys. Finally, Hoof 'n Paw's In the Buff was named Grand Futurity Winner by judge Martha Beale.

Breeder-judge Richard Beale put up Whitecliff's Alexis, owned by Wilna Coulter and handled by Frances Powers to Best in Sweepstakes over a large, quality field. Best of Opposite Sex in Sweeps was Shalimar's Kori of Taliko, handled by his breeder Karl Geletich.

Judge Robert Ward chose as his WD Polar Mist Great White North, shown by the breeder, Lynette Hansen, owned by M. Towriss-Smith of Canada. RWD was Chatka of Jerlaine, owned by Jerry and Elaine Ruettiger and bred by Don and Judy Anthony.

WB was Pemstar's Fantasia, owned by John Donner. Sea-Sun's Poki Ahu Mokhana, owned by Rosemary Jones, was RWB.

Ch. Whitecliff's Alexis, owned by Wilna Coulter, was Best in Sweeps at the 1986 SCA Specialty under judge Richard Beale. Bred only once, Alexis produced three champions in a litter of five and was still winning BBs and Group placements at age nine. *Callea*

Best Sled Bitch was Ch. Wolf River's Terra. Best Brood Bitch of the fifteen entered was Ch. Seamist's Diamond Dazzler, bred by Archie Peil and Danny Middleton and owned by Sue Hurst and Anne Peil.

Best Sled Dog was Wolf River's Drumlin, owned by Kay Hallberg.

Best Stud Dog and Best Veteran was Ch. Blue Sky's Smiling At Me, born in 1977, bred and owned by Elizabeth Lockman.

Best Veteran Bitch was Ch. Moonlighter's Ima Spark O'Bark, the 1985 BISS from the Veterans class!

Best Brace was owned by Wood, McClellan and LeCour, was Ch. Gandalf Wizard of Elmfield and Ch. Elmfield's Mountain Magic, litter brothers born in 1983.

The Awards of Merit were Ch. Image's the Barrister (Dukes); Ch. Moonlighter's Ima Spark O'Bark (Lensen); Ch. Wolf River's Terra (Hallberg); and Ch. Blue Sky's Breaking Away (Hooyman). The WD were Polar Mist Great White North; Ch. Statussam's Troublemaker, (Torres) and Ch. Whitecliff's Layka Karu, (Powers).

BOS to BB was Ch. Sambushed Spoonful O Sugar, bred by Elizabeth Metz and owned with her by Wayne and Jeanne Nonhof.

BISS was Ch. Whitecliff-Bykhal's Puck Karu, bred by Bonnie Giffin and owned and handled by Frances Powers.

The 1987 SCA National (the 56th)

About the time of the 1987 SCA National in New Hampshire, some changes in personnel and places happened. It was the first National held in the East since 1975.

The fifty-sixth National was held on the lavish green lawns of the Anheuser-Busch Brewery in New Hampshire. It was dedicated to the memory of Aljean Mason Larson, daughter of Agnes Mason of White Way, a brilliant horsewoman and handler of Samoyeds and Dobermans. Aljean was pictured in the catalog winning Best Team in Show with Samoyeds under judge Louis Murr about 1940, in Long Beach, California.

In memory of Phoebe Castle Faulmann (1951–87), she was pictured in the catalog with her Best Bred-by in 1983, Ch. Heritage Debra Gale.

The Minuteman Samoyed Club acted as host, and the Greater Pittsburgh Samoyed Club supported.

Carol Chittum judged the Futurity and put up Blue Sky's Dapper Dan, bred and owned by Dr. P. J. and Liz Hooyman. Dr. Marion Jerszyk judged Sweepstakes and put up Blue Sky's Dazzler, bred by Dr. P. J. Hooyman and E. Hooyman and owned by the breeders and J. and S. Bennett.

The exhibitors came from every point of the compass, and catalog advertising was an intriguing showcase of the Samoyed at the time.

From Canada came the High Scoring in obedience, Nepachee's Music Man, owned by Betty McHugh.

Best Stud Dog was Ch. Blue Sky's Breaking Away, by Ch. Ice Ways Ice Breaker ex Blue Sky's Pound Cake, owned and handled by Elizabeth Hooyman.

Veteran Bitch was Ch. Sulu's Mindy's On My Mind, owned by Barbara Arnaud, the Braviroffs and Ms. Lockman.

Sled Dog Bitch and Sled Dog Dog were both won by Kay Bailey Hallberg, with Ch. Wolf River's Terra and Ch. Wolf River's Drumlin. Drumlin was also Best Veteran.

My Way's Bear Elegance was Best in the Bred-by-Exhibitor classes. She was owned by Kathie and Randy Lensen.

The German Shepherd Dog authority, Helen Miller Fisher, judged the Regular Dog classes and gaited her Sams with as much diligence as could be expected from a Shepherd judge.

Winners Dog and Reserve both came from Open Dogs. These were Kondako's Show Biz (Richardson) and Blue Sky's Dazzler (Bennett and Hooyman), respectively.

The Samoyed authority, Duvella Kusler, judged the Regular Bitch classes, which were huge!

Winners Bitch and Best of Winners, Daska Farm's Frosti Tibbu owned by Eloise Spiegel, came from Open as did the Reserve, Windy Ridge Chablis Sumerhill, owned by Karen McClain and bred by the Studebakers.

Duvella Kusler stepped into the enormous ring to judge the huge field of champions present. It was a sight to behold all those immaculate Samoyeds on spacious green turf. After completely examining and gaiting every contestant—some more than once, the final moment came. BOS to BB was Ch. Whitecliff's Layka Karu, owned by Frances Powers, co-breeder Kathryn Molineux.

BISS was awarded to Ch. Windsongs Classic Composer, bred by Mary Kistner and Charlotte Koehler and owned by Pat and Gary Griffin.

The 1988 SCA National (the 57th)

National Specialties flourished in size and glamour from a one-day event to three days and later—with the addition of the board meetings and annual meetings of the SCA membership, the "National could last five or six days." Now with Agility, Herding, plus other activities, they may last a week. Of course, one might always choose which part to attend if such a choice works into the scheduled events.

One of the last lower key Nationals was in 1988, which took three days. It was hosted by the four Samoyed Clubs in southern California: Los Angeles, Orange County, San Diego and Southern California, using a theme of Westward Ho! Jeanne Nonhof, president, and Kay Hallberg, secretary, praised the event for the many satisfied participants.

There were 100 entries in the Futurity for Phyllis Brayton, a Siberian Husky breeder and an AKC judge. There were 132 entries for Kay Bailey Hallberg to judge, and twenty-six entries in Obedience for judge Harlowe C. Jahelka.

John Studebaker judged Dogs and Intersex and gave WD to Ann Bark and John Jermyn's Seawind's Mister Mister. Lynette Hansen's Polar Mist Law Breaker was Reserve Winners Dog.

Keke Kahn judged the Bitch classes and put Kolinka's Mischievous Molly, owned by Joyce Curtis and Marguerite Baird, to Winners. Reserve Winners Bitch was Sanorka's Kotton Kandi for breeder-owner Janice Hovelmann, handled by Carrie Parma.

Best Veteran Dog, out of fourteen, was Ch. Whitecliff's Gainsborough, owned by Wilma Coulter.

Best Veteran Bitch was Ch. Denka's Diamond Tiara, CD, bred by Garey and Cookie Hayden.

For BISS, John Studebaker put up Ch. Kolinka's Quilted Bear, owned by Eugene and Joyce Curtis and Marguerite Baird. As he was also the sire of the Winners Bitch, the entire Specialty took on an added luster for all concerned.

With eighty-four Specials in competition for Best of Breed along with the WD, WB and two Veterans, there were many more worthy candidates than the BISS winner. Awards of Merit go to a percentage of the entry. On this day the AMs were Ch. Image's the Barrister (Duke); Ch. Whitecliff's Alexis (Coulter); Ch. Sitkin's Simply Scrumptious (Luna); Ch. Northwind's Rising Star (Halmi/Feinberg), winner of the World Show in Israel; Ch. Blue Sky's Dazzler (Lockman/Bennett); Ch. Crizta's Li'l Drummer Boy (Bennett/Schultz); and Ch. Artic Brite Truly Scrum Shus (Hoffecker Osterreich).

For BOS, John Studebaker chose Ch. Kipperic Heritage Heroine (Hodges/Faulmann).

The Stud Dog class was won by Ch. Trailblazer Circuit Breaker (Mears/Cox), by Ch. Ice Way's Ice Breaker. Second was Ch. Andromeda Tugger of Crush (Ward/Bark), by Ice Way's Ice Crush. Both were grandsons of "Painter."

Am., Can. Ch. Windsong's Classic Composer (Ch. Kipperic Jaksun ex Ch. Windsong's Sleigh Belle), owned by Pat and Gary Griffin and bred by Kistner and Koehler. Although "Bach" tragically died at age four, he was BB at the SCA National in 1987 and had one all-breed BIS and five Specialties. Happily, he left eleven champion offspring. *Kim Booth*

Ch. Kipperic Heritage Heroine, owned by the late Phoebe Faulmann and her breeders, Don and Dot Hodges. "Phoebe" was a multiple Specialty winner, was BOS at the 1988 SCA National and had a 1988 all-breed BIS. *Bonnie*

Ch. Crizta's Cover Girl, CDX, TT (Ch. Ice Way's Flash Cube ex Snoko's Nishi of Silveracres), owned by Gini Addamo and Dany Canino and bred by Teena Deatherage Schulz. "Lace" was actively campaigned in Obedience and conformation in the mid-1980s. *Rich Bergman*

The Brood Bitch winner was Ch. Snowstar's Eilonwy O'Maikai (Weissman).

Puppy Sweepstakes was judged by breeder Kay Hallberg who chose Crizta's Capri of Bakari (Schulz/Gallien) for Best. Owned by breeder Teena Deatherage Schulz and Steven Capri, she eventually became Steve Gallien's foundation bitch.

The Futurity was judged by Phyllis Brayton who chose as Grand Futurity Winner Shandiin's Likan (Brown).

Mi-Sam's Compound Interest (Ronald) was Best Intersex from the 9–12 class; Statussam's Yogi Bear (Torrez) was Best Intersex Dog (9–12).

The two 15–18 Futurity winners were Ch. Frostyacres Mlle Dancing Bear (Stohl) and Polar Mist Law Breaker (Hansen).

In Obedience, Jake Jahelka judged the highest scoring Champion of Record to be Ch. Crizta's Cover Girl, CDX (Addamo/Canino). High in Trial was Ch. Elmfield's Applause, CD, owned by Gail Sheridan.

This fifty-seventh Specialty show held in Ontario, California, was in memory of Dan Morgan, a Samoyed breeder and AKC judge. His widow, La Vera, continues supporting the Samoyed breed in northern California.

The 1989 SCA National Specialty (the 58th)

The 1989 SCA National was held in Plymouth, Michigan, October 3–5, hosted by the Samoyed Association of Metro-Detroit. An astounding entry of eighty-eight titlists were entered in the parade at the close of the Specialty—the biggest parade ever held. There were 954 dogs entered, and with double entries (including Obedience and Non-Regular classes) it totaled a record 1,069!

Many that would become stars began their careers here. Some perished, like Kathy Metter's Futurity winner Denka's Teddy Bear, under the wheels of a car—the ageless problem of gates left open.

Some past stars, like Am., Can., Ber Ch. Polar Mist Dr. Pepper, (Ronald/Hansen) won the Stud Dog class under Jane Forsyth. He ties the record for SCA Specialty wins with ten BISS. His co-owner, John Ronald, does hold the all-time owner-handled record for SCA BISS with Dr. Pepper.

Ch. Sambushed Spoonful O' Sugar (Nonhof/Metz) won the coveted Brood Bitch class.

The 169 entries in the Regular Dog classes were judged by Jane Forsyth. Her WD, from Open, was Silver Sarks the Main Event (Schryer). RWD from American-bred Dogs was Snowstar Alsa Casanova (Binkley).

The bitches were judged by all-rounder Joe Gregory, who placed Flying Cloud's Song of the Sea (Norris/Bark) WB from the 6–9 class and Best Puppy with an AM for good measure. RWB, also from the 6–9, was Westwind's Ring Side Gossip (Malueg).

To great applause, Ch. Orenpac's Chaena (Gaskin) was chosen Best Veteran Dog. The same response met the Veteran Bitch, Ch. Nuvak's Rising Star (Rost).

Ch. Sambushed Spoonful O'Sugar, owned by Jeanne Nonhof and Elizabeth Metz, was BOS at the 1986 SCA National. This bitch produced outstanding puppies in addition to having a great show career.

Ch. Whitecliff's Layka Karu, bred and owned by Frances Powers, began her star-studded show career early by winning the Futurity and Sweepstakes at the 1985 SCA National Specialty. This lovely, multiple Group winning bitch was also BOS at the 1987 National. She was initially handled by her breeder-owner and later handled by Betty Arnold Chamberlain. *John Ashbey*

Sled Dogs first was Ch. Wind River Talkeetna Karibou, CD (Dannen). Sled Bitches first was Ch. Wolf River's Terra (Hallberg).

The thirteen Awards of Merit went to the WB, Best Puppy, Flying Cloud's Song of the Sea; Ch. Northwind's Rising Star (Halmi); Ch. Elfenbein Mauyak of Pachali (Islam); Ch. Silver Sark's The Swan (Hackbarth, Roder, Blacakbourn); Ch. Char-Soo's Bonanza of K-Way (Krauss/Kersten); Ch. Orion's Pascha of Oakhurst (Hurst); Ch. Orkdomain's Return to Sender (Cooper); Ch. White Magic's Grand Illusion (Dinger); Ch. Kazakh's Wennisericio O'sno Dawn (Waldman/Sorrentino); (Ch. Whitecliff's Miss Klassy Karu (Leone); Ch. Krystal's Treasure of Gold (Golden/Mears); Ch. T-Snow Star's California Girl (Herrmann); and Ch. Sambushed Spoonful O' Sugar (Nonhoff/Metz).

It was a bustling show. It was Gary Griffin's first time as SCA auction-eer. He became a master of the art through the years at every National. The auctions brought out tantalizing objets d'art, draining pocketbooks while adding fun for everyone.

Besides trying to pinpoint the expensive areas and regroup committee responsibilities, the SCA's board discovered it needed to exert more discipline in planning for each National. Although the local groups or clubs bid to host the event, it remains the responsibility of the SCA to approve the plans sub-mitted. It requires checking enthusiastic plans that can be nice but unrealis-tic. So rules, rules and more rules were discussed (mostly by mail) because there are so few meetings of either the board or the SCA membership. Fi-nally the rules were approved by the board, headed by Gen. Merrill Evans, and Marilyn Gitelson made a complete set of rules for each board member. Occasionally groups go back to square one to improve, and so did the Samoyed club of America.

The Sweepstakes for the Fifty-eighth National were judged by breeder-judge Dorothy Hodges of Kipperic Samoyeds. There were 175 puppies and young dogs entered. Dorothy awarded Best in Sweepstakes to Trailblazer Patent Pending (Krause). BOS was Ch. Orion's Bud Light of Polar Mist (Hurst).

Am., Can., Mex., Int. Ch. Orion's Bud Light of Polar Mist, was the top winning Samoyed dog in America in 1991 and the top producing Samoyed dog in America in 1993. A BIS winner, "Bud" is the sire of twenty champions.

The Futurity, judged by Mark Russell, had 136 entries, and the Grand Futurity winner was Denka's Teddy Bear (Metter). BOS went to Kamelot's Danish Maiden (Brown) who became a Group winner bitch, which is sometimes harder to do for the fairer sex. Interestingly, in retrospect, Takenak's Make My Day placed behind Teddy Bear. Make My Day, called Cally, became a big winner whose name will come up later.

The 1990 SCA National (the 59th)

The Fifty-ninth Specialty show, Obedience Trial, Sweepstakes and Futurity was held in Birmingham, Alabama, with Peggy Goodwin as chairman. It was held indoors in a great facility adjacent to the headquarters hotel. It did not take long for the "country Sams" to learn about the fancy contraptions, to ride the elevators and enjoy all the human and canine camaraderie going on around them.

Mrs. Betty Arnold Chamberlain, who established her kennel, Solitaire, in 1971, judged the Futurity of 106 entries. Best PD Intersex was Kondako's Queen of the Nile (Richardson/Swartz). Best PB Intersex was Orion's Devil in Disguise (Hurst/Gowen). Best 12–15 Dog was Millcreek Typhoon of Oorhame (Crawford). Best 12–15 Bitch and Best Intersex was Polar Mist Northern Spirit (Rigby), who topped the field to become the Grand Futurity winner.

The Sweepstakes was judged by Thomas J. Quigley, in purebred dogs since 1950. There were 158 entered. Sultry's Platinum Blonde (Billings) was Best in Sweepstakes with BOS going to Tarahill's Rue the Day (Wagner).

Jeanne Nonhof, the well-established, respected breeder-judge for the event, was columnist for both *AKC Gazette* and the *Samoyed Quarterly*, member of SCA since 1962, past president, and board member at the time. Jeanne says, "Given the choice between judging, breeding or showing, I would unhesitatingly choose breeding for therein lies the real challenge. The weaving of pedigrees and the care for careful animal husbandry which produces great specimens is infinitely intriguing to me."

In the regular Dog classes, Mrs. Nonhof chose the Bred-by Exhibitor entry Alever's Custom Cruiser (Rittberg).

RWD was Hoof 'n Paw's Knight Shadow (Bennett/Ward-Fanning).

With six Veteran Dogs entered, the Canadian entry, Ch. Orenopac's Chaena (Gaskin), was first.

Sled Dog was won by Ch. Gandale Wizard Of Elmfield, CD (Wood/McCellan).

Samuel Pizzino, AKC multiple Group judge, was responsible for the 159 regular and nonregulars in the Bitch classes. His choice in Veterans was Ch. Polar Mist Ice Vixen (Hansen).

Sled Bitch winner was Ch. Tundra Wind's Glacier Lily (Dannen).

Winners Bitch from Open was Nordic's Kismet O' Cynosura (Mathews, Skinner, Brummet).

RWB was Sultry's Platinum Blonde (Billings), the winner of the Sweep-stakes.

Jeanne Nonhof, judge of Intersex and Best of Breed, had 104 Specials entered, and adding the veterans and winners from classes, she had an impressive array of quality.

BOS and winner of the Brood Bitch class was Ch. Sitkin's Simply Scrumptious (Luna). Scarlett, as she was called, was #1 Samoyed Bitch, All Systems, in 1989.

BISS was Ch. Candenza Khasi O' Southland (Bullard), bred by Betty Powell and handled expertly by Glenn Lycan. The authors held Khasi in high esteem and consider him a true White Water Samoyed.

It was at this special event that a novice Sam owner "made the big trek" to Alabama from California—with her young dog Viktor. At some point during the trip, Judy Harris and Viktor parted company. Judy spent hours calling and searching for Viktor, who seemed to be on some other flight. Judy was frantic. He was finally grounded in Dallas at the point of the connecting flight, and the story had a happy ending. Sadly, this is not always true. Louise O'Connell (whose dogs died from overheating in the cargo hold) can say from experience that air travel with your dog can be precarious. Airlines may try—but not all succeed. Phyllis Benton with ADOA keeps the nose to the grindstone *watching* to improve air travel.

The 1991 SCA National (the 60th)

The 1991 SCA National was held in Colorado on the grassy turf of the Denver Hilton South. It was dedicated to the memory of John Helinski, a hardworking Samoyed person for thirty years. His wife, Bernice, continues and judges the breed now. Their Wynterkloud name was well known. Five hundred Sams were entered with 963 entries for the late Judge Thomas Mayfield for bitches and Intersex, and for John Connolly Dogs in the Regular classes.

Nancy Johnson judged the 162 Sweepstakes entries. Best was Saratoga's Speed of Sound (McAllister/Nieman), handled by Scooter Nieman, the Nieman family's proficient Junior Handler.

Mary Morstad judged 122 in Futurity. Frostyacres Borne Blonde (McFarlane) won the 6–9 Intersex; Tega's Joe Knows (Campbell) won the 9–12 Intersex; Moonlighter's Ima Grand Kid (Nonhof) took Junior Intersex; Junior Dogs went to Saratoga's Speed of Sound (the Sweepstakes winner) and Orkdomain's Prime Time (Cooper).

The Grand Futurity Winner was Tega Joe Knows, handled by John Coloma.

Judge Tom Mayfield's choice for WB was the lovely Canadian-bred Takenak's Ms Charity Bear (Jocelyn). RWB was Silverplume Chelsea Morning (Schopfer). Mr. Mayfield chose as Best Puppy from the classes Hoof 'n Paw's Midnight Maxx (Loper).

Ch. Shadow-Wood Sis Boom Bah, bred by Patti Rassmussen and Betty Arnold Chamberlain (handling), was BOS at the 1991 SCA National. *John Ashbey*

The top winners stand out by themselves. However, a few contenders who, except for the blink of an eye or a twist of a toe, may have been one of those toppers. The Award of Merit is a provision for their recognition. We have given the names of Samoyeds who have been honored with AMs at previous Specialties, a list of extremely fine specimens. A certain percentage of AMs are made at the close of choosing all the BESTS. Those seeking suitable stud dogs or perhaps trying to lease a bitch or study bloodlines and what is being produced by whom may find that the "winners" do not fit their breeding programs. They may find the bloodlines of a "runner up" more compatible for specific, planned breedings.

Two Veterans were honored with the Award of Merit at this Specialty. One, Ch. Orenpac's Chaena (whelped 10-27-80), owned by Dr. and Mrs. Robert Gaskin, was by the famous stud Ch. Ice Ways Ice Breaker from the dominant English import Ch. Kiskas Karaholme Cherokee. All these dogs made an impressive, dominant impact on the worth and quality of the Samoyed gene pool as they sired during the decade of the 1970s. The

This was just a part of the Best of Breed class at the 1991 SCA Specialty, in Denver, Colorado. With 116 champions present for breeder-judge, the late Tom Mayfield, it was a thrill to be part of such an exciting happening.

Veteran Bitch winner was Ch. Seamist's Raven of Wolf River (whelped 5-18-83), bred by Archie and Anne Peil, by the most influential Ch. Sassillie's Merlyn of Vicrian ex Ch. Seamist's Lavender and Lace, owned by her handler Kay Bailey Hallberg.

Awards of Merit at this National went to Ch. Polar Mist Code Breaker, Ch. Tarahill's Everybody Duck, Ch. Kipperic Sparksun, Ch. Shalimar's Kori of Taliko, Ch. Polar Mist First Stryke, Ch. Crizta's Capri of Bakari, Ch. Kondako-Crizta's Broadway Baby, Ch. Sitkin's Simply Scrumptious, Ch. Bramblewood's Naughty Nadia, Ch. Mystical's Memories to Cherish, K-Ways Rainbow Connection, Ch. Windy Ridge's Starlite Express and Ch. La-Ray's Sugar Mishka.

For BISS in this SCA National, Tom Mayfield pointed to Ch. Sassillie's Change of Heart (Cheesman/Horton).

BOS was Ch. Shadow Wood's Sis Boom-Bah (Rasmussen/Arnold).

An exciting spectator from Capetown, South Africa, was Lieselotte Egeles. The catalog showed the picture of her dog, Ch. Ikwezi Ice Bear, definitely English in type with a tremendous coat. She offered material for our book from Ivy Kilburn-Scott who also lived in Capetown.

The 1992 SCA National (the 61st)

In 1992, the SCA National Specialty was held in Mars, Pennsylvania. The Sweepstakes was judged by the well-known Siberian Husky authority Thomas L. (Tommy O') Oelschalager, who wrote the following critique (in condensed form) of his winners:

Being involved in the sport of purebred dog shows brings countless opportunities. . . . On September 30, 1992, one of the highlights became a reality, judging the Sweeps at the 61st SCA National. Jill Smoot asked me to write my thoughts:

Puppy Dog 6–9 months, 1st Hoof 'n Paws Knight in Flight (Carr). I believe this dog came into the ring first in line and if my memory is correct he never left first. This puppy carries himself quite nicely and uses his front to his advantage. He has a gleam in his eye of confidence and assuredness; how appealing to me in a young dog.

Puppy Dog 9–12 months, 1st Dancing Bear Color Me Bad (Stohl). I was thrilled to see him propel himself with such correct side gait, what I look for in side movement. . . .

12–15 month Dog, 1st Windy Ridge's Great Expectations (Studebaker). Strong and guiding himself around the ring with no exertion, a telltale sign of a sled dog. . . . This dog is an athlete! He carries no extra baggage.

15–18 month Dog, 1st Ch. Hoof 'n Paw's Rambling Knight (May/ Ward)., Stands over his ground well and a pleasure to watch him come and go.–His head is what I believe you all refer to as a "Bear Head" with a wonderful, pleasing look to his face. [*Authors' note:* Not all Samoyed fanciers use the term *Bear Head.*]

Puppy Bitch 6–9 months, 1st Tall Oaks Tattle Tale (Miller).
. . . the look of an angel; such beautiful Arctic eyes and such properly set ears . . . I must also mention second in this class, River City's Irish Holiday (Taylor). She ran with the wind. These two presented one of the two hardest choices of the day.

One note on this class as a whole. Twenty-eight entered, zero absent. I was very alarmed to see so many BIG, UNFEMININE bitches. The future of the breed lies heavily in the young bitches. I would be careful. [*Authors' note:* Excellent—ditto this caution.]

Puppy Bitch 9–12 months, 1st Devonshire's Holiday Magic (Garrett). There is an aura to this bitch that absolutely captivates me. She has the proper outline and all of the parts fit. She comes and goes wonderfully soundly and around was a pleasure. She could keep that same pace for hours; a must for a sled dog.

Bitch 12–15 months, 1st Dancing Bear Meesha Of Amsden (Landgraf).This bitch wears one of the most beautiful coats I have seen. It glistens like diamonds, a tribute to her owners and their ability to maintain it. She has great legs and freedom in her stride.

Bitch 15–18 months, 1st Azteca's Gypsy Rose Lee (Fiano/ Luna).
This bitch gave me the "look" . . . great mobility . . . I loved her type.

When I brought my eight first place winners back into the ring for Best in Sweepstakes, I had NO idea who would win. Here before me stood eight animals that were all capable of winning Best. As I stood back and looked at them all, I had a comfortable feeling that here stood eight young Samoyeds who offer great hope for the breed. They all presented correct outlines and style. Most certainly movement . . . was utmost in my mind. They had to have soundness and endurance. In the end, the 9–12 puppy bitch, Devonshire's Holiday Magic, demanded the top award. She never faltered, and the 6–9 puppy dog, Hoof 'n Paws Knight in Flight with his amazing determination seizing Best of Opposite.

With America's space program landing the toy-like Land Rover on the planet Mars on July 4, 1997, we look back with awe at the theme of the 1992 National, "Out of This World '92," which was inspired by its location in Mars (Pennsylvania). It was hosted by the Greater Pittsburgh Samoyed Club and supported by the Potomac Valley Samoyed Club with Joan Rea as chairman. A total of 492 Sams were entered with 877 entries for author Dolly Ward, who later wrote:

> My task was to find as much Arctic type with as much soundness of limb and mind; and as proficient a characteristic gait of the breed as possible in the Total Dog, with a proper 60 percent–40 percent head and "Sammy-Ed" expression! The degrees of each of these qualities vary individually as well as in combination thereof and therein lies the criteria for judging each exhibit on the day.
>
> We all realize also that exact health, attitude, and exuberance may alter slightly from day to day or hour to hour even with the well trained or most proficiently handled.
>
> A few years ago, I thought our breed was in trouble. So many were just plain white dogs; the only quality in common was their color. But I worry no longer for the good outweighed the poor by far. There were no poor bites and only a few round eyes. The most important quality of good solid temperament prevailed. I heard no growls, saw no fights, even after so many hours in crates, traveling conditions on the road and without the usual exercise. Yes, Antarctic Buck, you would have been proud of your descendants.
>
> The fact there were so many above average, it did not make my job any easier. No one judging this day could not have found excellent exhibits deserving to win.
>
> So, taking the catalog in hand and looking up the numbers from my notes, I made the following comments:
>
> Without the final cut, I still had most deserving exhibits and would only cut again because of the need to retain only the final fourteen which provided eleven Awards of Merit, excluding BB, BOS and BW. In fact, regrettably, I could not keep, for lack of performance and condition, the 1990 SCA BISS "Khasi," whom I had admired so much in the past, and on whom I was co-owner at the 1988 SCA National.
>
> There were several I have awarded Group firsts or placings I had to let go. There were a couple of class dogs who had NO COAT, and while I'm not "gung ho" on coat, there does need to be some covering to win at a National!
>
> At nine and one-half (9½) years, the Veteran Bitch, Terra, was in top condition, mentally and physically, obviously typey and a just off square silhouette in proper proportion. Fifty-five percent leg length at the elbow, angle of neck carriage lined with stifle and she out-gaited every other

exhibit. Breeder-owned-handled by Kay Hallberg, a true breeder of working dogs that show. Ch. Wolf River's Terra was the feminine Sammy BISS and most importantly—Terra was FEMININE!

I had some provocative choices. I would like to prove that I found Ch. Wolf River's Terra all by myself. Although Bob Ward awarded her First in Veterans Sweeps out of a hearty 28 entries, and John Ronald selected her out of Veteran Bitches, but it was my pleasure to have awarded Terra an all-breed BIS some years ago; and now the coveted Top Spot of a National BISS.

Studying the sire and dams of the entries, it shows Terra contributing extraordinarily well in the whelping box as well as the show ring, the ultimate award; the reason for dog shows. Of Terra's 12 offspring, eight became champions.

At four years, the highly campaigned, widely winning Specials Dog, Cheryl Wagner's, Ch. Tarahill's Everybody Duck was BOS to BB presented by Tarahill's manager/handler Chris Jones. I forgave some lack of neck and smidgen lack of leg length because he was spectacular and exciting with the thickest type of coat, which was groomed to perfection.

WD and BW was Samusz's Spectacular Bid (Bednarczyk). A well trained, imposing 2 1/2-year-old of good size and good length of leg. Very easy going, balanced gait, at which he could perform hour after hour. He might even look better with less coat, but his Sammy expression really asked for it and he was totally masculine.

Reserve WD was another two year old, Risuko's Silver Warrior (Miller), a most pleasing, masculine dog with Sammy characteristics, a standout from the Open Dog class.

There were some most promising younger dogs who will be turning on for future judges as I could see their possibilities in spite of their immaturity.

The winners of the Sled Dog and Sled Bitch classes, Ch. Wind River Talkeetna Karibou, CD and Ch. Tundra Wind's Glacier Lily, both owned by Kent and Donna Dannen, were considered closely until the final cut, lacking a bit only in that finished look.

I watched for temperament especially which is a feature that does not jump out at one necessarily, but reveals itself in subtle ways during the examination of body and gaiting. It is fascinating to see how dogs relate to their handlers be they owners or agents.

The Best Puppy in regular classes came from 6–9 Puppy Dogs—a joy to behold. He had such confidence and together with being well made, he moved out with full extension and matching drive to his fullest potential. He was Hoof 'n Paw's Knight in Flight (Carr). He was pushed to this win by the 9–12 Puppy Bitch, Devonshire's Holiday Magic (Garrett). She had excelled in winning the Futurity under judge Judy Mears, the Sweepstakes under judge Tommy Oelschlager and RWB under judge John Ronald.

Igloo's Unfounded Stealth (Seman), lovely and promising, had a champion litter brother in the Parade of Titlists. Stealth later finished and won a BB at Westminster.

Best in Bred-by Exhibitor classes was Windsong Valentine (Kistner—Koehler). She was stylish and sound in both static and kinetic balance. From the candid snapshots I brought home, she looked much like the BISS Terra in profile and stance.

Two of my favorite non-regular classes are the Stud Dog and Brood Bitch classes. I was pleased to see it scheduled *before* Best of Breed Competition. The Stud Dog class was truly magnificent to see although a bit harder to manage even in the large, carpeted ring. Judging 75 percent on the get and 25 percent on the stud, one looks for consistency in what is produced; how well the get excel in anatomical structure, movement and type.

First in Stud Dog was Ch. Moonlighter's Grandstander with Ch. Moonlighter's Ima Grand Kid and Windy Ridge Sizzlin' Chajita Grandstander and Grand Kid both earned Awards of Merit! These were absolutely faultless unless you are a little "picky!"

Second was Ch. Romsey's Lord of the Rings, (Benton) with his get, litter mates and AMs Am., Can. Ch. Takenak's Make My Day and Am., Can. Ch. Takenak's Ms. Charity Bear. The dog excelled in fantastic static beauty, true Sam expression and the bitch moved out the better of the two, a cast of perfection if you could absolutely blend the two!

Third Ch. Image's the Barrister, CD (Duke) who proudly headed two quality exhibits. It is important to read again the sires and dams behind these studs placing.

Fourth Ch. Samtara Striking Reflection, (Kersten) whose get might have been more impressive with two get instead of all five get present.

In that Stud Class there were eight more entrants and even with two absent, it showed a ring full of hope, plans, goals, and . . . Samoyeds.

The team of four was absent but the matched Braces, who are judged on similarity in form and function, were topped by the Canadian entry of Am. Can. Ch. Takenak's Ms Charity Bear and Takenak's Mad About You, (Jocelyn). Second was Ch. Gambir's Ace in Lace Kanduit and Kanduit Boomerang Back in Lace, (Malone/Klaiber).This brace was matched well in size and gaiting.

The Veterans Dog class had an entry of eight with two absent and the first place was the most animated of all the entries. Ch. Silverecho's Sensuous Teaser, (Carden/Billings) All were in good company and some showed age a bit more than others, but all were delightful. At almost 8½ years, Teaser still had his figure, bounce and an extremely white coat. He seemed to be laughing all the time; it was a pleasure to have him as a deserving AM.

I have one suggestion to future National Chairmen; be sure the superintendent provides arm bands with BLACK NUMBERS which are easier to read than slim penciled numbers. I doubt if the spectators could look up dogs "by the number." Even prescription "sun glasses" would not have helped here!

List of Award of Merit Winners, in no particular order, but as they appeared in the "judges" book.

1. Winners Bitch—Frosty Acres Nakyska O'Sansom (B)

2. Ch. Frosty Acres Golly Ms Molly (B)

The two Frostyacres girls were quite similar and certainly a credit to the breed. The WB came from a strong field of competition and was appealing, but lost BW to the WD because his masculinity feature is something the male side of our breed needs. It is hard to keep the masculinity defined and maintain the beauty our breed characteristics demand. That is a fine line. *Coarseness or greater size is not masculinity.*

3. Ch. Takenak's Ms Charity Bear (B)

4. Ch. Takenak's Make My Day (D)

5. Ch. Moonlighter's Ima Grand Kid (B)

6. Ch. Moonlighter's Grandstander (D)

7. Ch. Images the Barrister (D)

Such universal type as to be highly regarded across the world. Gorgeous face, front, and manner. A pleasure to award him yet another Award of Merit. He must be making a collection of AMs. (As will be seen later, this turned out to be a prophetic observation.)

8. Ch. Hoof 'n Paw's Drifter (D)

Was magnificent, and I judged him highly. He won the Minnesota Specialty en route home after the National. Drifter was the answer to type and soundness, that age old discussion, which is more important? Well really, it is the total dog!

9. Ch. Kondako's Queen of the Nile (B)

10. Ch. Orion's Bud Light (D)

A solid Samoyed type; moving to perfection. Always a soft spot in my heart for Bud, a grandson of our Painter. In trying to be as objective as possible, one would be less than honest if he did not appreciate quality seen developing from his bloodlines. A deserving male always well-presented and another to whom I have awarded a BIS.

11. Ch. Silver Echo's Sensuous Teaser (D)

The Veteran dog who KNEW he was only about a year or two, shining in his showmanship (probably topping everyone in this department). Here also true to universal Samoyed type. They'd love him in England and Australia, probably have loved him in Canada. A son of Dr. Pepper. What more can I say? He and his handler presented a beautiful "team picture." Excellent head! Showing his age a bit more than Terra.

So, Ch. Wolf River's Terra met them all, standing and gaiting. Batting her eyes in femininity, Terra said to me, "I met all my worthy opponents." Then ever so quietly she communicated, "Why not me? The old bitch, beating any dog, running the legs off of most of them, giving 'em a what for in harness, holding my head high for the show ring and whelping and caring for more good Samoyeds; doing my best in the "box." Dolly thinks, "Indeed. Why not!"

Congratulations Terra, you deserve BISS, 1992.

Signed the contented judge

As one of the authors who was honored by being invited by the Samoyed Club of America to judge Intersex at its 1992 National in Pennsylvania. I will quote from our *Club Bulletin* (the official magazine of the SCA) with the permission of the editor, Jill Smoot, who wrote the following about the SCA National:

For those of you could not attend the Specialty, you missed an OUT OF THIS WORLD TIME (that was the theme of this National held in Mars, Pennsylvania, near Pittsburgh). Joan Rea, Show Chairperson, is one organized woman. . . . The entire committee did a superb job. Ross Chapin provided one of the highlights of the entire show. Picture Ross stewarding for Dolly, Best of Breed cuts have been made, there are lines and rows of dogs everywhere. Ross positions himself center ring and in a very authoritative voice says, 'I want the head bitch to the front of the line and who comes walking down the line, not too sure they want the title of HEAD BITCH, but Karen McFarlane and Molly! The gallery roared! For those of you who did not attend the banquet because you thought it would go on and on, Judy Bennett zipped through the Awards. She asked Sharon Hurst if she wanted to say anything after receiving Ch. Orion's This Buds for You Top Dog Award and all Sharon could do was sob, "I can't," while dripping tears of joy all over husband Jim, and breeder Lynette Hansen. The best part of the evening was Dolly Ward's speech. Dolly mentioned that perhaps Lina Basquette might have given us a better show but Dolly danced to the podium to the music of "HELLO DOLLY." She then remembered something she needed which was in her purse. Husband, Bob, produced the purse, then she rummaged through three zippered compartments looking for what turned out to be SUNGLASSES. It seems Dolly had a real problem with the round eyes on the Sam on the Pittsburgh club's logo. So she donned her sunglasses. To top it off Sandy Dukes, SCA President, presented Dolly with a stuffed Sammy with ROUND BLUE EYES, complete with sunglasses. Everyone was hysterical. Dolly then pulls out her notes and announces to the crowd, "I have all your numbers." Blackmail instantly registers in the minds of many. Dolly's commentary on her notes kept everyone laughing, she was definitely on a roll.—Jill Smoot

The Futurity

Judy Mears of Colorado Judged the Futurity and wrote:

There can't be a greater honor and compliment than to be selected to judge the Futurity by the breeders of SCA. I believe that those who care about and plan breedings, also nominate the litter to be shown with the best that is produced.

The first impression of the entry had to be the high quality of puppies that are coming out to be shown. Temperament is good, type and balance overall is good. I don't remember seeing a bad topline or a poor tail set.

Heads ranged from short and broad with a lot of stop, to the longer style with less stop. I feel both fit the standard as long as they are balanced with the body style. There were a few bad bites in both styles of head.

Carpet is very poor footing for showing dogs. Dogs' feet do not get proper traction on carpet and if there is any tendency to flat, splayed feet, it SHOWS on carpet. There were very poor puppies with poor feet. I could count the bad rears on one hand. The breed as a whole has nice rear movement going away and from the side.

Fronts (shoulder set) and chest shape were the most common problems that I saw. Many puppies either had a very steep shoulder and upper arm or a terrier type shoulder. Neither will give the light, free, ground covering movement that a Samoyed should have.

The two who were in the ring for Grand Futurity Winner were truly outstanding. Both Devonshire's Holiday Magic and Samtara N K-Way Gorgeous Girl excelled in showmanship, movement, balance and condition. Both had lovely heads and faces. My final choice went to the puppy who had the better fitting coat. I liked the way the topline flowed from back of ears down the neck and back to the tail. It's a joy to have to be picky to fine detail to reach the final winner. Devonshire's Holiday Magic.

The 1993 SCA National (the 62d)

The 1993 SCA National at Santa Rosa, California, was hosted by the "Nuts Bunch"—Marilyn Gitelson and Gail Speiker plus the Show Committee of the Samoyed Club of America.

There were 400 Samoyeds present that year. A special event that took place at the annual meeting was the premiere of the new AKC video on the breed. Karen McFarlane was chairperson of the video committee, and the result was accepted heartily without division. Kathy Hritzo Heimman handled all the entries invited to participate in the taping of the video.

Brian Phillips, longtime professional handler, judged the Veteran Sweepstakes. Once again (repeatedly it seems) the ageless Ch. Wolf River's Terra won Best Veteran, with Best Opposite Veteran going to Ch. Hoof 'n Paw's Knight Rider.

Mr. Phillips also judged the Sweepstakes and for Best Puppy put up Hyalites Classical Jazz (Stolba); BOS was Polar Mist Mover N-A Shaker (Hansen).

Carol Ann Montgomery chose Kamelot's Southern Belle Best Intersex 6–9 (Elvera/Brown); Reserve went to Elfenbein White Barracuda, out of twenty-four entered; Best 9–12 went to Hoof 'n Paw's Here Comes the Knight (Ward-Fanning/Bennett); and Reserve went to Dushals Trailblazer of Seelah (Mears/Cox).

Best Intersex 12–15 was Whitecliff Rossia Express Karu (Ow-(Wilson/Powers); Reserve was Whitecliff Britta Karu (Giffin/Powers); Best Intersex Fifteen Months and Over was Artic Mist Rocket of Saratoga (Kelley/Nieman/Bateman).

Grand Futurity Winner was Hoof 'n Paw's Here Comes The Knight.

An unusual feature of the 1993 National was that the three judges who had been selected and invited by a vote of the entire SCA membership did not know their assignments before the show. At the annual meeting, the night before the show, from *out of the hat*, the assignments were drawn by lot. Each judge drew a slip of paper, and when all were ceremoniously selected, a hush of silence fell on the gathering. What was the outcome?

Luckily Robert Page really wanted to do bitches. Peggy Adamson wished to do dogs, and Mary Morstad was ecstatic to receive the tiny piece of paper inviting her to judge intersex—Best in Specialty Show. So each judge was happy. Who knows what each exhibitor really thought? It was something different for this era. Not since 1948, almost fifty years earlier, had such a "Lotto Drawing" taken place. At that event, the Interstate Samoyed Club, Cleveland, Ohio, the three judges who drew lots at ringside were Marie Meyer, James Trullinger and Mrs. F. H. Beddow.

The late Peggy Adamson was enchanted doing her first Sammy National and said it "was like a gift from the Gods." She wrote:

> I drew dogs. This was lucky for me since nearly all my judging would be on Thursday. I could then spend the rest of the time as a spectator, eating, drinking and inhaling Sammies every waking minute. Pure heaven. The boys were washed and squeaky clean. Because I am so allergic to chalk, this made me very happy. . . . The legs were usually well boned and sturdy but not many were 55 percent. I was surprised at the number of lovely shoulders, but short upper arms. I always wonder why the Standard makes no mention of the upper arm. Its correct length is so essential to a good front. "WHISKERS? ALL DOGS SHOULD HAVE THEM!" Only a brute would cut off a cat's vibrissae—why should we do it to dogs. Note: only one SAM was missing his whiskers. Excellent scissors bites. Only two with misaligned incisors.

Peggy Adamson was impressed with her ten-month-old puppy, "so fresh and wonderful. What a great name Polar Mist Mover N A Shaker. I wonder if the next ten years will treat him as kindly as the ageless Terra?"

Her WD, BW and eventually Best Bred-by Exhibitor in Show came from "depth of quality teeming with potential champions. . . . When he stopped he came back into a perfect stance . . . he stood facing me, his eyes looking right into mine . . . nothing challenging about it. He was actually half smiling, intent look with a quizzical gleam in his eyes. . . . That pixie! He was trying to mesmerize me and I couldn't take my eyes away (Sams are the only ones I've ever seen do this)." He was Moonshadow's Magician by Ch. Orion's Bud Light of Polar Mist out of Ch. Moonshadow's Pegasus (Howard); RWD was Moonlighter's Knokyursoksov (Ruettiger).

Judge Mary Morstad wrote in her critique that "this was one of the greatest thrills in the dog world for me," and she did judge Best Bred-by and Best Puppy in Show and finally BISS.

The following Awards of Merit were made: Ch. Hoof 'n Paw's Knight Drifter, Ch. Tega's Joe Knows, Ch. Frostyacres Golly Miss Molly, Ch. Kondako's Queen of the Nile, Ch. Tarahill's Everybody Duck, Ch. Hoof 'n Paw's Wild Rose Knight, Ch. Takenak's Ms Charity Bear, Ch. Saratoga's Sonic Boom and Trailblazer Spruce Kiva.

BISS for the second time was Ch. Sassillie's Change of Heart (Cheesman/Beard/Horton). Morstad said, "He has matured well since he won the 1991 Denver Specialty. . . . He has good type and balance, and a great attitude."

Highest Scoring Dog in the Regular classes and Highest Scoring Champion of Record was Ch. Sansaska's Treasurer Chest, UD (Bunner).

The 1993 Annual Awards were presented at the SCA banquet, thereby adding to the excitement of the event. Top Winning Dog was Cheryl Wagner's Ch. Tarahill's Everybody Duck with Agent, Chris Jones. Second was Ch. Tega's Joe Knows, with breeder-owner-handler, Gail Campbell.

Top Winning Bitch was Janice Hovelman's Ch. Ren-J's Go Go Dancer, handled by Jimmy Moses, PHA. No second.

Ch. Sassillie's Change of Heart, BISS at the National in 1991 and 1993. "Chance" is pictured with breeder-judge Mary Morstad and owners Mary Beard-Leal, Carol Cheesman and Kathy Horton.

Am/Ber Ch. Tarahill Everybody Duck (Ch. Tarahill's Son of a Duck ex Ch. Tarahill's Can Do Too), owned by Cheryl Wagner, was #1 Samoyed in 1992 and 1993, retiring with fourteen BIS. A multiple BIS and BISS winner, he was twice BB at Westminster and BOS at the 1992 SCA National. Chris Jones, Kennel Manager for Tarahill, handled him to his illustrious record. *Booth*

Top Brood Bitch was Sno Questor's Callico O' Ren-J, James and Renee Miller. Second was Ch. Char-Soo's Bonanza of K-Way, Kathleen Kersten and Wanda Krauss.

Top Stud Dog was Ch. Orion's Bud Light of Polar Mist, owned by James and Sharon Hurst. Second was Am., Mex., Int. Ch. Sunburst's Torch of Liberty, owned by Lia and Larry Benson.

Top Sled Dog was Ch. Tundra Winds Mtn. Thunder, CD, WSX, owned by Connie Rudd.

Top Sled Bitch was Ch. Tundra Wind's Glacier Lily, WSX, owned by Kent and Donna Dannen.

Top Obedience Samoyed was Ch. Sansaska's Treasure Chest, UD, owned by Barbara and Larry Bunner.

Top Junior Handler was Heidi "Scooter" Nieman.

The 1994 SCA National (the 63d)

The 1994 SCA National was held in La Crosse, Wisconsin. Fred Stohl and the committee planned for "everything," including weather. The Midwest had been in a great deluge that year, and after the big rains, it was fortunate that the Mississippi stayed within its banks for this special show. Dubbed "PURELY CAPTIVATING," the logo showed only the Sammy's black eyes, black nose and black lips—nothing more! This most effective, striking design was fired onto ceramic trophy cups, bowls and candle holders and was printed on T-shirts.

Karen McFarlane jollied the welcoming by passing out "dinosaur" stickers to veteran SCA members and "puppy" stickers to the novices attending. It helped set the tone for congeniality. Everyone had a great time, while the board met laboriously in person, as they do once a year.

Herding instinct and Agility tests were conducted, as well as Therapy Dog testing, weight pulling, Flyball, Seminars and the Annual meeting. You name it, and it was held, including a Top Winning Dog party given for "Buddy" by Cheryl Wagner after the Awards banquet.

The Futurity was judged by breeder Lynette Hansen Blue. In Puppy Dogs Best Intersex was Anadyr's Bourbon Street; Best Puppy Bitch 9–12 months was Cloudnine's Penny's From H'Vn; Best 12 under 15 months was Vanderbilt's Break the Seal; Best 15 and up was TNT Radiant Crystal Image; and the Grand Futurity winner was Cloudnine's Penny's From H'Vn (Stutzman/Cherne).

In her critique Lynette wrote that the fronts needed work, that rears had improved and that she had seen a lot more drive; she felt the breed was coming along nicely.

Don Hodges, breeder-judge, commented similarly on his Sweepstakes entries. We may, therefore, consider working on breeding better fronts in the future, while guarding everything else as well!

Best in Sweepstakes was Artic Cross Chances Czar (Dunkle).

The plum assignment of any National Specialty is judging Intersex, which includes all champions entered as well as the Winners Dog and Winners Bitch, Sled Dog and Bitch, and Veteran Dog and Bitch for the final selection of Best of Breed or BISS, followed by Best Puppy in Show and Best Bred-by Exhibitor. This honor was bestowed by the committee on Mr. Edd Bivin.

An orderly ring was filled with hopefuls that were gaited many times— down, back and around. After a thorough inspection of each exhibit before him, including checking the mouths for complete sets of teeth, Judge Bivin pointed dramatically to Gail Campbell showing Ch. Tega's Joe Knows. He wrote later, "My Best of Breed is very balanced, of proper proportion, bone to size to size, and length of leg. He is very sound coming and going, and going around. He does not have a big coat. He has a very nice coat of good durable texture. He is a pretty headed dog with adequate expression and pleasing going around the ring."

For Best of Opposite Sex, he chose Ch. Solitaire's Shaboom of Bykhal, bred by Sterling and Patty Rassmusen and Betty Chamberlain, out of Shadow Wood's Sis Boom Bah by the same sire as the BB, Ch. Bykhal's American Dream.

BW and Award of Merit was the WB sent up to Edd Bivin by Mardee Ward-Fanning. Finishing her championship at this event was Ch. Operoh Whispering Mariah. "Harley" was bred by Cindy Williams (Operoh) and owned by Stephen and Michelle De Pina.

RWB was Saratoga's Lost Aviatrix (Neiman). Veteran Bitch was won by that "incomparable girl from Wolf River, Terra." Sled Bitch was Ch. Tundra Wind's Arctic Gentian (Dannen). Brood Bitches was a most exciting class with the ring positively filled with sixteen matrons, each present with two of their get. Topping this breathtaking, quality group was Frostyacres Hot Salsa (McFarlane/Overman).

All dog classes were judged by Duvella Kusler, whose WD was Classic Edition Too Legit to Quit (Patterson/Heathcote), who completed his championship with this good win.

RWD was Tarahill's Duck 'Em-N-Leave 'Em, (Renfro Polydys). A big upset in Veteran Dogs saw Ch. Kondako's Show Biz (Richardson) defeating the "usual winner" Sandra Duke's "Bear"!

The Sled Dog class was won by Ch. Sno-E's White Hot Mogul (West). Stud Dogs with twenty-one entered was won by Ch. Nordic's Magic Hobby Horse (Skinner/Brummet).

Finally, Edd Bivin chose as Best Puppy in the regular classes Cloudnine's Penny's From H'Vn. Best Bred-by Exhibitor was Saratoga's Lost Aviatrix and Best Junior Handler was "Scooter" Neiman.

Awards of Merit went to Ch. Tarahill's Everybody Duck; Ch. Hobby Horse Nordic Mischief; Ch. K-Ways Star Dancer of TNT; Ch. Winterway's Jeopardy; Ch. Takenak's Make My Day; Ch. Frostyacres Golly Ms Molly; Ch. Frostyacres Borne Blonde; Ch. White Magic's Sorceress; Ch. Moonlighter's Ima Grand Kid; plus the Winners Dog and Winners Bitch.

The 1995 SCA National (the 64th), Reported by Jill H. Smoot, *Bulletin* Editor

The Samoyeds of the world congregated in Austin, Texas, in 1995 for the SCA National Specialty Deep in the Heart of Texas. They started arriving on Saturday afternoon, and by Monday the headquarters were graced by white fuzzies with smiling faces. The weather cooperated, blessing us with sunny skies.

Along with the dogs came the Fancy decked out in their western finery. Joan Auld and her group put on a Texas-style Specialty and were congratulated. The vendors lined the halls surrounding the ballroom and tempted our checkbooks with many Sammy items.

In addition to the conformation and obedience judging, many events were available to challenge the multipurpose side of the Samoyed. Sammy people and their dogs could participate in weight pulling, Therapy dog work, instinct testing, pack hiking and Agility.

Human participants could sharpen their skills in the show ring by taking the handling seminar, scoop golf balls in the relay race, learn about spinning Sammy hair, and dress up with their dogs in the Sammy fashion show.

While some were visiting and shopping, many made good use of the dog wash in preparation for the judging. Don Winslow and his group provided the tubs and water in return for a donation to the rescue fund. The level of anticipation rose as the puppies and junior dogs were being prepared for the Futurity and Sweepstakes. The blow dryers kicked on in the grooming tent, and soggy puppies turned into show dogs before our eyes.

The Monday Futurity and Sweeps judges, breeders Connie Konopisos and Chris Middleton, had the insight to get past the excited puppy part and found some very nice dogs. The Grand Futurity Winner was Oakbrook's Panning for Gold (Stevenson). The Best in Sweepstakes dog was Mystical's O My Sweet Master (Amest/Schold).

The Obedience ring was in full swing with some Sammies proving that it really can be done!

Tuesday found all the class dogs ready for adjudication by our AKC delegate, John Ronald. John, also a Sammy breeder-judge, was very pleasant with the exhibitors and very gentle with the many untrained dogs in his entry. John finally resorted to crouching on the floor and making noises so the dogs would look at him instead of their handlers. Sometimes it worked and sometimes it didn't. Overcoming all the obstacles, John found his WD, Wolf River's Diamond Dust (Hallberg).

Wednesday brought the girls to the ballroom. John was not crippled by his cowboy boots, and he ably worked his way through the bitches as effortlessly as he had done the dogs the day before, bestowing WB to Polar Mist Cover Gyrl of Lazy S (Hermle).

The Wednesday evening auction brought everyone back to the ballroom. There were some lovely offerings, including a one-of-a-kind figurine from Tom Mayfield's collection, a print of the *Sammy in the Cloud* from the 1994 Specialty, which brought quite a bit more than its original price. We were offered hand-crafted quilts, spun Sammy hair items and darling puppy prints, to name just a few. Finally, came a beautiful stained-glass treasure, hand-crafted by Marita Lawrence.

Marilyn Gitelson and her group hosted a judges' breed seminar. Anyone interested in becoming a judge was invited to sit with mentors and benefit from their knowledge. The Standard was discussed in depth, and dogs were supplied for the "hands-on." Everyone came out enlightened. The consensus of those present after watching the dogs and bitches was that the quality of dogs is finally improving, and the girls have lost a little.

Thursday morning found champion dog's and bitches lined up outside the ballroom and down the parking lot for the eagerly anticipated Intersex classes. Most were anxious to get in the ring because they had been waiting in their crates all week. The ring stewards instructed the competitors about how the judging would proceed, and everyone filed into the ring, for the official check-in. After all were accounted for, the bitches left the ring and Michele Billings started examining her dogs. After making several cuts, she excused the dogs and moved on to the bitches. She worked confidently and with humor and found her winners. BB was awarded to Ch. Promise's Silver Bullet (Cassidy); BW was the WD Wolf River's Diamond Dust; and BOS went to Ch. River City's Irish Holiday (Smoot/Green). In Mrs. Billings's personal comments to me, she said she was impressed by the depth of quality she found in her entry. She feels the males are improving, which she said she is finding in many other breeds, and they "held their own." Overall, the quality ran very deep, and our breed is in good shape. So the 1995 "Texas" National ended with the awards banquet and a climate of happy celebration.

The 1996 SCA National (the 65th)

The Sixty-fifth Annual National Specialty Show, Obedience Trial, Agility Trial, Sweepstakes and Futurity of the Samoyed Club of America was held in Puyallup, Washington, October 9–12, 1996. Show chairman Cheryl Loper did a fabulous job of guiding many helpers to create the "National that will be remembered."

The hand-crafted souvenir Sammy papoose lapel pins were a lasting mark of a great event planned and executed from the heart. Even the Best In Show judge, Marilyn Gitelson, was presented to the assembled in a sled pulled by Maxx, Jason Loper's Agility and Weight Pulling champion. Mrs. Gitelson commented that such an "arrival" helped ease the usual tensions associated with such a prestigious event.

Breeder-judge Wanda Krauss presided over the Sweepstakes and wrote:

6–9 Dogs—Sancha's Starry Knight stood out in his class for his balance and ease of movement. 9–12—Dogs, Moonstar Hollywood Knight HNP had excellent proportions. . . . His brother, Moonstar's Cold Smoke HNP, was in better coat and prettier, but I chose the dog whose structure will make him the better dog longer. 12–15 Dogs, Image's Bear in Mind, demonstrated his superior set of both shoulder and croup by his effortless movement. If these dogs were horses, this is the one I would choose to ride all day. . . .

6–9 Bitches—Sancha's Splash of Stardust was clearly the best built being both well balanced and well angulated and she had it all together this day. 9–12 Bitch, Sylvan's Skylark is not only very technically correct but also showed great self confidence and spirit in performance . . . She was my Best, primarily due to her marvelous expression. 12–15 Bitches—Shaman's Comes Singing took the win in this class due to the excellent, smooth blend of neck into body and proper rear stride placement.

Best of Opposite went to Image's Bear in Mind (Dukes). From his gorgeous eyes, excellent coat texture, to his free and long stride and superb rear drive, he shows promise to take center stage.

Frances Trojan, long time SCA Secretary, judged the Futurity. From an array of superior exhibits Chinook 'N' Tundra Wind's Skyrocket, (McAllister) was chosen the Grand Futurity winner.

In her critique, Ms. Trojan commented as follows:

The presence of light eyes on a few was disturbing although there were not enough to call it a trend. . . . Coats were not penalized because youngsters of the ages being shown are likely to be in various stages of hair loss. There were some too tight tail sets. This may be due to many judges INSISTING on having the tail tight over the back most of the time instead of as the standard says, "over the back at least once. . . . "

The critique presented by Marilyn Gitelson, Intersex judge, was glowing regarding her "thrill of a lifetime" to judge Best of Breed, in "her favorite part of the country" and hosted by one of the best Sam clubs, Washington State.

To be able to get 96 Specials in the ring with room to spare had to be a first—with thanks to Genia Cox, Chief Ring Steward, and hats off to B. J. Moses for the fabulous ring. . . . My final twelve (6 dogs, 6 bitches) were truly outstanding representatives of the breed.

The BB bitch, Ch. Hoof 'n Paw's A Rose Is a Rose, stood out as soon as she walked into the ring. Ana, as she is called, had a lovely feminine head and expression, beautiful outline, was in superb condition, moved flawlessly and never stopped showing

Though only about half in coat, what she had was exactly correct: a dense undercoat with stiff, silver tipped guard hairs showing through. She absolutely shone throughout the day, and got better and better. She is the epitome of a Samoyed bitch.

If you had told me at the beginning of the day that I would select an eleven year, eleven month old dog for BOS, I wouldn't have believed it with the dogs in the ring but the Senior Veteran winner, Ch. Image's The Barrister, made it so easy to do. He got better and better. In wonderful condition and coat, he gave everything he had with all his heart, and asked for the win.

Where do we need to improve? Proportion. Proportion. Proportion! Too many are still too long backed; too many are still lacking on leg length. Fronts have improved, but have a ways to go. Chest depth was lacking on many dogs. Rears are not as good as they were. Eye shape and placement need work. Breed to get the proper coat; don't rely on the scissors. And clean the teeth. Too many were shown with dirty teeth!

And thanks (I think) to the creators of the "MOOSE." [*Authors' note:* A cardboard replica on wheels that was rolled in to be judged by the Intersex judge in the SPECIALS ring! And Judge Gitelson went over the entire moose, asked him to gait and the handler, Jason Loper, complied most seriously, so the Moose was judged, although he lost to the bitch!!]

Awards of Merit were presented to Ch. Wolf River's Diamond Dust (Hallberg); Ch. Midnight's Sun's Second Chance (Horton); Ch. Promise's Silver Bullet (Cassidy); Ch. Sno 'n Sno's Clr 'n Present Danger (Jureziz Studebaker); Ch. Hoof 'n Paw's Wild Rose Knight (Ward-Fanning/Bennett); Ch. Polar Mist Cover Gyrl of Lazy S (Hermele); Ch. Takenak's Mad About You (Jocelyn); Ch. Saratoga's Arctic Tern (Lyles/Neiman); Ch. Saratoga's Lost Aviatrix, CD (Neiman); and Ch. Polar Mist Society Girl, CD (Hansen-Blue).

Obedience HIT was Charok's Aslan Country's Dream, CD, AX (Crawford).

Agility Trial winner with a perfect 100 was Silveracres Fantasee (McLaughlin/Peterson).

Some of these winners are pursuing their Working Certificates, and many are establishing themselves as sires and dams of note with numerous champion offspring. Many American dogs have been campaigned in Canada and finished their Canadian championships. Conversely, Canadian dogs have finished their American championships. Ch. Hoof 'n Paws Wild Rose Knight is the premier "gopher getter" on a five-hundred-acre ranch. Ch. Polar Mist Cover Gyrl of Lazy S is the chief baby-sitter for her two- and four-year-old human kids and frequently masquerades as their steed. Ch. Images The Barrister road works his devoted breeder-owner-handler a mile or more a day. None are pampered, spoiled or high-strung show dogs, nor are they kennel dogs left to suffer boredom. All are cherished members of their families. Also of interest is the fact that only three of these eighteen SCA winners were sold by their breeders to other Sammy fanciers. The remaining fifteen dogs are solely owned or co-owned by their breeders. Not surprisingly, given the close family ties of the winning dogs, a few breeders produced more than one of the 1996 SCA winners. Don and Heidi Neiman lead the group as breeders of three: Stud Dog and two AM winners. Lynette Hansen-Blue along with Marge Goodenough bred the WD and an AM winner. Margaret and Leslie Jocelyn produced the Brood Bitch and WB. Lee Wacenske produced the winning littermates of the Veteran Sweeps, and Mardee Ward-Fanning bred the BB and an AM winner.

Of the 1996 entry in general, our judges commented that fronts and side-gait have improved greatly. Areas that still need work include emphasis on producing better rears, achieving more leg length and shorter backs, correcting eye shape, size and placement and striving for proper coats. Scissors sculpting is not desired when showing Samoyeds, but cleaning their teeth would be a definite plus.

My thanks to the Sammy owners who sent detailed information and loving comments on their dogs' many accomplishments. My thanks also to those judges who supplied the rationale behind their placements.

WESTMINSTERS

When it comes to dog shows, Sammy people are thoroughly dedicated to their annual SCA National Specialty. Probably they are no more enthusiastic about their Specialties than fanciers in any other breed about theirs.

The National provides those special classes—Sweepstakes and especially Futurities. Breeders proudly bring the results of carefully planned matings to these competitions. These continuing efforts to produce the most nearly perfect Samoyeds ultimately serve the best interests of the breed. Then, to a person, the growing friendships promoted by seeing the gang annually is mentioned at the top of lists of "why we attend Nationals."

Then there is Westminster, the big show in the Big Apple every year around Valentine's Day. This is "le grande social" dog show. There are many parties, Specialties and visits with old friends in the dog sport. Those who do not attend may see the Groups and BIS on television but miss the electric atmosphere. Here Sammies are shown as part of the total all-breed format. Without trying to offer a complete record of Westminster BB Samoyeds, we mention the names of more recent winners of the coveted Best of Breed at the "Garden," as Westminster is often called because it has been held in Madison Square Garden exclusively since 1915.

In past Westminsters, the Samoyed's banner has been carried by Richardson's Ch. Kondako's Sun Dancer; the Hritzos' North Starr's King's Ransom and his son, Ch. North Starr's Heir Apparent, with a Hritzo winning in Junior Showmanship; Frances Power's Ch. Whitecliff's Layka Karu; and Jack Price's Ch. Bubbles LaRue of Oakwood, later placing second in a strong Working Group. From the west, Ch. Hoof 'n Paw's Tasha of Sacha's Knight and Ch. Hoof 'n Paw's In the Buff made the grade. Jack Feinberg's Ch. Northwinds' Running Bear and later Esther Halmi's Ch. Northwind's Rising Star took Westminster BBs. Cheryl Wagner's Ch. Tarahill's Casey Can

The "Sam-a-'yed" showing off its reach, drive and style in the Group ring at Westminster. Do you recognize this dog without its handler? Do you know the year? *Holloway*

Do, and later Ch. Tarahill's Everybody Duck shown by Chris Jones also joined this exalted company.

In 1994, Leah Seman and Barbara Brisgel saw their Ch. Igloo's Unfounded Stealth take the top breed spot, while in 1995, the Veteran, Ch. Kazakh's Lucky Duck, owned by the Waldmans, turned back the challenge by a field of younger rivals for Best of Breed.

In 1996, a stunning array of top Samoyeds from all over the United States graced the ring. The final choice for Best of Breed was Ch. Shada Silver C's Just Ducky, owned by Donna Thornton and Sharon Parker. The Best Samoyed at the 1997 Westminster show was Ch. Hoof 'N Paws A Rose Is a Rose, owned by Jeff and Nan Bennett, Dolly Ward and Mardee Ward-Fanning and handled by Robert Chaffin.

Many notable dogs and handlers have taken turns gaiting around the vast, green-carpeted Group ring at Westminster with an audience of millions watching through the eye of the television camera.

All-breed dog shows, Specialties and Obedience Trials are held all over the United States throughout the year. It is a hobby that piques the competitors, gratifies the animal lover and occupies the family that pursues this healthy, fascinating sport.

chapter 5

Background of the Samoyed Standard

An explanation of the whys and wherefores of a breed Standard is due the reader who is new to the purebred dog sport.

For each breed recognized by the American Kennel Club, there is an officially approved Standard by which the breed is judged. The American Kennel Club does not write these Standards. They have been either propounded and formulated by the parent breed clubs or adopted by these parent clubs from Standards of other countries.

Obviously, much research and discussion has been required in each case to construct a description of the breed on which a large majority of the parent club, breeders and owners can agree. In other countries, each breed club does its own policing, and changes in the Standards can be more easily effected. In the United States, however, after winning the approval of a majority of the parent club, proposals for change are then submitted to the board of directors of the AKC. If the proposal is tentatively approved, it is published in the *AKC Gazette*, the AKC's official magazine, to bring it to the attention of any owners or breeders who were not aware of the intended revision. After ample time, the proposal is again presented to the AKC board of directors for approval.

There are few breed Standards that can claim the completeness of that used to measure and evaluate the Samoyed. As you will see, only a few changes have been made since the breed was recognized. The dog described in the American Standard today could well be the expedition dog that modeled the first Standards.

There have certainly been no changes in structure, coat or disposition. As in its native habitat, the Samoyed remains a friend of man, a hunter, a protector, a herder, a beast of burden and a draft animal.

133

Ch. Starchak, CD, at eighteen months (c. 1945). Note the good body on an out-of-coat male, the correct underjaw and the proper proportion of muzzle in relation to overall length of the wedge-shaped head (40 percent muzzle to 60 percent skull). Observe also the correct shoulder placement and set of tail.

The question of the use of the Samoyed has long been a matter of controversy. Is it a herd dog? Is it a sledge dog? Is it a guard dog?

It may be said generally that all working dogs were originally hunting dogs. Certainly this is true of the remaining breeds still in their native form and not reshaped by man. Our research shows that the true Samoyed dog was a hunter for his master. It was not possible for nature to create him as strictly a herd dog. The animals to be herded in his native land were reindeer, but they did not live in the deep snow country because of the lack of forage and moss. And the Samoyed was not designed as a sled dog by Mother Nature. While his natural attributes lend themselves to draft work, the Samoyed was put to this use by man and not by birth. When exploration was the "in" thing, the northern dog, used to the climate and lack of food, filled a need for the explorers, who lacked other means to conquer the frozen lands.

Early Samoyed breeders met with great resistance to breed popularity when people admiring the "white teddy bear" puppies discovered that the breed had been used for sled work in the arctic and mistakenly regarded them as "fierce and savage beasts descended from wolves." To counter this reputation, many original breeders felt that the herd dog aspect was the one to foster, as who would ever identify a Collie tending his flock, and nuzzling a lamb, as a "fierce beast?"

There have been many other breeders who have just as loudly proclaimed their Samoyeds' abilities as draft dogs. In the early days in England, even the Kilburn-Scotts trained their dogs as sled dogs until the English laws prohibited it. The sled dog activities were carried on in America and Canada by the majority of early breeders and large kennels. The Reids (Norka Kennels), the Romers (Yurak Kennels), the Seeleys and the Pinkhams all worked their dogs in harness in the early 1920s and 1930s and thus bred for sledding abilities. The kennels of Ernie Barbeau, Harold Haas and Agnes Mason continued to breed for sled work in the 1930s and 1940s. In the 1940s and 1950s, breeders such as the Weirs and Gleasons in the Northwest, the Ralph Wards and the Seekins in New York, Juliet Goodrich and Harold Danks in the Midwest and the Wards, Witchers, Van Sickles, Burrs, Keepers, Allens and Bristols, King, Goldwater, Tom Witt, Breckenridge and especially Mel Fishback in the West, all trained Samoyed sled teams leading to the birth of the Organization of Working Samoyeds created by Mel Fishback.

Appreciating this background, a Standard was written to include all the aforementioned qualities except that of hunting. Mr. Kilburn-Scott cited the Samoyed's ability as a herder and sled dog in his first Standard description in 1910, and this description of points has been little changed since. Size is the usual point of difference among breeders and countries, but isn't size a question in many breeds?

The Samoyed Standard serves the purpose of maintaining a natural, original type of animal. It is not a created breed. Its characteristics have been developed over centuries of living with simple nomadic peoples who had no outside contact with other tribes and thus no interbreeding of their dogs with others from other areas. The Samoyed was one of the family; he provided an extension of the master's hands and feet. His disposition had to fit into the communal society. As a result, his character is as splendid and pure as his shades of snowy white coat.

THE EARLY STANDARD

Ernest Kilburn-Scott, responsible for so much of the beginnings of the Samoyed in the Western world, formulated a first Standard for the breed in the early 1900s. This Standard was quite closely followed when the official English Standard was adopted in 1909 and 1911 with the formation of the first Samoyed associations in England.

The Standard as formulated by Mr. Scott read:

Colour. Pure white; with slight lemon markings; brown and white; black and white. The pure white dogs come from the farthest north and are most typical of the breed.

Expression. Thoughtful and remarkably pretty in face; fighting instincts strongly pronounced when aroused.

Intelligence. Unusual intelligence, as shown by the many purposes for which dogs are used by the Samoyede people and the ease with which they can be taught tricks.

Size and Weight. Dogs 19 to 21½ inches at the shoulders; bitches 18 to 19½ inches at the shoulders; *weight* about 40 lbs.

Head. Powerful-looking head, wedge-shaped, but not foxy. Wide and flat between ears, gradually tapering to eyes; stop not too pronounced; absolutely clean muzzle, not too long, with no lippiness; strong jaws and level teeth. The nose may be either black or flesh-coloured.

Eyes. Very expressive and human-like, sparkling when excited; set obliquely and well apart. Eyes should be dark for preference, but other colours are admissible.

Ears. Pricked, set wide apart, and freely movable; set slightly back in contradistinction to the ears of the Eskimo and Chow-Chow, which are forward; shape triangular, and not too large; tip slightly rounded.

Body. Body shapely, but not cobby, with straight back; muscular, with deep ribs; chest wide and deep, showing great lung power; straight front and strong neck.

Legs. Good bone, muscular and not too long; thighs well feathered; forelegs straight; hindlegs sinewy, and set for speed.

Feet. Long, and slightly spread out to get good grip; toes arched and well together; soles hairy and well padded to give grip and protection from ice and snow.

Brush. Long, with profuse spreading hair; carried over back or side when on the alert or showing pleasure; when at rest, dropped down, with slight upward curve at end.

Coat. Long and thick standing well out all over body, especially along back; free from curl; undercoat very soft and woolly; large, bristling ruff, hair on head and ears short and very smooth.

The Standard was little changed through the years. There were occasional efforts to expand or change it, such as in 1948 when an attempt was made to require that the coloration of the nose and pigmentation be black, thereby eliminating all throwbacks to the original dogs, which had had light and liver points in many cases. In 1900, Major F. O. Jackson had proposed that "the typical Samoyede should be pure white and have a flesh-coloured nose." In formulating the Standard, Kilburn-Scott had not gone as far as that, because there were many good dogs with a little lemon color about the ears and with black noses. Actually, the black nose and dark eyes add greatly to the expression, making some of the faces of the dogs almost humanlike.

The Americans, Canadians and Australians all originally adopted this English Standard with minor variations.

THE REVISION OF THE AMERICAN STANDARD

In 1945, there had been constant complaining about poor judging of Samoyeds throughout the United States. It was felt that the Standard was inadequate. Many judges had expressed their thoughts that the Standard was in some parts unwieldy and in other parts too flexible for uniform judging.

As the breed was increasing in numbers and being exhibited in areas where it was previously unknown, the parent club president, S. K. Ruick, appointed Mrs. Agnes Mason to be chairman of a Standard Committee, with the purpose of revising the Standard. The members were Helen Harris, Berta Ruick, Lucile Miller, Martha Humphriss and Louis Smirnow. Countrywide participation in local discussion groups aided the committee. The committee worked to form an illustrated Standard, but the American Kennel Club advised that illustrations should be used as an aid rather than as part of the actual Standard.

Comments, examples, measurements and photographs were exchanged across the country. In 1946, the size specifications were altered, with suggested heights for bitches raised from 18–20 inches to 19–21 inches, and the dogs from 20–22 inches to 21–23½ inches. This was done when more than fifty champions were measured, and it was found that there were only four within the previously suggested heights.

In 1952, Mrs. Mason added the breeder-judges Robert Ward, Vera Lawrence, Joe E. Scott, C. H. Chamberlain and Miles Vernon and the breeders Gertrude Adams and B. P. Dawes to the committee. Mrs. Mason, now president of the parent club, appointed Mrs. Adams to be committee chairman.

A reopening of the issue of the height of bitches as suggested by the breed Standard occurred in 1953. The problem was that the membership had voted by mail (133 yes, 25 no) to raise the height of bitches to 22 inches because there was a desire to have it theoretically possible to have some bitches and dogs of the same height. There is no overlapping in either the American or the English Standard. Many breeders and judges believed that in natural growth, some are always the same size regardless of sex, like other breeds and animals.

Work toward the new Standard continued. The committee prescribed percentages to be used in the new Standard in an attempt to avoid indefinite phrases such as moderately long, or medium, or shorter than. Precise angles and degrees for measurement came from hundreds of measurements taken of actual dogs and from many photographs of past celebrated dogs. The

An example of proper shape and proportion in a Samoyed male. The model fairly exudes correct breed type.

actual number of degrees used to set the lay-back of shoulders and angle of the stifle, for example, were based on the average of many measurements.

A great deal of opposition was encountered by the committee in setting a description of the head. Many believed that if percentages were used or if the muzzle were defined as big, medium, or short, we might be "keying" to one particular strain or individual. The description of the muzzle in ratio to the skull was finally adopted because it allows for variation in size as well as slight variations to fit the balance of the dog being judged. The head should be 60 percent skull to 40 percent muzzle. A description of the style and expression of the head creates perhaps the greatest divergence of opinion among breeders in all breeds. Each is much attached to his or her own "linebreeding," which stamps the slight variation in heads. No matter what, however, the head must conform to the characteristics of the breed and harmonize with the overall balance of the dog.

The committee, after reading comments from all sections of the country, decided to drop the weight suggestions of the old Standard. Weight is a variable, based on condition and health, and since the Standard explores soundness and movement in such detail, it was felt that correct substance should be recognizable to the breeder or judge.

Disqualifications were held to a minimum by desire of both the Standard Committee of the Samoyed Club and of the American Kennel Club. It was felt that a fault that would properly disqualify an animal should be quite objective, quite disabling, quite permanent and quite foreign to the breed.

Great variance in size is not foreign to any breed although objectionable to many breeders. It was decided to state in the Standard that penalties should be assessed to the extent to which the dog appears to be oversize or undersize, according to suggested heights.

The greatest dissent came over disposition. This has always been the greatest asset of the breed. Even the earliest accounts of the explorers mentioned how they could detect the Bjelkiers from the other dogs in the dark because they would be poking and nuzzling for attention and affection. They would be the dogs first on the sleeping bags, seeking human companionship. The dogs were able to run in groups. These qualities endeared the breed to the early breeders, and there are many who still prize this trait above all others in the breed. However, to disqualify permanently for misbehavior in the ring has a note of finality about it that is hard to accept, based as it is on a brief moment's determination. *Really, it is up to the breeder to eliminate this fault in training and in choosing the sire and dam of a litter.* A severe penalty is assessed in the ring for such behavior and should prevent such animals from winning and thus being desired as breeding stock.

The new Standard was approved by the American Kennel Club in February 1957. It had thus required eleven years of work and research and writing to reach an agreement within the parent club for this revision.

A further change was made in 1963. The point scale to assess a value for each area of the Standard met with great resistance by both the club members and the American Kennel Club. Some members felt that this created a system where some would ignore the whole dog because it was found to be lacking in one area. In other words, the point scale promotes "fault judging" rather than assessing the whole value of the dog on his good qualities and nearness to the Standard. After much discussion, on the recommendation of the Standard Committee—confirmed by a vote of the membership of the Samoyed Club of America—and with the approval of the board of directors of the American Kennel Club, the entire point scale was dropped in 1963.

The final addition was in 1993 with a vote of the entire membership of SCA, "Whiskers are not to be removed."

It is an oxymoron that the title of this book is the *new* Samoyed, as chosen by the publishers, because on reading it, longtime Samoyed lovers everywhere will discover there is little if anything new about this breed. The "stars" may change, but the type, temperament and activities of this breed remain the same. We believe the Samoyed clubs of the world protecting this breed should be infinitely congratulated and lauded because the Samoyed breed was not polluted by novice owners in power positions, would-be "improvers" or "political" shakers promoting change for the sake of change.

chapter 6

Official AKC Standard for the Samoyed

As submitted by the Samoyed Club of America and approved by the American Kennel Club, September 29, 1993.

GENERAL CONFORMATION

(a) **General Appearance**—The Samoyed, being essentially a working dog, should present a picture of beauty, alertness and strength, with agility, dignity and grace. As his work lies in cold climates, his coat should be heavy and weather resistant, well-groomed, and of good quality rather than quantity. The male carries more of a "ruff" than the female. He should not be long in back as a weak back would make him practically useless for his legitimate work, but at the same time, a close-coupled body would also place him at a great disadvantage as a draft dog. Breeders should aim for the happy medium, a body not long but muscular, allowing liberty, with a deep chest and well-sprung ribs, strong neck, straight front and especially strong loins. Males should be masculine in appearance and deportment without unwarranted aggressiveness; bitches feminine without weakness of structure or apparent softness of temperament. Bitches may be slightly longer in back than males. They should both give the appearance of being capable of great endurance but be free from coarseness. Because of the depth of chest required, the legs should be moderately long. A very short-legged dog is to be deprecated. Hindquarters should be particularly well-developed, stifles well-bent and any suggestion of unsound stifles or cowhocks severely penalized.

General appearance should include movement and general conformation, indicating balance and good substance.

(b) **Substance**—Substance is that sufficiency of bone and muscle which rounds out a balance with the frame. The bone is heavier than would be expected in

140

RELATIONSHIP OF BONE STRUCTURE TO THE OUTLINE OF BODY AND COAT

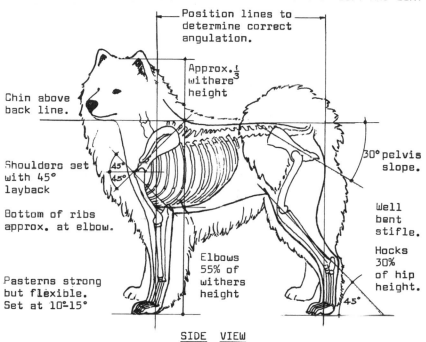

Position lines to
determine correct
angulation.

Approx. $\frac{1}{3}$
withers
height

Chin above
back line.

Shoulders set
with 45°
layback

Bottom of ribs
approx. at elbow.

Pasterns strong
but flexible.
Set at 10°-15°

45°
45°

Elbows
55% of
withers
height

30° pelvis
slope.

Well
bent
stifle.

Hocks
30%
of hip
height.

45°

SIDE VIEW

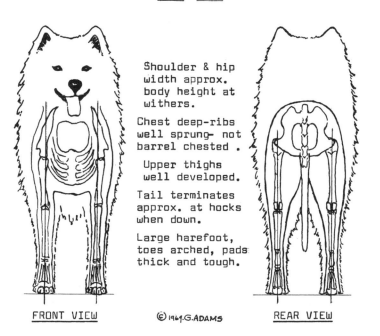

Shoulder & hip
width approx.
body height at
withers.

Chest deep-ribs
well sprung- not
barrel chested .

Upper thighs
well developed.

Tail terminates
approx. at hocks
when down.

Large harefoot,
toes arched, pads
thick and tough.

FRONT VIEW   © 1969.G.ADAMS   REAR VIEW

a dog of this size but not so massive as to prevent the speed and agility most desirable in a Samoyed. In all builds, bone should be in proportion to body size. The Samoyed should never be so heavy as to appear clumsy nor so light as to appear racy. The weight should be in proportion to the height.

(c) **Height**—Males, 21 to 23½ inches; Females, 19 to 21 inches at the withers. An oversized or undersized Samoyed is to be penalized according to the extent of the deviation.

(d) **Coat. (Texture and Condition)**—The Samoyed is a double-coated dog. The body should be well-covered with an undercoat of soft, short, thick close wool with longer and harsh hair growing through it to form the outer coat, which stands straight out from the body and should be free from curl. The coat should form a ruff around the neck and shoulders, framing the head (more on males than on females). Quality of coat should be weather resistant and considered more than quantity. A droopy coat is undesirable. The coat should glisten with a silver sheen. The female does not usually carry as long a coat as most males and it is softer in texture.

(e) **Color**—Samoyeds should be pure white, white and biscuit, cream, or all biscuit. Any other colors disqualify.

MOVEMENT

(a) **Gait**—The Samoyed should trot, not pace. He should move with a quick agile stride that is well-timed. The gait should be free, balanced and vigorous, with good reach in the forequarters and good driving power in the hindquarters. When trotting, there should be a strong rear action drive. Moving at a slow walk or trot, they will not single track, but as speed increases, the legs gradually angle inward until the pads are finally falling on a line directly under the longitudinal center of the body. As the pad marks converge the forelegs and hind legs are carried straight forward in traveling, the stifles not turned in nor out. The back should remain strong, firm and level. A choppy or stilted gait should be penalized.

(b) **Rear End**—Upper thighs should be well-developed. Stifles well bent— approximately 45 degrees to the ground. Hocks should be well developed, sharply defined and set at approximately 30 percent of hip height. The hind legs should be parallel when viewed from the rear in a natural stance, strong, well-developed, turning neither in nor out. Straight stifles are objectionable. Double-jointedness or cowhocks are a *fault*. Cowhocks should only be determined if the dog has had an opportunity to move properly.

(c) **Front End**—Legs should be parallel and straight to the pasterns. The pasterns should be strong, sturdy and straight, but flexible with some spring for proper let-down of feet. Because of depth of chest, legs should be moderately long. Length of leg from the ground to the elbow should be approximately

55 percent of the total height at the withers—a very short-legged dog is to be deprecated. Shoulders should be long and sloping, with a layback of 45 degrees and be firmly set. Out at the shoulders or out at the elbows should be penalized. The withers separation should be approximately 1–1½ inches.

(d) **Feet**—Large, long, flattish—a hare foot, slightly spread but not splayed; toes arched; pads thick and tough, with protective growth of hair between the toes. Feet should turn neither in nor out in a natural stance but may turn in slightly in the act of pulling. Turning out, pigeon-toed, round or cat-footed or splayed are *faults*. Feathers on feet are not too essential but are more profuse on females than on males.

HEAD

(a) **Conformation**—Skull is wedge-shaped, broad, slightly crowned, not round or apple-headed, and should form an equilateral triangle on lines between the inner base of the ears and the center point of the stop.

Muzzle—Muzzle of medium length and medium width, neither coarse nor snipy; should taper toward the nose and be in proportion to the size of the dog and the width of the skull. The muzzle must have depth. Whiskers are not to be removed.

Stop not too abrupt, nevertheless well defined.

Lips—Should be black for preference and slightly curved up at the corners of the mouth, giving the "Samoyed smile." Lip lines should not have the appearance of being coarse nor should the flews drop predominately at corners of the mouth.

Ears—Strong and thick, erect, triangular and slightly rounded at the tips; should not be large or pointed, nor should they be small and "bear-eared." Ears should conform to head size and the size of the dog; they should be set well apart but be within the border of the outer edge of the head; they should be mobile and well covered inside with hair; hair full and stand-off before the ears. Length of ear should be the same measurement as the distance from inner base of ear to outer corner of eye.

Eyes—Should be dark for preference; should be placed well apart and deep-set; almond shaped with lower lid slanting toward an imaginary point approximating the base of ears. Dark eye rims for preference. Round or protruding eyes penalized. Blue eyes *disqualifying*.

Nose—Black for preference but brown, liver, or Dudley nose not penalized. Color of nose sometimes changes with age and weather.

Jaws and Teeth—Strong, well-set teeth, snugly overlapping with scissors bite. Undershot or overshot should be penalized.

(b) **Expression**—The expression, referred to as "Samoyed expression," is very important and is indicated by sparkle of the eyes, animation and lighting up of the face when alert or intent on anything. Expression is made up of a combination of eyes, ears and mouth. The ears should be erect when alert; the mouth should be slightly curved up at the corners to form the "Samoyed smile."

TORSO

(a) **Neck**—Strong, well-muscled, carried proudly erect, set on sloping shoulders to carry head with dignity when at attention. Neck should blend into shoulders with a graceful arch.

(b) **Chest**—Should be deep, with ribs well-sprung out from the spine and flattened at the sides to allow proper movement of the shoulders and freedom for the front legs. Should not be barrel-chested. Perfect depth of chest approximates the point of elbows, and the deepest part of the chest should be back of the forelegs—near the ninth rib. Heart and lung room are secured more by body depth than width.

(c) **Loin and Back**—The withers forms the highest part of the back. Loins strong and slightly arched. The back should be straight to the loin, medium in length, very muscular, and neither long nor short-coupled. The dog should be "just off square"—the length being approximately 5 percent more than the height. Females allowed to be slightly longer than males. The belly should be well-shaped and tightly muscled and with the rear of the thorax, should swing up in a pleasing curve (tuck-up). Croup must be full, slightly sloping, and must continue imperceptibly to the tail root.

(d) **Tail**—The tail should be moderately long with the tail bone terminating approximately at the hock when down. It should be profusely covered with long hair and carried forward over the back or side when alert, but sometimes dropped when at rest. It should not be high or low set and should be mobile and loose—not tight over the back. A double hook is a *fault*. A judge should see the tail over the back once when judging.

(e) **Disposition**—Intelligent, gentle, loyal, adaptable, alert, full of action, eager to serve, friendly but conservative, not distrustful or shy, not overly aggressive. Unprovoked aggressiveness to be severely penalized.

DISQUALIFICATIONS

Any color other than pure white, cream, biscuit, or white and biscuit. Blue eyes.

chapter 7

Commentary on the Current Standard

All AKC member clubs are represented at meetings of the governing body by their elected delegates. At the helm of the Samoyed Club of America ship for many years was the invaluable John Ronald. He always presented the Samoyed case with diplomacy and force to the forefront at the AKC.

In the mid-1980s, the AKC and the other major national registries of the world felt that greater global uniformity of breed Standards would help judges, exhibitors and breeders make their contributions to purebred dogs. The AKC felt it should format its breed Standards so that whatever Standard one read, it would flow in the same order as any other Standard.

The Samoyed Club of America and many other parent breed clubs felt that the current format they had was as important as the wording of the Standard. They felt the order of items described in the Standard gave one a sense of the relative importance of those items. For instance, one Standard may first describe heads, whereas another would initially mention movement, implying that these features were of primary importance in each Standard.

The Samoyed Club opposed reformatting its Standard and asked John Ronald to protect its right to keep the Standard as it was. Ultimately, John proposed and got passed an amendment to AKC's Constitution that guaranteed that, notwithstanding anyone's desire to change a Standard (including the AKC), no changes can be made without the parent club's approval. The AKC abandoned the move to reformat Standards a short time later.

Several years later John learned that the AKC had quietly been copyrighting the Standards in its registry. The parent breed clubs, including the Samoyed Club of America, were concerned because according to the AKC's constitution, they (the parent clubs) were responsible for their Standards and felt they would be unable to protect and control them if someone else controlled the copyright. This issue has never been completely resolved. However, the AKC

145

agrees the parent clubs are responsible for the Standards and has promised that the AKC's copyrighting will in no way limit the parent clubs' use of their own property.

Regarding the topic of general appearance, "general appearance" is an attempt to picture the dog as he evolved in his native habitat—a dog for hunting, herding and hauling—and the natural attributes that made him survive in that severe, barren and cold climate. The Samoyed must be strongly built and agile.

The coat possesses density and quality to withstand not only weather and cold, but also the formation of ice that would prevent movement and threaten survival. The spiky, stand-off guard hair keeps the snow and ice away from the undercoat. The white coloration, which is most natural to Northern Arctic animals, conserves warmth. Studies have shown that the makeup and color of the fur from Arctic animals prevents the conduction of heat from the body. Inexperienced people feel that such a thick coat must entail a lot of suffering in hot weather. Wrong! Nature automatically substitutes a lighter overcoat every spring; such a body covering is as effective an insulator in the summer to repel heat as it is in the winter to ward off cold. It has been proved beyond any doubt that the Samoyed, Arctic dog though he is, can withstand hot weather. You may see him in Africa, Puerto Rico, the southern United States, South America and Japan.

The head described is the typical wedge of the wolf, the bear, the fox, the ermine and the seal, which provides the powerful jaws and the ability of the teeth to rip and tear that a hunter must have. The eyes, through centuries of squinting in the bright Arctic sunlight, have the slightly slanting Mongolian look so necessary to survival. Note that the ponies taken on the polar expeditions, whose eyes were without this feature, all suffered from snow blindness and became quite helpless.

The ears are extremely functional and movable to avoid freezing and are heavily haired inside and out for protection. Do you know that there are no long-eared animals in the Arctic regions? In cold weather long-eared dogs have a tendency to form blood blisters in their ears, with subsequent freezing and formation of gangrene.

"Expression" is the sum total of the appearance created by the set of the eyes, the tilt of the ears, the size of the mouth and the upward curve of the lip line. A Samoyed must have tight, close flews. The right expression has an intelligent, penetrating look, with a devilish, quizzical attitude that says to you, "Well what do we do now?" The Samoyed faces the world cheerfully, confidently and with a frank candor that is unmistakable. He returns your gaze squarely, honestly and without a trace of calculation. He has nothing to conceal.

The centuries-long association with humans, living in the huts and "chooms" of the Samoyed people, has created a disposition and expression unmatched by any other breed. The primitive harshness one might expect in both man and dog is subordinated to kindliness and friendship.

The dense undercoat is a vital part of the Samoyed makeup, but it is wrong to blame the lack of an undercoat for the lack of a stand-off outer coat. True, the perfect coat is composed of both the under and outer coats, but when the outer coat is of a proper texture, it stands up unaided by the undercoat even during periods of heavy shedding. It is a matter of texture, not length. The outer coat must be harsh to enable it to stand up. When you pat or dab the open palm of your hand flat on the guard hair, it should bend under pressure and spring back to the upright position immediately on release. The hair should appear to protect the animal, like the quills of the porcupine, from weather, dirt, snow and wetness. The profuse coat does not lay down unless it is of improper texture. A flat-lying coat is just about as poor a coat as a Samoyed can have. This type of coat is useless for the life that the Samoyed is born to lead and for the work it is supposed to do.

The proper Samoyed coat shakes free of water after swimming, does not permit snow and ice to pack into it and freeze, and shakes free of dirt and mud when the dog rolls itself dry in straw or grass. *Quality of texture and type of coat are more important than quantity.*

All details of body and leg structure listed in the "General Appearance" section of the Standard are for that all-purpose animal—the hunter, the herder, the hauler. These details give us a nimble yet sturdy dog that will not give up in the snow or during extended pursuit of game.

THE "3-H" DOG—HUNTER, HERDER & HAULER

The concept of substance is misunderstood in Samoyeds when individual dogs are praised for possessing massive bone. Substance goes with soundness and, in its broadest sense, indicates that the dog shall be so constructed as to be capable of doing his native job well. The Samoyed is only a fast sled dog when he is first a fast herder. Too much of what is written leads one to believe that the Samoyed should be massively boned. This great emphasis on "good" and "heavy" bone emerged because of the fine-boned and weedy-type specimens exhibited in the early 1900s. Many of those owners assumed that bone on the Samoyed would be like that of an Eskimo or a Chow Chow. Once Mrs. Kilburn-Scott said, "If a dog possesses unusual bone, he is right-off type." A working dog with too heavy bone lacks speed, agility and grace to do his work as a herder, hunter or sled dog.

Picture the Samoyed people hunting wild reindeer in Siberia. They build a corral with large wings of fences to guide the herds into the corral traps. Men and dogs spread out in a huge fanlike net and drive the reindeer into the trap. The reindeer are quite fast and nimble. The men and dogs chase them for most of the day and sometimes for several days. Think of the nimbleness and endurance that is required to run on ice and snow. This certainly is no occupation for a Newfoundland or a Chow Chow.

Personally, from working dogs in teams, we know that the exceptionally heavy-boned dogs have actually passed out after several hours of intense work; likewise, smaller dogs have given up and have been brought home on the sled. One would know better if one follows the accounts of the explorers and the dogs that best survived their journeys. Not the largest and not the smallest, but the dogs weighing fifty-nine to six-nine pounds were the last to be in harness. Strangely enough, in the sport of Greyhound racing, rarely are dogs over seventy pounds or under fifty-five pounds found at the tracks. It is not because larger and smaller do not exist, but because there is an optimum size for strength and speed.

If our ideal Samoyed is to be graceful as well as beautiful, it must have sufficient body length to permit graceful movement. A compact body does not lend itself to good action, and using either males or females of this kind for breeding is to accentuate a fault of cobbiness.

"Torso" includes the neck, chest, loin and back. We should begin with the neck and agree that, as we are describing neither a racer nor a draft animal, the neck should be moderately long. An animal, when he runs, uses the length of the neck to balance itself while at the gallop; therefore, a racing animal has an extremely long neck, whereas the draft animal has a short neck to consolidate strength at slower speeds. The Samoyed shall therefore have a proudly arched, moderately long neck, set for speed but not racy.

The definition of chest has caused much difficulty among owners because the phrase "broad chest" has often appeared. Even in the Standard some misinterpretation occurs. The dog's front is not his chest; this is his front or brisket. The chest rightly is at the lowest point between the front legs. The breadth is measured more by the spring in the rib cage. The barrel-chested effect is to be avoided to eliminate the comparison to purely draft animals. The approved Standard is quite explicit and clear on this point.

The loin and back are well described in the Standard, but the important part they play in producing a proper topline could be expanded. The Samoyed's topline is level except for the slight rise at the withers and slight slope at the croup. The full view of the topline may give the impression of quite a slope to the topline, but this is caused more by the arch of the neck and the rounding out by the proper coat, which grows with a maned effect over the shoulders. There is a slight arch over the loin.

The Standard's description of the tail is excellent, but mention should be made of the disastrous effect on dogs in the Arctic lacking the proper loose tail to protect themselves while sleeping. The explorers who docked their dogs found that within three weeks their dogs had died of pneumonia. *Tails too loose or too tightly curled are incorrect.*

The description of disposition is fairly thorough in the Standard. The unadvertised ability of the Samoyed to get along in groups in kennels and at shows benched without dividers was a standardized fact for more than sixty years. No one thought much about this quality; it just happened. But unfortunately, in some instances, it does not happen now. We in America do not emphasize this strongly enough now. It seems that which we most take for granted is the last to be missed.

Special features in the Standard that must be observed while judging are tail up and over the back at least once, moveable ears for protection and a topline that is neither too steep from front to rear, nor too high in the rear. The gait in action, never clumsy, must be a graceful, natural trot that indicates an eagerness to move. In other words, does he want to move?

Note: One of the greatest values of the Standard is that it provides a measure for evaluating your dog. Never evaluate your dog against another dog. The approved Standard has been developed by many breeders of long experience and approved by the AKC. They based their observations on the Standards originally set down by men who knew the dogs under working conditions and the observations set down by explorers.

THE CONSIDERATION OF SIZE

Are dogs larger or smaller now than they were in the past? Neither, for Fridjof Nansen listed his males as averaging fifty-nine pounds in working condition and his bitches at fifty pounds. Records show that Antarctic Buck was the tallest dog of the breed in 1909, and most of the descendants spring from him. He was reported by some at 21.5 inches, and some at 22 inches measured at the shoulder, not at the withers. (In America, we measure at the withers—the highest point of the shoulder.) In 1925, the English Ch. Snow Crest was reported at 23 inches and weighed seventy pounds. In 1930, English Ch. Kara Sea was measured at 22.6 inches and weighed sixty pounds. The English import Ch. Tobolsk measured 23 inches and weighed sixty-five pounds in 1922. At the same time, the English import Ch. Donerna's Barin was reported to be 22.5 inches tall and weighed sixty-five pounds. In 1948, Irish import Ch. Snowland Stara, the first champion in the British Isles after World War II, was 23.5 inches tall and weighed sixty-eight pounds. In 1954, the imported Ch. Raff of Kobe was 23 inches tall and weighed over ninety pounds before he was placed on a strict diet by his new owners, the Powells.

The Samoyed is a herding, hauling and hunting working dog. He needs a heart-shaped body, with well-sprung ribs. The lowest point of chest approximates the elbow. The measurements here are averages from the detailed measurements of more than fifty champions. Even the known details of the great champion of more than fifty years ago, Ch. Kara Sea, are included. Showing his similarity to dogs of today, Kara Sea's length of leg from elbow to ground (E–G) was 55 percent of his height at the withers (22.6 inches).

These opinions, no matter how varied, return us to the matter at hand. How do our present-day Samoyeds measure up to the Standard? All breeders have experienced what happens when they lose sight of the original purpose of the breed and overemphasize something else. When size goes beyond nature's standard or the animal is bred smaller, many difficulties arise.

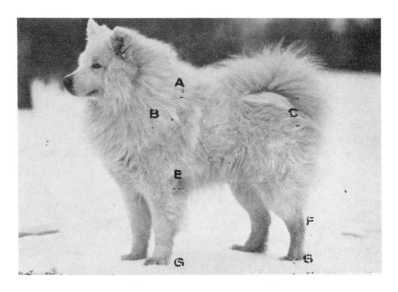

Ch. Dobrynia, owned by the Very Rev. Msgr. Robert F. Keegan

Height at Withers (A–C)	19"	20"	21"	22"	23"	24"
Length (B–C) Shoulder point to hip point	20.25	21.50	22.50	23.00	24.25	25.00
Height at rear	19.25	19.75	20.75	22.00	22.50	23.50
Barrel or circumference	24.50	26.00	26.75	28.00	28.50	29.00
Pastern or ankle	3.50	3.75	4.00	4.25	4.62	5.25
Depth of chest	8.50	9.00	9.25	9.50	10.25	10.75
Length of ear	3.10	3.25	3.375	3.50	3.87	4.00
Distance between eyes	1.87	2.00	2.00	2.12	2.25	2.25
Length of head (occiput to tip of nose)	8.00	8.12	8.37	8.50	19.00	9.50
Length of muzzle	3.25	3.37	3.50	3.87	3.90	4.125
Hock to ground (F–G)	5.75	6.00	6.25	6.50	6.75	7.00
Leg length (E–G) (elbow to ground)	10.45	11.00	11.55	12.10	12.65	13.20

Proportion of boning, soundness, disposition and the like are affected. As a result, the dog can no longer do the job intended by nature.

Large Sams may be quick and agile. Small Sams may be clumsy and slow. Or the reverse may be true. The key to correctness is *agility,* and we must keep the correct, stable companion-like disposition. Good temperament is to be prized above all!

A LOOK AT TEMPERAMENT WITH
TERRY BEDNARCZYK

Temperament embodies the heart and soul of our Samoyed breed. Behavior is the window to temperament. We evaluate a dog's temperament by its behavior. Temperament is what we live and work with in our dogs, and it is the mechanism that allows the lead dog and team, the competitor, the herder, the weight puller, the Obedience or Agility dog to give that 110 percent (or 50 percent) in its performance—despite working conditions.

Our breed is a hearty breed. It has had to be hearty to survive and to perform the variety of working requirements of its native people in their rugged environment. Our breed had optimum opportunity in being extremely well socialized with its people in addition to ingraining the attributes of hunter, herder and hauler. This uniqueness of its life's demands and requirements has created the basic Samoyed character, personality and temperament. It is a temperament that encompasses a very loving and people-oriented animal, yet a hearty and confident canine that should not back down from a challenge.

Our Standard states that our breed's disposition should be "intelligent, gentle, loyal, adaptable, alert, full of action, eager to serve, friendly but conservative, not distrustful or shy, and not overly aggressive. Unprovoked aggressiveness to be severely penalized."

It's distressing to see our breed display questionable behavior or temperament—inside or outside the ring. Seeing a top-winning breed champion standing in the ring with a silent display of raised lips and bared teeth or with an open, unprovoked challenge to other canine competitors in the ring is cause for concern regarding the shape of our breed. Then to have this individual promoted and rewarded by judges—despite untypical behavior (temperament) displayed in the ring is unconscionable. At the other end of the spectrum, it is just as disturbing to see an individual react frantically to a friendly stranger's approach and to seek only the confines of its crate so it can mentally survive whatever is going on around it. What about the dog that panics when the owner is no longer visible? These situations can only have deleterious effects on our breed.

What is even more disturbing is that it suggests that maybe we have overlooked something very important in our breed and breeding programs. In a pursuit to achieve the pinnacle of physical perfection, have we left behind possibly the most important attribute that endears this breed to so many of us—its temperament?

We, as exhibitors and breeders, are the real-life judges inside and outside the ring. We have the ability to influence the shape of our breed. As breeders, are we truly giving equal emphasis to the mental and physical attributes in our prospective litter? Do we properly prepare the individual dogs we breed for the forthcoming events of their lives by environmental influences and proper placement?

A puppy goes through four critical growth periods very early in life—birth to sixteen weeks. Those growth periods can have critical and lasting effects on an individual's adult behavior and social relationships. Social behavior is developed in dogs as it is in people. Despite genetics, environmental influences in learning can enhance or suppress an individual's genetic makeup. The following are the major growth periods.

Birth to three weeks: This time frame can vary slightly, however, a helpless newborn at the end of this period can see, hear and is mobile—a relative toddler ready to embark on new adventures.

Three to seven weeks: During this period the brain and nervous system are developing, and by the end of this period a youngster has the capacity of an adult but not the experience. Socialization with both people and their littermates is vital. Puppies learn a tremendous amount of behavior interaction and appropriate social roles with one another and their mother at this time, which is critical to normal development. The dominance order is started, and it is an excellent time to introduce play training. During this time weaning takes place, and the mother leaves puppies for extended periods.

Seven to twelve weeks: This is the best time to form the human-dog relationship as well as to begin training. The type of relationship, trust and attachment made by the puppy at this time can greatly affect its attitude toward people and situations as well as acceptance of direction and education and training. Considerable teaching and play-training done at this time becomes the foundation of the youngster's life education. A balanced social interaction with people and its littermates is even more vital. Placement in the new home is usually done during this time, around the eighth and ninth week.

Twelve to sixteen weeks: A puppy has experienced tremendous physical and emotional growth in just three months. Socialization needs to continue with new experiences and people. This period can be considered as the cutting period when the puppy declares its independence. This can also be the time when owner and dog decide who is boss. A puppy at this stage is a young adult that still needs to be provided safe opportunities for experiencing life's challenges and opportunities to quench curiosity and enhance learning.

This brief overview of these critical growth periods can be further broken down into almost weekly subsets and overlapping periods of mental, physical and emotional growth. However, once these periods have passed, they are gone forever.

ADDITIONAL READING AND
REFERENCES

Wendy Volhard, "Drives—A New Look at an Old Concept," *Off-Lead* (September 1991–October 1991).

Elizabeth Randolph, *How to Help Your Puppy Grow up to Be a Wonderful Dog* (New York: Fawcett Crest Books, 1987).

The Art of Raising a Puppy, The Monks of New Skete (Canada: Little Brown & Company, 1991).

Clarence Pfaffenberger, *The New Knowledge of Dog Behavior* (New York: Howell Book House, 1963).

Jack Volhard and Melissa Bartlett, *What All Good Dogs Should Know—The Sensible Way to Train* (New York: Howell Book House, 1991).

The American Temperament Test Society, Inc. (ATTS, Inc.), P.O. Box 397, Fenton, Missouri 63026; (314) 225-5346.

The American Kennel Club, AKC Canine Good Citizen® Department, 5580 Centerview Drive, Suite 200, Raleigh, North Carolina 27606; (919) 233-9780 to order free information kit or to purchase test kits; (212) 696-8322 for questions regarding the program.

Therapy Dogs International, Inc., 6 Hilltop Road, Mendham, New Jersey 07945; (201) 543-0888.

The German Shepherd Dog Club of America, Robert Penny, Chairman & Chief Tester—Temperament Committee, Sierra Madre, California 91024.

The Samoyed Club of America, at the AKC's request, chose a committee to create a video to explain and illustrate the Samoyed Standard.

chapter 8

Judging the Samoyed

THE ARCTIC BREEDS—DIFFERENCES AND SIMILARITIES

The following excerpt is adapted from an article written by the authors, which appeared in *Kennel Review*. It is included here by special permission.

Both alphabetically and three dimensionally, we put the Samoyed exactly between the Alaskan Malamute and the Siberian Husky. All are distinctly individual Arctic breeds. Everyone has some pet peeve and ours is to have either judges or exhibitors subjectively or objectively classify the Samoyed as a fluffy, non-working or Fancy Dog. The Samoyed should be able to perform his legitimate work even if he does not have to work anymore. Function dictates form and so we should be able to assess the differences among these three Arctics; as their functions are not the same and neither are their forms or gaits.

Yes indeed, the Samoyed is the medium (although the Siberian Husky talks medium and moderate a dozen times in its Standard). The Samoyed is a bit larger than the Siberian Husky but smaller than the Alaskan Malamute. The Samoyed bone is less than required for a good Malamute but heavier than that required for a good Siberian. Samoyed bone should never be so bulky as to make a coarse, non-agile Samoyed. The Standard says "The Samoyed should never be so heavy as to appear clumsy, nor so light as to appear racy." A SAMOYED IS AGILE: a hunting, herding, hauling work dog or companion. He should never be a watered-down freighting Malamute nor a beefed-up racing Siberian.

His color is not just white. The color of Samoyeds varies in all shades of white to buff, often with deeper shading of lemon or buff, especially around his ears.

Regarding proportion, the Samoyed is similar to the other two breeds under consideration. He must have 55 percent leg height as measured from ground to elbow, or elbow to ground, depending upon the way your artist's

There can be no mistaking this typically masculine head. *Kitten Rodwell*

eye views proper proportion of leg height to overall height of the dog at the withers. Every Samoyed Standard (American, English, New Zealand, Australian and Canadian) states: "Because of the depth of chest required, the legs should be moderately long, a very short legged dog is to be deprecated."

The Samoyed is not square, he is "Off-Square." The function of this form is to allow balance of running power enabling maximum reach in the forequarters with corresponding driving rear power. To quote the Standards again: "A short coupled loin would make him practically useless for his legitimate work, but at the same time a close-coupled body would also place him at a great disadvantage as a draft dog. Bitches may be slightly longer in back than males."

It is the Samoyed proportion of 55 percent (elbow to ground) for leg as compared to the remaining 45 percent (elbow to top of withers) with the correct 45 degree shoulder layback that gives the shape of the Samoyed, built for endurance and snow conditions.

There is no disqualification, either under or over, as to size (as there is in the case of the Siberian Husky) but rather a recommendation in the USA of 21–23½ inches for dogs and 19–21 inches for bitches, measured at the withers, with deviations to be penalized according to the extent of the deviation. Note that foreign Standards differ: the Swedish/Norwegian/

Finnish is 22–24 inches males and 19–22 inches bitches. The English/ Canadian/Australian is 20–22 inches for males and 18–20 inches for bitches. When judging the breed in any country or any state, we find the Samoyeds are really all the same with the same varieties of sizes, shapes, heads, coats, and gaits.

The Samoyed head is his stamp of distinction and sets him apart from every other breed. The "lighting up of the face with the smile" is a total picture created from the thick well-set ears, the curved mouth and lip-line and the dark brown eyes. Combined with the typical outgoing temperament and stable personality, all that produces the typical expression of the breed.

The temperament denotes the style of the pack animal, and here is a likeness rather than a difference in the Northern breeds. The Arctic breeds must get along with an established pecking order of the group in order to work together. As these three breeds are natural dogs as opposed to man-made breeds such as the Doberman Pinscher and German Shepherd Dog, they do possess likenesses as well as differences. All three have weather-resistant coats, double coats which include the soft downy undercoat and outer coat standing off from the body which is designed to repel snow and water.

The texture of the Samoyed coat is of greater importance than the quantity of hair. Pressing the palm of the hand against the vertical hair, the coat should feel spiky to the touch. Any indentation made in the hair should bounce up like a spring recovering. Buff color in exhibits should be used in the breeding program to preserve this proper quality of coat texture and therefore we achieve the creamy white to buff to silver white colors.

These eight-week-old puppies exhibit desirable Samoyed pigment. Correct pigment, or "black points," should be evident by eight weeks. Black points are defined as black eye rims, lip lines and nose.

Samoyed pasterns should be mentioned as being different from those of the other two breeds. In the Malamute, pasterns are more upright as are the Siberian's (which Standard also mentions flexibility). However, the pastern of the Samoyed approaches a 15 degree angle on its way to being as flexible as that of the German Shepherd Dog, stated as 25 degrees. This flexibility enhances the quick motions of herding-type activity. Some Samoyeds may be criticized as being "down in the pastern" when in reality it is not the bone angles but the leg-feathering which is a deceiving illusion. A thorough judge will fold back all of the leg feathering on Samoyeds, Collies and Shelties to ascertain the proper angulation of the pasterns.

The Samoyed's snow shoe foot is different. It is a hare foot, longish, strong, not splayed, with hair between the toes. His foot type could mean either salvation or demise on the trail, in the wild or in the show ring!

With all the differences among these Arctic breeds, there are also fundamental likenesses. None of these breeds should ever be barrel chested. Their work requires great endurance; therefore, for maximum lung and heart performance, these vital organs must be encased in the heart-shaped rib cage described in the Standard; rather than any round-shaped, "watermelon" body. Depth of chest reaching to the elbow is vital.

While all three breeds carry their tails over their backs, each does it in a different manner. Actually all northern animals either carry their tails over their backs or in a high plume or else they have no tail or a very short tail; also all northern animals have shorter, thicker ears than animals native to moderate climates. Examples are: the fox, ermine, Arctic hare, polar bear, mink, lynx, Siberian Husky, Samoyed and Alaskan Malamute. The eyes of all are protected from snow-blindness by shape and design.

The Samoyed carries his tail over his back and it must touch and drape over either side. One should be able to slide a hand between the tail and back at the root, when judging, to insure that it is not a "snap-tail" which would indicate a flat croup and straight stifles. The Siberian carries his tail in a "flag" without touching his back while moving or standing. Malamutes should carry their tails as a waving plume. So much depends upon structure for any of the breeds from tail set to tail carriage, i.e., low tail set with much angulation; high tail set or snap tail with straight stifles and flat croups, with no reach, extension or drive.

The Samoyed's loose tail with its profuse feathering can be observed to be over his nose and face while curled-up and sleeping. History books quote that this is the way he filters the harsh Arctic cold and thus breathes air rather than frost (or possibly big-city pollution). His tail tells you his mood of the moment as it wags gently or vigorously while "talking."

The ears have great mobility for all three breeds. Up when alert, down and folded well into their ruffs when running, working or sleeping. All of this from their native land where large, thin, immobile ears would be damaged by freezing temperatures. The Samoyed's triangular ears are set closer together than the Malamute's, but not as high as the Siberian's. Their size should match the wedge of the head. The length of the ear when folded toward the muzzle should approximate the distance to the inner corner of the eye. Puppy ears may seem large but remember the adult coat and ruff will round out the wedge.

Can there be any doubt that Bobmardon's Mint Julip's happy smile is exactly what the Samoyed Standard calls for in the section on Expression?

None of the Arctic breeds should have a round eye! Sammies have a kind of isosceles triangular-shaped eye, set in a slight slant (quite like the eye of a good Collie). (*Note:* all dogs have round eyes, it is merely the shape of the eye rim that is distinctive to each breed. Very few Standards mention this fact; the Shetland Sheepdog and Great Dane Standards are exceptions.)

Northern breeds' eyes should not be sunken or protruding and never be too close together. Remember they are designed to live with bright snow and ice glare. Standards call for dark eyes which does not mean black. Dark brown eyes give more expression. Blue eyes disqualify the Samoyed and the Malamute but not the Siberian.

One great difference in the three breeds is the preparation for the show ring. All have double coats, but the Samoyed's coat is both longer and without markings. It must be thoroughly combed prior to a bath. For its denseness, it must be blown dry after the bath, followed by brushing and a complete comb-out. All of this special show preparation should be done at least two or three days before the event, in order for the coat to revert to its proper texture. Proper nutrition and sufficient brushing weekly should care for the Arctic coats. Of the three Arctics, only Samoyed coats have no doggie odor. As judges, we expect to have any exhibit presented clean and well groomed, and hope they each meet their Standard.

[*Authors' note:* Supplementing our own observations, we here present observations on judging by some other respected authorities.]

JUDGING SAMOYEDS

by Derek G. Rayne

As a judge of all Working breeds for over sixty years, I have seen many changes in all of these breeds.

In evaluating any Working breed, type and soundness do not always go hand in hand. A lovely head often rests on poor shoulders! The most common fault in many Working breeds is poor shoulder placement. In short-coated breeds, poor shoulder placement is visible to the ringside. In coated breeds, such as Samoyeds, a judge may have to use his hands or wait till the dogs are moved in a circle when the lack of reach will be noted.

We have more good Samoyeds than we had sixty years ago, almost every section of the country has dogs of quality. Unfortunately, with the increased popularity of many breeds, a judge has to go over a lot of mediocre dogs; the percentage of good dogs does not increase with the size of entry.

In 1978, I had the honor of being one of the judges at the Samoyed National Specialty Show in Portland, Oregon. During that weekend, I became aware of two things that should be of concern to the Samoyed breeders. Some dogs are too large and some are too small. Correct size and uniformity is very important to a breed. The second item of concern I observed was the loss of

An example of typically feminine head type and expression modeled by Ch. Hoof 'n Paws Drifting Snow.

An example of exquisite male head type and Samoyed expression modeled by Ch. Sanorka's Moonlight Gambler.

the true "Sammy" expression. Many dogs had light eyes with a hard expression, and others had non-typical heads.

Some years ago, I wrote that if a dog is looking over a fence and only the head is silhouetted against the sky, the viewer should be able to distinguish a Siberian Husky from a Malamute or an Elkhound from a Keeshond, without seeing the rest of the dog. Of course, this holds equally true for a Samoyed. The head is the character of the breed and should never be sacrificed for soundness or showmanship.

[Derek G. Rayne is one of a small group of distinguished judges approved to pass on all AKC-recognized breeds.]

THE IMPORTANCE OF PRESERVING SAMOYED TYPE

by Edna Travinek, Retired AKC Judge

A strikingly handsome dog. An appealing and feminine bitch. Both possess the ideals of type, soundness, balance and style.

Essentially an Arctic dog noted for its functional versatility, the Samoyed has, over the years, managed to retain its basic type—established years ago by its pioneer breeders.

Perhaps the Sam's lesser popularity with the public has proven to be an advantage in preserving the overall type, especially when we consider the obvious breakdown that has taken place in other functional breeds through mass production and/or lack of constructive study of suitable bloodlines.

A change in Samoyed type that I have noticed is a tendency toward cupped, tight feet. This is correct for the Great Pyrenees but not for the

Ch. Images The Barrister, CD, in a graphic demonstration of classic reach and drive.

Sam, which is supposed to have the hare foot, or as some might choose to call it, "snowshoe" feet.

The Samoyed Standard requires well-bent stifles. There is a tendency toward straight stifles, if not the actual occurrence of straight stifles. Although excessive grooming can also give the illusion of straightness. Thus it becomes important for the judge to get fingers beneath the carefully treated and brushed hair to determine correctness of stifles. And, we are aware of the shoulder problems confronting dog breeders today to some degree, including those who work with Samoyeds.

By its Standard, the Sam is classified as a herding/sledding dog. Therefore, the functional Sam is a moving Sam which should be equipped with a 90-degree angulation, both fore and aft. Such a structure will provide a good reach in front and a strong drive in the rear—suggesting a smooth, well-oiled machine capable of covering much ground.

We cannot change the skeleton, but the gait can be improved by roadwork with a car or bike and the Sam on a line for those who lack space at home. A daily trot at a set speed will condition the dog and do wonders for slack muscles and will hold the framework in place. Start slowly with a quarter of a mile and build up to a few miles. The entire dog will benefit, physically and mentally, including his trademark—the Sammy smile.

[Mrs. Travinek was a highly respected judge of all Working breeds.]

TWO EXCERPTS FROM A 1930 CRITIQUE

by Miss J. V. Thomson-Glover, an English Judge

A born showman looks about him, proudly interested in everything within range. I do not care to see Samoyeds standing about, or tailing around like a flock of sheep. People think a dog shows well if it stands motionless, with its eyes glued to whatever the handler has in his hands.

An eye entirely foreign is creeping into the breed, and perhaps novices do not realize how much beauty and Samoyed character is thus lost. [*Authors' note:* And this problem was creeping into the breed in the 1980s; and alarmingly, round eye shape has sprung into Sams in the 1990s].

Hear, hear!

SAMOYED HEADS

Mrs. Ivy Kilburn-Morris was among the most respected figures in the breed. She had indeed grown up with the breed, identifying with it over eight decades. She had long been concerned with Samoyed heads and wrote:

> I find many of these changed and not of the original type, resembling more the Chow or Keeshond. In some cases the true Samoyed expression is entirely lost. The fault lies in the structure of the foreface: the skull above the eyes is too broad, the stop rather too pronounced, the muzzle too short and the mouth too wide and "lippy." Sometimes the eyes are too large and prominent, more round than almond-shaped, or badly spaced. These changes give a hard expression, foreign to the breed.
>
> There is also another type of incorrect head, where the eyes are inclined to be too close together, and there is not sufficient stop. . . . No matter how good a dog may be in other respects, if its head is not correct, it is not a typical specimen.

The judge is employed to find the best dogs—not the smallest, not the largest—the best dogs!

Richard Beauchamp, editor-publisher of *Kennel Review,* in writing to breeders of the Bichon Frise, made comments that are equally applicable for breeders of the Samoyed:

> When size is significantly reduced in this or any breed for that matter, one does not reduce all body parts proportionately. I have found that as size decreases, the upper arm shortens and the shoulder straightens. The straightening of the shoulder, of course, gives the individual a longer back and a shorter neck. Reduction of length in the upper arm creates less front angulation in the rear quarters. It goes without saying that this seriously restricts the easy reach and drive which is the hallmark of the Bichon. (Or the Samoyed.)
>
> The judge who arbitrarily decides he is "for" or "against" the dog which falls toward either end of the ideal at the expense of the well-made dog is not serving the best interests of the breed, and is in fact simply gratifying his own personal preferences, which is not what good judging is about!

The Samoyed Standard states, "Double-jointedness or cowhocks are a fault." This photo clearly illustrates double-jointedness—unsound and unsightly.

The authors reiterate that a drag of the Samoyed breed is shortness of leg, and it should be penalized to the extent of the deviation. Ideally, the elbow should approximate 55 percent of its height at the withers. This lack of quality of proportion and lack of characteristic anatomy for the Samoyed if combined with poor coat quality will give an off-type Sam.

Additional cautions—Avoid both large coarse mouths that show sloppy flews and ugly faces! Finally, avoid breeding round eyes into the Samoyed, we so plead. With the AKC recognition of the American Eskimo Dog in 1995, it is important to be aware of the distinct differences between the Samoyed and the "Eskie." The Eskie is allowed in three sizes: Toy, Miniature and Standard. It is the Standard Eskie (fifteen—nineteen inches) that can most resemble the Samoyed. The disqualification of blue eyes and any color other than white or biscuit cream are the same as in the Samoyed. Therefore, it is paramount that the key distinctions in eye set and shape be very apparent to Samoyed breeders, judges and fanciers. Although the Eskie Standard has close similarities to the Samoyed Standard, *the eyes are quite different*. The Eskie Standard calls for "not fully round, but slightly oval . . . not slanted. . . . " The Samoyed's eyes are "deep-set; almond shaped with lower lid slanting toward the base of ears." The differences though subtle are extremely important to the *type* of each breed, Samoyeds versus American Eskimo Dogs.

Ideal Samoyed Movement

by Karl Michael Smith (Ice Way Samoyeds)

An outstanding moving dog is an exciting dog. His beauty and grace in the ring and in the field, his powerful driving rear, working in harmony with his fully extending front, thrill the knowledgeable exhibitor and spectator alike. The pride and satisfaction in owning such an animal transcends winning any prize or award. A Samoyed is a working dog and cannot be outstanding unless his movement is also outstanding.

The trot is the gait which most judges request when evaluating movement. This is a two-time gait: the left front and right rear moving together, followed by the right front and left rear. To insure perpetual support, the front foot moves slightly in advance of the back foot.

The trot is well suited for traveling on rough ground and over long distances at a moderate speed. It is the mode of travel used by dogs in seeking out wild game. It is also an excellent gait for assessing movement in its relation to structure; it shows the strong and weak points in a dog's moving parts more readily than any other gait.

A dog of correct structure, when moving at a brisk trot, will display a maximum amount of drive in the rear assembly. The thrust generated by this rear assembly is propelled through the loin, back and withers to the front assembly. If the shoulders are correctly placed, the shock passes through them with minimum effort, being absorbed by the muscles.

The forward motion generated by the rear assembly will shift the dog's equilibrium forward. The shoulder should open to the fullest extent possible to compensate for this shift; in other words, the front leg reaches forward as far as allowed by the shoulder angle. This can be best accomplished by a shoulder that is set at 45 degrees. The front leg should have good length in the upper arm allowing the front leg to reach out in a long stride close to the ground, thus countering the instability created by the drive of the rear. The neck and head will be thrust forward moving the center of gravity forward, resulting in acceleration and speed.

164

Correct movement, single tracking.

Correct movement, from the side.

To better understand the effect that structure has on a dog's movement we can divide the dog into three sections: the front assembly, the topline and body, and the rear assembly. Under actual conditions, the sections must work together in complete harmony.

FRONT ASSEMBLY

The front assembly consists of the scapula or shoulder blade. The shoulder is long and sloping and set at 45 degrees to the ground. The humerus or upper arm forms a right angle with the shoulder blade and is approximately the same length. The forearm joins the humerus at the elbow joint and is set at an angle of approximately 135 degrees. The pasterns are joined to the forearm at the pastern joint; they have a moderate 10–15 degree slope.

The front assembly has many functions. It supports about 63 percent of the dog's weight. It provides a portion of the propelling force, particularly on turns. The front assembly absorbs the shock delivered forward by the rear assembly, and it helps the dog maintain balance. A correct front assembly allows the dog to single track, offsetting lateral displacement or side-to-side movement.

The shoulder blade is the key to a good front. A sloping 45-degree shoulder allows for a longer, wider blade than does the more vertical 60-degree, straight shoulder. Muscle action is increased by the greater length of the blade; the greater width of the blade provides for larger muscles increasing muscle strength. The 45-degree blade lies alongside the thoracic frame. It moves in a longer arc than the 60-degree blade. It supplies more lift, and its movement is applied parallel to the line of locomotion.

A dog cannot reach past the angle of his shoulder. A 45-degree blade gives maximum reach. While the 60-degree blade results in more vertical forward motion, going up and down as much as forward, the 45-degree blade allows for a longer reaching, ground-covering stride—allowing the pad to hit the ground as momentum expends itself, minimizing stress on the front assembly.

The humerus or upper arm is approximately the same length as the shoulder blade. It is set at about 90 degrees to the blade, letting it extend further back on the body, allowing the longest possible arm without increasing the dog's height. The longer upper arm has a greater arc of travel, allowing for a longer stride. The longer arm increases the length of the triceps muscles and those activating the forearm. The arm's ability to absorb shock, to generate power and lift are all enhanced by its greater length.

When moving, a dog strikes the ground with the heel of his paw; the shock goes directly to the bones of the pastern. The pastern must therefore have a slight bend and not be rigid. Sloping pasterns will visibly differ from broken-down pasterns.

TOPLINE AND BODY

The topline consists of the head and neck, the back, which is divided into the withers, the mid-back, the loin and croup and the tail. The body consists of the chest, the rib section and the abdomen.

The head and neck together shift the center of gravity from side to side on turns. When running, the dog extends its head and neck forward; this creates instability by moving more weight forward and creates speed. If a dog wants to stop, the head and neck go up, throwing the center of gravity toward the rear.

The neck is an integral part of the front assembly. All the muscles that draw the leg forward, directly or indirectly, depend on the neck for support. The cervical ligament is the basic strength to the forward movement of the leg. The neck muscle, like all muscles, contracts two-thirds of the length of its fleshy part. To increase the movement of a part, you increase the actual length of the fleshy part of the muscle; to increase strength, you increase the area of the muscle.

The ewe, or concave, neck is caused by a weakness of the neck muscle and gives poor support in moving the leg forward. The bull, or short, neck shortens the length, and therefore the movement, of the muscles that control forward leg movement.

The withers lie behind the neck on the vertebral column. The first seven vertebrae are involved in shoulder action. They are different from the vertebrae composing the rest of the spinal column; they are longer and are pointed upward and toward the rear. They support the neck ligament and the muscles coming from the shoulder blade.

The mid-back consists of six vertebrae. The spinal column should be straight and form a line parallel to the ground while the dog is standing. The back should be level, but the back line shouldn't because the loin must have an arch.

The area of the loin consists of seven vertebrae. The vertebrae are inclined forward to give better support to the rearing muscles. The power generated by the back legs is passed through the loins and spinal column to the front assembly. The loins also help in handling the shock of the forehand landing. The loin does not receive support from any bones but is set with an arch like a bridge for strength. The slope of the croup and the tail set are good indicators as to the slope of the pelvis.

The chest and rib section are very important in the makeup of a correctly moving dog. To provide for a good single-tracking front, we trade width of chest for depth. The first four or five ribs should not be as "well sprung" as the rest. They should be more flat-sided to provide greater freedom of action to the shoulder blade. The deeper, narrower body is more efficient for work than the round, barrel-chested body. The former provides more heart and lung room and helps combat lateral displacement while moving. Heart and lung capacity is influenced more by the length of the rib than its mid-curve. Body depth should be measured through the ninth rib to get a more accurate idea of heart room. Tuck-up must be confined to the abdominal section.

The abdomen lies behind the rib section. The Standard calls for a tuck-up. During locomotion this allows the large muscles from the pelvis to the base of the ribs to operate in a straighter line than would otherwise be possible.

REAR ASSEMBLY

The rear assembly is comprised of the pelvis. The pelvis is set at about 30 degrees to the horizontal. The femur, or thigh, joins the pelvis at the hip socket forming a right angle and is about the same length as the pelvis. The stifle joint connects the lower leg to the thigh and is set at approximately 90 degrees. The hock joint joins the lower leg to the hock and forms an angle of about 120 degrees. The hock is set at a right angle to the rear pad.

The rear assembly lends support to the dog, but its main function is to generate power. The power delivered by the hind leg is in proportion to the difference in the leg's extended and contracted length during stride. This calls for a well-bent stifle, approximately 45 degrees to the ground to deliver sufficient drive. When sufficient drive is achieved, the leg is carried forward to where momentum is exhausted. Then the leg receives the shock of ground contact. Power is delivered from the time the leg becomes vertical until the pad is airborne.

The rear assembly is designed primarily for propulsion. While the front "fights" to maintain stability, the rear constantly creates instability. It is this process by which movement or locomotion is achieved. It is important that the stifle be well bent; this lengthens the femur and its corresponding thigh muscles. It also provides for longer muscles to the hock joint.

Just as you want the longer thigh for speed and power, you want the shorter hock for endurance. "Hocks close to the ground" reduce the load on the Achilles' tendon and by their shortness allow for a longer thigh.

The back leg is carried forward by muscles coming from the pelvis and attaching to the upper and lower thighs. The leg is drawn back by the strongest group of muscles in the rear assembly. The muscles come down from the pelvis and croup and wrap around the top of the lower thigh. This wrapping allows the muscle to draw the stifle joint back and also to straighten it. The muscles of the loin and back also enter into the action.

These muscles draw back the hind leg and are called rearing muscles.

A well-angulated stifle is one of the best ways to assure strong rearing muscles. This will lengthen the muscles, which gives more muscle action and provides for more muscle area with a corresponding gain in muscle strength.

BALANCE

Balance depends not only on the ratio of head size to neck length, neck length to back and leg length, depth of chest to length of leg and overall body length to height, but the angulation of the front assembly must be in symmetry with the rear.

In viewing the dog from the side, balance is not achieved if the shoulder and upper arm are well set but the rear assembly lacks angulation. The dog will have more reach than drive. Balance is also not achieved if the rear is well angulated but the front assembly is set more vertically. This dog will have more drive than reach. Either condition accounts for many gaiting faults.

In viewing the stationary dog from the front, the pad of the forefoot is set directly under the muscular support of the shoulder blade, and the rear heel pad is set directly under the pelvis joint. When the dog starts to move at a slow speed, this position does not change; but as speed increases, the pads converge toward a centerline beneath the dog, commencing a single-tracking action. The dog begins with static balance and moves into various positions of kinetic balance.

In conclusion, I must acknowledge, with regret, that some of the top winning Samoyeds in the country do not have the correct angulation called for in the Standard. For various reasons, they win despite this inadequacy. By doing their share of winning, the breeders and owners of these dogs do not find it necessary to breed for more angulation. But most people, once they have been fortunate enough to own and show a dog with correct shoulder lay-back and a corresponding well-angulated stifle, will never again settle for less.

REFERENCE

McDowell Lyon, *The Dog in Action* (New York: Howell Book House, 1950).

Seven eight-week-old "Orion" puppies owned by Sharon and Jim Hurst.

c h a p t e r   10

Selecting a Samoyed Puppy

The selection of the puppy is of paramount interest to both the Samoyed breeder and the buyer.

The prospective buyer should do the following:

1. Read all the material available about the Samoyed.

2. Write to reputable breeders asking for explicit information on their stock and its evaluated potential. The AKC and the Samoyed Club of America are both excellent sources for leads to reputable breeders.

3. Visit as many kennels as possible. Remember not every Samoyed breeder necessarily owns a large kennel; most do not.

4. Attend as many sanctioned matches, all-breed shows and Samoyed Specialties as you can. You will learn something every time.

5. Look at as many Samoyeds of all ages as possible.

6. At every opportunity, talk to Samoyed owners in depth.

If you live in a well-populated area, you may be able to select your own puppy from a litter. This may or may not be fortunate, depending on how well you have studied the breed.

If you live where no Samoyeds are being bred or shown, you will probably have to depend on a sort of mail-order business between you and the breeder. Again, this may or may not be fortunate, depending on how "good" the breeder is. *Beware.* Unfortunately, many breeders wish only to make a sale and may not know much more than you do about how to evaluate puppies.

If you want a pet Samoyed, first study the breed. Selection of a pet is as important as the selection of a show dog. You may end up with a dog that can be both, though you "do not plan to show." We think the ideal purchase

Samway's For Glamour Plus at seven and a half weeks is by Ch. Silvasam Ways to Win ex NZ, Aust. Ch. Samway's Miss Cover Girl. "April" lives with her owners, Mr. and Mrs. Jackson in Australia.

Four seven-week-old Syanaria puppies, bred by Peggy and Lloyd Winger in Australia.

This eight-week-old grew up to be called Bach, Am., Can. Ch. Windsong Classic Composer, SCA Specialty winner and noted sire, owned by Gary and Pat Griffin.

is a pet who may be shown or the show dog who may be your pet. Many Samoyed fill this dual role anyway, and they are quite good at it. Most people would not deliberately buy a Samoyed with an eye to "campaigning" this breed at shows all over the country unless the dog was also their pet.

The initial investment in a puppy or half-grown (six months to two years) Samoyed is the smallest expense, compared with the care, time and monetary and emotional costs you spend on your pet/show dog. It "costs" no more to raise your show dog than to raise your pet. The costs involved in entering the show game may be a tax write-off under "entertainment," as there is no better family sport than the dog game. It intrigues the children and their gray-haired grandparents. That is family togetherness.

A puppy is most frequently chosen at the age of eight weeks; but don't disregard the advantages of selecting a half-grown Samoyed. Starting with the head, notice the placement (not too close) and shape (almond) of the eye as well as its degree of darkness. Check the circumference of the muzzle, especially for depth and breadth on either side of the nose. A snipy muzzle when the pup grows up is most undesirable. Ears may not be standing yet, but check the thickness and strength of cartilage to determine whether the ears will "come up." Also check their placement on the head. Ears should not be too large or be set too low because this will detract from the Samoyed's unique expression.

Grasp the puppy's knobby knees to judge the extent of bone. If the knobs are missing, the puppy may lack bone and size. Knobs are more observable at about three to four months.

Hold the puppy securely around the chest and observe how the legs hang. Do they hang straight in both the front and rear? If they toe out while gaiting, the puppy may walk or stand improperly. Watch it move about. Does the pup walk and trot with some spring and rhythm of gait? Do the feet point straight ahead? Does the rear drive match the front drive, or is one too strong for the other?

A trio of Blair and Judi Elford's seven-week-old Vanderbilt puppies sired by Can. Ch. Moonlighter's Hi Speed Chase ex Can. Ch. Wolf River's High as a Kite.

Tail set is quite obvious, so see that it is not too low or too high. Measure the spring of the rib cavity with your hands. If you feel a barrel shape, don't choose that darling one if it's a winner you're after. If you feel a heart shape, it's probably going to be okay. All coats look fluffy in young puppies. If you can, check the sire and dam, better yet the grandparents, to predict the type and amount of coat the puppy will have.

Study the pictures again—imagine the dog without any coat. Proportion of length of neck and squareness of the whole puppy standing is a matter of how the parts combine to make the whole picture. Legs should not be short. We have included pictures that show puppies at different ages and what they grew to look like as adults. Take careful note of disposition. Never choose the shy one, the wetter or the withdrawn pup.

Children and puppies are one of life's greatest "go-togethers" when children are taught how to treat animals. Here, Blair and Judi Elford's son Casey and ten-week-old "Biff" (Vanderbilt's Balsam Furr) show how well the combination can work when parents do their homework.

Ch. Sansaska's Pandamonium (Ch. Frostriver's Toy Drum ex Hyland's Shalimar of Hilltop) at three months, owned by Derek and Marilyn Gitelson, went from a photogenic puppy to a successful producer and Specialty Brood bitch winner. *Jayne Langdon*

Even the best "puppy picker" can be disappointed, but evaluation of the ancestors and the puppy "on the spot" is the best you can do. In addition to the puppy's inherited potential, tender loving care, nutrition, exercise and some luck combine to give you the "pick of the litter."

And, of course, be sure that your puppy has had his protective inoculations: distemper, hepatitis, leptospirosis, parvovirus and such others as might be essential, depending on your location.

Some items to expect from the breeder to take home with you besides your new puppy include

1. The AKC registration application or certificate signed over to you, the new owner. A common error in terminology is the interchange of the words *papers* and *pedigree*. The AKC registration papers are issued from the litter number previously recorded by the breeder with the AKC. With a bill of sale, it is your evidence of ownership.

2. The pedigree is provided as a courtesy by the breeder to give you a document that lists the sire and dam, the grandparents and great grandparents—usually as far back as six generations. This is your puppy's

Am., Can. Ch. Nordic's Blue Ice Hobby Horse (Am., Can. Ch. Nordic's Magic Hobby Horse ex Ch. Nordic's Kismet O'Cynosura), owned by Gail Matthews, Dr. Shaunna Brummet and Jeffrey A. Skinner. A BISS winner, "Icy" was #2 Samoyed bitch and #8 overall in 1994. *Booth*

family tree! If an older dog or a puppy that is already named by the breeder changes ownership, you will need to send those papers to the AKC with a fee for transfer to your name as the new owner.

3. A reputable breeder will give you a record of the puppy's shots and dates of worming.

4. Also, he or she will provide a menu of the puppy's current diet and even asupply of that food to carry the pup in the new surroundings, thus avoiding potentially upsetting changes of diet and environment.

Provide a small chain collar, a leash and a Vari Kennel #400 crate (or similar). This size will be large and comfortable enough for a full-grown adult Samoyed.

The following chart, showing an average increase in weight of puppies through their first eight weeks, is based on statistics compiled by the authors.

Moonstar's Hollywood Knight HnP (Ch. Hoof 'n Paw's Wilds Rose Knight ex Ch. Hoof 'n Paw's Midnite Maxxine), owned by Daryl Getty and breeder Sakura Moses of the Moonstar Samoyeds. *Lindemaier*

Age	Average Weight
At birth	14–18 ounces
1 week	$1^{1}/_{2}$–2 pounds
2 weeks	2–3 pounds
3 weeks	3–4 pounds
4 weeks	4–5 pounds
5 weeks	5–8 pounds
6 weeks	$7^{3}/_{4}$–$8^{3}/_{4}$ pounds
7 weeks	9–12 pounds
8 weeks	11–14 pounds

The darkening of the black points, such as eye rims, nose and lips, varies greatly with the bloodlines but generally follow this pattern:

1. Rarely a few spotted noses at birth.
2. On the fourth day, a few eye rims will begin darkening.
3. On the fifth day, at least half the litter will have black eye rims and noses will appear smoky.
4. At one week, all eye rims appear dark and all noses are spotted with black. Now dark spots are showing on lips.
5. By the ninth day all eyes appear darker and ready to open but will probably not open until the thirteenth or fourteenth day.

Ch. Oakbrook's Panning for Gold, owned by Jane and Alan Stevenson, was the SCA 1995 Grand Futurity winner. *Rich Bergman*

Winners—Puppies grow up to do exciting things. Frostyacres Hot Salsa, owned by Bob and Karen McFarlane, won the Brood Bitch class at the 1991 SCA National. Her impressive offspring are Ch. Frostyacres Show Me O'Snowdahl, Ch. Frostyacres Golly Ms Molly, Ch. Frostyacres Borne Blonde. Ms Molly became a BIS gal twice. *Kohler*

Am., Int Ch. Samusz's Spectacular Bid, CD, TT/TC, CGC, HIC, TDI, owned, bred and shown by Terry Bednarczyk, was BOW at the 1992 SCA Specialty under breeder-judge Dolly Ward. In 1993 "Clifford," as a BIS and BISS winner, won the first Central Arizona SC Specialty, earning his CD title the same day. In 1993 he ranked in the top ten Samoyeds and was #8 Samoyed in Novice Obedience. Clifford has made a convincing mark in Obedience, Agility and Herding as well as in conformation. *Rich Bergman*

At age eight weeks, the following characteristics should be established enough to determine what they will be in the adult dog:

- Shape and set of eyes, color
- Biscuit shadings
- Size of ears and placement
- Set and carriage of tail
- Disposition (outgoing to timid)
- Bone (large knuckles for proper size)
- Gait

Cheri Hollenback's great-nephew, Jeff Stelzer, with "Kodiak."

Training to show like the big Sams helped this handsome youngster become Ch. Polar Mist Mover N A Shaker for his breeder/owner Lynette Hansen Blue. He was the SCA Best Puppy in 1993 and sired the Best Bred-by and RWD at the 1995 SCA National.

chapter 11

On Raising Puppies

by Susan North

The breeder's responsibility for raising puppies on a sound psychological foundation is just as great as his or her responsibility for raising puppies that are free from parasites and are inoculated against distemper. Emotional health is actually more precarious: a worm infestation can be treated, but a puppy that has not received socialization before the age of three months will be permanently crippled emotionally and can never realize his potential in forming a responsive relationship with a human being.

Based on the research of Drs. Scott and Fuller at Jackson Laboratory (I highly recommend their book, *Genetics and the Social Behavior of the Dog*; Chicago: University of Chicago Press, 1965) and the practical application of their conclusions at Guide Dogs for the Blind, described in Clarence Pfaffenberger's most interesting book, *The New Knowledge of Dog Behavior* (New York: Howell Book House, 1963), it is now possible for breeders to give their puppies the best possible head start by some simple training and experience at a very early age.

When you breed a litter, you are bringing lives into this world and must, I believe, accept total responsibility for them. Your pet-quality puppies have just as much right to your time and attention as the show prospect that you think will do all that winning for you. If you don't have time for the pet puppies, you really don't have time for the litter! Breeders too often assess their litters, picking out the show prospects and then ignoring the pets who are sold as quickly as possible with a minimum investment of time and money. Nothing could be more foolish or detrimental to the breed as a whole. The real public relations job in dogs is done by those pet puppies who in their daily lives have contact with many, many people, leaving a strong impression for better or for worse. By investing a modicum of time, you can build a firm emotional base for each of your puppies and help assure dispositions that will be a credit to your breeding in or out of the show ring.

Moonstar's Unforgettable HNP, from the second breeding of Ch. Hoof 'n Paw's Wild Rose Knight and Ch. Hoof 'n Paw's MidKnight Maxxine, was a standout as early as three weeks old. Owned by Sakura Moses and Mardee Ward-Fanning, "Natalie" offers graphic proof that "style and showmanship, if they appear at all, will be evident at an early age!"

Can. Ch. Polar Mist Break The Bank (Ch. Ice Way's Ice Breaker ex Can., Am. Ch. Polar Mist Saucy Minx), owned by Blair and Judi Elford and bred by Lynette Hansen. "Gucci" finished with a BIS from the classes.

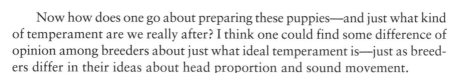

Now how does one go about preparing these puppies—and just what kind of temperament are we really after? I think one could find some difference of opinion among breeders about just what ideal temperament is—just as breeders differ in their ideas about head proportion and sound movement.

I personally feel that the 100 percent extrovert that sells himself so well to puppy buyers and judges alike is not completely desirable. A totally fearless dog, a dog without caution or reserve who is indiscriminately friendly with every passing stranger or a dog without nerves or sensitivity may be the handler's delight, but frankly he is not my idea of an intelligent animal. It is possible, I think, to have a dog that shows himself off proudly, a dog that is polite, manageable and sensible but still has his dignity and maintains his natural cautions about new people and new situations.

If you have a dog that is self-confident and secure and that knows he can trust you, you can ask him to do certain things. You can ask him to stand still in the ring while some stranger goes over him from top to bottom—and this dog will do it because he has learned to trust your judgment, not because he is necessarily delighted with attentions from a total stranger.

Friendship with an intelligent and aware animal must be earned. So I permit some reserve in my dogs; I welcome some selectivity in their friendships—I have great respect for each of my puppies as individuals and feel they are entitled to develop their own unique personalities. The training program that I follow with my puppies is not designed to turn out robots or totally uniform dispositions.

The idea, rather, is to take some time to explore with each puppy his or her own personality, to cultivate his or her particular potential at that so very critical early time when it is possible to do so very much.

Begin to prepare this ideal emotional climate with your bitch in whelp. She is all important—and if she is the right type of bitch (any others should *not* be bred), then she can give you a great deal of assistance with her puppies. She should be loved; she must be happy; she should have extra, tender attentions as well as extra calcium. She must be made to feel very, very special—and when it is time for her to whelp, you *must* be there because this is a joint venture.

You begin with the puppies at birth, not waiting until that almost magical twenty-first day when the puppies first find the world opening up to all their senses. Touch, taste and smell are somewhat operational at birth, although most neonatal behavior is a matter of reflex response. The newborn puppy is certainly concerned, however, with food and warmth, so I supplement all my puppies with a bottle even when this is not indicated by the size of the litter or the condition of the bitch—feeling that by this bottle feeding you begin a regular, pleasurable human contact.

The tactile sensitivity of the tiny puppy is quite developed, and I like to handle my puppies constantly, beginning immediately to turn them gently on their backs. To lie on one's back is to be utterly defenseless, and by making this a routine exercise that is pleasurable from the beginning, you start the bond that will become absolute trust. One can spot at this time the puppies that resist—and these will invariably be the same puppies who will have an initial freeze reaction to a new situation, the puppies with an additional emotional vulnerability that will need a bit more work along the way.

Do not, however, confuse sensitivity with shyness and instability. A sensitive and aware intelligence, a curiosity and a certain wariness are necessary for survival. A dog totally without caution or that is insensitive to its surroundings is not equipped to care for itself in any type of living situation. The path from the crate to the exercise pen three times a day is *not* a living situation, and *no* dog should be so impoverished as to think it is!

Up to the fourth week the routine is just daily contact and handling. Raw meat is first fed from the fingers—and what a treat that is, again supporting the concept in that tiny head about pleasurable human contact. As the babies begin to eat out of a pan, I accustom them to my "puppy call"—I prefer a clucking noise with lots of "puppies, come"—and within a few days this call brings them instantly and eagerly to their feet. And you've gotten still another lesson across.

At four weeks I take the babies one by one and put them in a strange place. I leave them in the position they automatically assume, usually a sit, and move two feet away, coaxing with my puppy call. Up to this time the puppies have known only the place in which they were born, and it is very interesting to see their reactions to totally new surroundings. Some puppies will vocalize immediately and constantly, and in my experience, these are the puppies that will continue to have a great deal to say throughout their lives. Some puppies back up rapidly in an escape reaction. Others, the more dependent types, come directly to the one familiar object—my shoes—and refuse to budge, while others pick themselves up and march off in a show of great independence.

I *never* allow any of the puppies to become fearful. For the first time in their lives, they are consciously faced with a totally new problem, and the experience that I want them to have is *not* fear but rather that of conquering their first anxiety and being reassured by human contact.

Even the simple training that I do with my puppies involves problem-solving behavior on their part; from a number of responses that they could make, they learn to select the one that most quickly brings them praise. At four weeks I start with light puppy collars and brief periods in a crate, always in groups of two or more because isolation at this stage is very frightening. Between six and twelve weeks the real training begins. This training period establishes for the puppy a time when it is removed from the dominance of its mother and the interaction with its brothers and sisters and is taken off to be your very special dog, the center of your attention. I snap a light lead on the collar, under the chin, and the puppies usually trot right along. You never run into the resistance that you encounter if you put off lead training

Ch. Crush's Kalim of Whitecliff, owned by Bud and Beverly Norris and Ann Bark, was BISS at the 1989 SCA National under judge Joe Gregory. *Kim Booth*

Ch. Candenza Khasi O'Southland, owned by Lynn and Richard Bullard and bred by Betty Powell, was BISS at the SCA National in 1990 under breeder-judge Jeanne Nonhof. *Dana Alverson*

until three or four months. You support the puppy with your clucking noise or whatever sound you prefer—and because that sound has always meant "On your feet and good things coming," the puppy will be happy and willing to follow you. Once in a while you run into a pup that is not going to cooperate and sits down solidly, refusing to budge. *Let him sit;* he'll soon be bored with that! And when he moves, go right along with him. Soon enough he'll be going along with you.

Introduce the sit, the stand, the stay—always briefly and without force. When the puppy is headed for me anyway, I introduce the "Come"—again no forcing, no dragging, no corrections, just suggestions about what the puppy was about to do anyway! At this point you get the feeling that this baby is training you.

Now if this sounds like I'm suggesting that you make a lot of spoiled little darlings who get praised for doing exactly what they wanted to do anyway,

Ch. Polar Mist Cover Gyrl of Lazy S, TDI, CGC (Ch. Winterfrost's Gyrfalcon ex Ch. Polar Mist Champagne on Ice), owned by Nancy Hermle and bred by Lynette Hansen Blue and Marge Goodenough. "Shelby" completed her championship from the puppy class with WB and Best Puppy at the 1995 SCA National in Austin, Texas. *Mikron*

Ch. Wolf River's Diamond Dust (Ch. Wolf River's Drumlin ex Ch. Seamist's Raven of Wolf River), owned, bred and shown by Kay Hallberg, was BW to finish at the 1995 SCA National Specialty under Michelle Billings. *Mikron*

let me correct that impression. I do indeed believe in discipline. An undisciplined dog is not a secure dog because he does not know what you want and constantly has to face your displeasure. Moreover, an undisciplined dog is a danger to himself. There are several stern corrections that I impress on these baby minds, and there is no nonsense about it.

One of the most critical of these lessons regards electric cords. I lay an inviting length of cord on the living room rug and bring the puppies in one by one. Invariably they go for the cord, and when they do, *pow*—a loud "No" and a good shaking by the back of the neck. (This shaking by the back of the neck is instant canine communication for "Don't try that again.") I make this lesson a harsh one, knowing it must be effective once and for all. I also allow puppies to almost dash out the door on their own impulse— and quickly and firmly close the door right on them, holding them there for a few struggling seconds—and the babies generally wait for an invitation from then on.

We also give a lesson about cars. The puppies are allowed to wander in front of a car with its motor running, and when the puppy gets to the critical spot, a loud blast on the horn is usually enough to convince him to avoid the front ends of cars with their motors running.

If I had a swimming pool, I would also include a lesson on how to swim and how to find the steps. As it is, I can only warn new owners of the peril that swimming pools represent to dogs and that this important lesson will be their responsibility.

The word *no* is completely eliminated from teaching. If the puppy is wiggling and refusing to stand, just keep repeating the Stand command, telling the puppy what you want, *not* telling him that he's not doing what you want. The no is reserved for specific crimes such as chewing on the couch, puddles on the rug or biting ankles. The gnawing and biting that reaches a peak in the seven- or eight-week-old puppy can be stopped quickly by returning the pressure on the jaw when the puppy takes your hand in his mouth. Immediately the puppy will only be interested in spitting you out, and if you hang on for another few seconds, he'll be so delighted to get you finally out of his mouth that he will not be apt to chew on you again.

Once the puppy is going well on the lead, he is exposed to different kinds of terrain, flapping canvas, lawn mowers and bicycles. He learns to go *over* small obstacles and go around others; he goes under ladders, in and out of doors and up and down stairs. Inside the house he meets the vacuum cleaner, noisy pots and pans, electric trains and assorted household confusions.

By this time he is lying happily and quietly on his back for a tummy rub, and it is a simple matter to teach him to lie on the grooming table with which he is already familiar from his regular brushings. He has had his mouth examined constantly and has been given his calcium pills regularly so that his taking medication never needs to be a problem.

In the sixth week I teach the "Carry" command, and it doesn't matter to me what object the puppy likes to walk around with—a ball, a glove, a stick—anything that delights a particular puppy enough to make him hold his head proudly and trot around on the lead showing off. You are building neck and head carriage control in the best possible way with this exercise and are laying the groundwork for the retrieve, which is the next lesson.

The retrieve is a most important exercise psychologically. It involves the puppy going away from you, off on his own toward an object he likes, then returning with his treasure to share it and please you. Some puppies make an immediate and instinctive retrieve. The puppies that at four weeks reacted to the new surroundings by clutching your shoes will now be the puppies that love you so much they can't bear to leave you long enough to run after the ball. But they will learn, so make the task as simple as possible. Run with the puppies, pick up the ball and give it to them, praising them effusively for carrying it around. By the ninth or tenth week you will see a dramatic grasp of this exercise and should have a whole litter of willing retrievers.

Am., Mex., Int. Ch. Sunburst's Torch of Liberty (Ch. Sansaska's Mark of Evenstar ex Crizta's Tonda of Havipai), owned by Lia and Larry Benson. A BIS and BISS winner.

Ch. Cloudnine's Penny's From H'vn, owned by Jan and Kent Cherne and Mark and Diane Stutzman, was the SCA Grand Futurity winner in 1994. Nancy Golden handled "Penny," a "Gabby" daughter to this coveted win. *Mikron*

d'Keta's Snezhok Blue (Ch. Sanorka's Moonlight Gambler ex Am., Can. Ch. d'Keta's Kira O'Silverthaw), owned by Ivan and Elena Kuzmenko, went Best in Sweepstakes over forty puppies at the SC of Washington State 1995 Specialty under Elizabeth Gonzales. *Snezhok* means snowball in Russian, his Russian family's idea of a perfect name. *Callea*

Like any pack-oriented animal, like man and like monkeys, dogs learn by example and imitation. You probably have older dogs whose behavior is exemplary in one way or another; use these aunts and uncles to help educate the babies. An older, steady dog on a grooming table will quickly teach a youngster about "sitting out," and you reinforce the example by the already familiar "Stay" command. Take the puppy in the car with a calm rider so the puppy learns to sit quietly and wait patiently while you go into the store.

I also accustom the puppies to going around with me off leash. At this age they are still very dependent and will naturally follow. If the first freedom off leash doesn't occur until they are older, you will run into the smart alecs that run off to be chased, and you've allowed an unnecessary bad habit to begin.

At ten weeks I separate the puppies into individual crates for a daily nap, giving each an incredibly succulent round bone, trying to make the isolation as pleasant as possible. By three months all the puppies are happily sleeping alone at night in crates and are naturally housebroken.

I keep mothers with puppies much longer than the general practice because I feel a good mother is such a good influence. Of course by six weeks, mothers do not care to be with their babies *all* the time, nor is it good for the puppies; but I do arrange it so that mothers and puppies spend some time together every day.

As for coat, I sacrifice it—on both mothers and puppies. Coat can always be grown, but puppyhood lasts only a matter of weeks—at the most months, and this should be a time for playing and running and exercising emotionally and mentally as well as physically. The show puppy that is isolated at three months for the sake of coat is cheated out of a very important part of life, and you can't ever make it up to the dog. The business of showing comes soon enough, and I won't have my puppies robbed of their childhood just to make them into hairy child stars.

As the interaction between the puppies themselves increases, the order of dominance in the litter becomes apparent. I try to minimize the dominance. I keep more toys available than there are puppies. Dry food is available at all times, and when the meat meals are served, I feed singley or in amiable groups of two. If fighting occurs, I shake both puppies by the scruff of their necks and insist on immediate friendly contact. I am not interested in argumentative behavior, and I do not want the fighting pattern to begin.

If one puppy is noticeably subordinate to all the others and is becoming timid, I remove the pup before he or she comes to view defeat as inevitable. Often an older, outgoing puppy won't compete with a timid one but will take care of the pup instead and pass on some of the already established confidence. It is most important to avoid any sense of failure. One of the most interesting discoveries made at Jackson Laboratory was that once a puppy has learned to fail, he or she becomes reluctant to try even a simple problem. Success seems to breed success, and what you want to accomplish is to convince the puppy that he or she is self-reliant and can handle the world.

My approach to all this is admittedly unscientific. I have no test cases; I don't withhold socialization from a control puppy to prove a point. These are not dogs in a laboratory, these are my babies—and I want the very best for every one of them. With every new litter I find different things that are helpful, a refinement of technique here and there, a new lesson that comes to mind.

It is not possible, of course, to foresee or simulate most of the new situations that your puppies will encounter in their new homes. But what you can do is give them a framework of reference: They will know that they have encountered new situations in the past and have been able to cope with them. You will have built their self-confidence to a point that they can adjust and take things in their stride. Because you protected them from failure during those sensitive weeks, they will not be imprisoned by doubt and anxiety but instead be eager to tackle new challenges with confidence and assurance.

chapter 12

Special Care for Samoyeds

Start your good care from puppyhood with daily observations. Look at your Sammy's eyes. Open her mouth to look down her throat. Examine her teeth. This is training for both owner and dog.

Periodically take her temperature with a rectal thermometer. Grease the bulb end with petroleum jelly before inserting it gently, and hold about two minutes. Normal is about 101 degrees Farenheit.

Here is "Samoyed-assisted" handicapped therapy demonstrated by the late Frances Roe. Together with Pat Enselm, Eleanor Cragen and Wilna Coulter, Frances founded the San Francisco Samoyed Rescue, through which Samoyeds have found new homes since 1973. Ninety-nine percent of the rescued animals have been spayed or neutered by the Rescue, which is supported by an annual all-breed charity match. There are no paid employees, and all proceeds go directly to aid Samoyeds.

The bond between our dogs and us sometimes shows itself in unusual forms. If Charlene Taren had not used her head (keeping it above water and not panicking), this story might have ended far differently. Charlene and her Samoyed "Dolly" were walking near City Park Lake in Fort Collins, Colorado, when Dolly slipped her leash, mischievously took off after a flock of Canada geese and fell through the frozen surface of the lake. Charlene, horrified, went to her pet's rescue but fell into the 37-degree icy water herself. Dolly, at forty-five pounds, was able to pull herself out, and local firemen rescued Charlene after fifteen harrowing minutes. Ironically, Dolly was out of Lynthea's Miss Conduct by Ch. Ice Way's Ice Breaker. What's in a name? *William Posell, chief photographer,* The Coloradan

If you are with the dog daily, you are more able to observe abnormalities of appetite and energy, dull eyes, a funny cough or indications that could be the forerunner of serious problems requiring a visit to your veterinarian.

With sound nutrition and adherence to cleanliness and definitely your attention, your Samoyed will thrive. Keep the dog clean through grooming, care and careful attention to the cleanliness of her living quarters.

SOME GENERAL HINTS

We are not the first to recommend that you depend on your veterinarian for proper diagnosis and treatment of your Samoyed health needs. But there are a few helpful hints about home care that, with common sense, might save you a trip to your Samoyed's doctor; even your veterinarian will appreciate it. First, take her temperature, and with any rise or fall call your veterinarian. Otherwise, follow these tips.

- For upset stomachs: Feed charcoal biscuits—and keep the milk of magnesia handy.
- For simple diarrhea: Use cooked rice instead of kibble.
- For eye care: Apply boric acid solution and an opthalmic ointment.
- For cuts or wounds: Apply hydrogen peroxide followed by Panolog spray (Pfizer). To stimulate hair growth and prevent scars, apply vitamin E daily.
- For ear trouble: Treat with Furacin powder after cleaning with alcohol on cotton swabs (gently). Others recommend Panolog ointment, which is fine for any skin irritation.
- For nerves from thunderstorms: Administer *a mild tranquilizer from your vet* and some love.
- For an ounce of prevention: On returning home from a show, it is good practice to wipe off feet with Lysol or Clorox solution.
- For fleas: From your vet, For FLEAS program (monthly pills) and Advantage (monthly drops). Also, keep the yard sprayed.
- For a fussy eater: Cooked chicken and rice are a good combination to help put on weight.
- For baths: Stuff ears with cotton, and put a drop of mineral oil in each eye to prevent irritation from soap.
- Provide proper shelter and ventilation. From the Oahu Samoyed Fanciers' Amy Sakata, breeder, comes a warning that is as true anywhere in the world as it is in Hawaii: "Do not leave your Samoyed inside your car for any length of time. (This is especially important in the summer but is a rule that can well apply all year round.) Even though you roll the windows down six inches or so, it is not enough. Try sitting in a car yourself with the windows down six inches, and notice how hot it becomes. Too many dogs have died as a result of prolonged unattended stays inside a hot car."
- Prepare drinking water while traveling: To prevent diarrhea from drinking strange water when you are not able to give your dog his usual drinking water, simply add one teaspoon of lemon juice to a pan of water, or purchase distilled water.
- A suggestion for summer travel: Fill a plastic milk jug half full of water, and freeze it. Cut holes in the sides and place it in a pan. As it melts, the dogs will have cool water.

- Preserve bait liver for traveling: Handlers keep their bait for a long time on long trips. Boil beef liver, cut it up in strips and bury the strips in salt in a container with a lid. Refrigerate. For use, take out what you need and wash off the salt.

DROP EARS

Ears usually come up, but if you are impatient and want to help, wait until after teething, when the dog is about four months. Barbara Hayward suggests the following method, recommended by her veterinarian: Buy Kire-felt at your druggist. A brand name is Dr. Scholl's™. Cut it to the desired shape of the ear. Peel the plastic off the adhesive back and tape it into the inside of the ear. Then tape the entire ear around with adhesive tape and leave it on for five to ten days. It's important that the ear be held absolutely erect. Repeat the "bandaging" if necessary until the muscle is strengthened so the pup will hold it up by herself.

If the drop ear is prevalent in the entire litter or in several litters of the same stock, one had better look to a change of bloodlines to eliminate this serious fault, for although the Standard does not say a drop ear is a disqualification, it does say the ears shall be erect. Ears should be erect before the dog is shown. It is not a universal problem, but breeders must be aware and eliminate the fault by avoiding stock throwing soft or drop ears.

CRATES

A crate is a prerequisite to safety. In the car, your dog will be comfortable, and windows may be opened wider for she won't be jumping out to follow you. A crate is indispensable for the Samoyed bathed, groomed and ready for the show. It is her place, and she likes it. It helps keep her clean. If her crate is left on the floor with the door ajar, you will find your dog will walk in to lie down for a catnap. We prefer wire crates to solid metal ones.

DEWORMING

Recommended ages for having stools checked by the vet are four weeks, eight weeks, twelve weeks, six months and one year. A twice-yearly check for the adult Samoyed is adequate under normal conditions. Either have your veterinarian worm your dog, or use only the medication and the dosage he prescribes for the type of worms.

IMMUNIZATION

Veterinarians vary on this subject, but suffice it to say your Samoyed must have shots for distemper, hepatitis, leptospirosis, parainfluenza, rabies and, since 1978, parvovirus, at the proper times your vet advises. If such problems as Lyme disease, kennel cough and heart worm are endemic in your area or if you will be showing where dogs exposed to such conditions are present, speak to your veterinarian about protection for your Sammy.

SAMOYED NUTRITION

Eileen Whitlock-Kelble, professor in Home Economics at the University of Tulsa, writes of the early native diet of northern breeds:

> In both the Arctic and the Antarctic, especially where the terrain is variable, unknown, or treacherous, the dog-drawn sledge still provides a valuable means of transport. Although these lands support a varied wild life, it is often necessary to travel long distances with no resources other than those that can be depoted or carried.
>
> Fresh meat in the form of white whale, walrus, seal, or bear have always formed the basis of the northern dog's diet. Perry stressed that the dog's food was meat and meat alone. Croft suggested six pounds of fresh meat, with extra blubber if necessary, as the ideal daily diet during cold conditions. Lindsay emphasized the importance of feeding fresh meat before starting on long sledge journeys.
>
> Dried fish, especially cod or halibut, has been widely used. Mawson estimated that two pounds of dried fish represented six pounds of fresh fish (which he felt was an adequate daily ration). Thomas recommended two or three pounds of dried fish with two pound cubes of blubber, though he felt that a full diet of seal meat is preferable.
>
> Pemmican as a sledging ration is prepared both locally and commercially. It contains 66 percent protein and 33 percent fat and its preparation consists of lean beef, dried and pounded, mixed with fat. Although it is considered one of the best rations available, all authorities agree that it should be supplemented with fresh meat as frequently as possible. A diet of 100 percent pemmican usually results in persistent diarrhea.
>
> On the trail the usual practice is to live off the land except for depoted rations. Fresh meat under those conditions can become a precarious luxury. Many explorers who have relied on game found themselves and their dogs in very short supply. Nansen, who used Samoyeds, was reduced to feeding dog to dog until he was forced to consume the remaining dogs himself.
>
> Some authorities, however, maintain that no matter what he is fed, the husky dog appears to thrive. Some of the early explorers gave little thought to the problems of feeding their sledge animals which resulted directly in the failure of several of the expeditions. Scott, for example, who also used Samoyeds, admittedly was not an expert on the subject of dog handling. Food for the dogs on his Discovery expedition was a ration of $1\frac{1}{2}$ pounds of deteriorating stock fish daily. For the later Terra Nova expedition the ration was $\frac{2}{3}$-pound biscuit. When the dogs became "quarrelsome and fickle" he finally realized that they were underfed. After much soul searching, he decided to feed dog to dog. According to his reports, the "dogs never

pulled their own weight and left each member of the party with an uncon-
querable aversion to the employment of the dogs in this ruthless fashion."

When Amundsen compared the unhappy experience of Scott's expeditions to his own, he determined that it was the master who had not under-
stood the dogs. On his own expedition he provided seal meat and dried
fish in addition to the pemmican, and all this was supplemented with fresh
dog meat. Twenty-one of the fifty-two dogs returned from his expedition
"bursting with health and putting on flesh."

Subsequent expeditions included those of Mawson, Shackleton, and
Byrd, the British Grahamland Expedition, the Norwegian, British, and
Swedish Expedition, and the Commonwealth Transantarctic Expedition,
all stressed the importance of supplanting the diet with fresh seal meat and
blubber whenever possible.

More detailed works on the nutritional requirements of sledge dogs
began with the building of a permanent population of Antarctic sledge dogs
in 1945. It is now estimated that adult working sledge dogs require between
3,000 and 8,000 kilocalories per day, dependent largely on the extent of
their activity. Seal meat, although it is composed almost entirely of protein
(33%) and fat (66%), still appears to be the ideal diet for sledge dogs.

However, in the United States today the typical Samoyed is not a sledge
animal. His role is that of family caretaker, companion and member of the
family. Therefore, his needs are not identical to those of the working sledge
animal.

Jeff Bennett, founder of Nature's Recipe and an avid Samoyed enthusiast, writes about the current philosophy of commercial pet food.

Just as humans have come to understand, "you are what you eat," the past
20 years of veterinary science has extended this truism to the pet world—
"your pet is what you feed it." The more we examine the pathology of pet
disorders and deficiencies, the more we are discovering that the basic elements of nutrition—vitamins, minerals, enzymes and hormones—are woe-
fully inadequate in the average pet diet. Not only have most commercial
foods missed the mark, pet breeders are recklessly reproducing genetic defects that make balanced nutrition and good digestion even more difficult
to obtain.

My introduction to the subject of pet nutrition came in a desperate
attempt to rescue my own pet from suffering. My Samoyed, Tasha, became
sick with hot spots, itching and intestinal problems when I consulted with
Alfred J. Plechner, D.V.M., who suggested that food allergies could be the
root cause of this illness. Together we concocted a vegetarian diet that
brought about immediate improvement! The more I delved into the atro-
cious state of the pet food industry, the more I realized that someone needed
to intervene. Following the first vegetarian diet, I developed the first lamb
and rice commercial pet food and Nature's Recipe went into business. Since
those early days we have discovered critical information about the deficiencies in most pet nutrition and the importance of diet in pet health.

CREATIVE LABELING

There are no federal guidelines regulating quality in pet foods and labeling that describes "beef," "fish" or "chicken." A closer look at most food labels reveals the key word "by-products" that describes everything from horns, hoofs, bone, intestines, waste, beaks and feet. Animal by-products that are rejected by human use because of disease or spoilage are readily shipped to some pet food manufacturers. As a result, the protein and mineral content that you would expect from a "beef" dinner is nonexistent and may, in fact, be detrimental to the health of your pet. Pesticides, additives, color-enhancers, sugar and other harmful or artificial ingredients also load the deck against providing basic nutrition for your animal.

SYMPTOMS OF NUTRITION PROBLEMS

The most widely recognized symptoms of nutrition problems are skin diseases and bowel irregularities. Pets that scratch incessantly, bite, lick and develop open sores and enlarged nodules are commonly diagnosed with some type of allergy. In addition, vomiting, diarrhea and odorous stools are commonly treated by a change of diet. Lack of vitality, increased appetite accompanied by weight loss and dull eyes and coat also indicate that there is a problem with the nutrition and digestion. But there are other symptoms that may be more surprising. Sudden behavior changes, seizures, bronchitis and kidney diseases may also have their roots in inadequate nutrition. Proper diet has been known to eliminate these diseases entirely.

WHAT'S MISSING?

Although many pet foods include vitamin additives in their mixes, these can lose their potency as a result of heat, moisture, light and oxidation. This loss of vitamins only increases when large amounts of food are bought at once and stored over a number of weeks. To counter this loss, food should be purchased in smaller quantities and kept in a closed container.

Along with vitamins, minerals—particularly zinc and calcium, phosphorus, iron, copper, potassium, magnesium and iodine—are critical to combat disease and should be in sufficient amounts in pet foods as a supplement to nutrition. Chelated multimineral compounds are available in powder or tablet form that can be added to food or water. Natural B-complex vitamins contain yeast, so supplements should be synthetic. Vitamin C enhances the function of the adrenal glands and, therefore, the overall digestive and absorption capacity of your pet.

It doesn't take much to keep your pet healthy, active, allergy-free and content. Common sense tells us that the vitamins and minerals missing in most pet diets need to be added daily to keep a good nutritional balance.

EVERY DOG NEEDS A "SPECIAL" DIET

These days, there are still some very active dogs being bred for sledding, herding, hunting, police work and guide dogs. These dogs, serving their original functions, are bred to be strong, vital, healthy, muscular and active. Genetic weaknesses are bred out of these dogs, and they remain capable of processing foods and of normal digestion.

However, most dogs in the world have been recklessly bred for looks, according to whatever fad or fashion is current. Many of these mutations are accompanied by limited digestion, impaired adrenal glands, respiratory problems, immune deficiencies and general ill health. So pervasive is this lack of concern for animal health that many experts agree that more than 70 percent of all breeds are simply incapable of normal digestion and combating allergies. Some project the eventual destruction altogether of cats and dogs through incurable genetic defects that are allowed to perpetuate unheeded.

A good hypoallergenic diet offers balanced nutrition, avoiding troublesome foods such as milk, yeast, corn and chemical additives. More and more specialized pet foods are being developed that can conveniently provide this type of diet for your pet on a daily basis. Ask your veterinarian or pet store owner for advice. The addition of chicken, brown rice, lamb and cottage cheese needs to be accompanied by careful observation to detect allergic responses. Snacks, chew sticks, biscuits or treats are out! Table scraps of green vegetables, fish oil and breads can be added to the regular diet, but not meat products. Meals should be given two or three times daily to aid digestion, rather than in one large portion. Mineral supplements if needed should be given daily.

Nutrition in animals is finally being recognized as a key factor in many, many ailments. But most pet food manufacturers or food purchasers have not yet made the commitment to the cost and care needed to provide a healthful diet for our animals. Your pet is what you feed it. With just a little bit of care, the love, attention and loyalty that you enjoy from your pet will continue for many years in the life of your family.

SKIN ALLERGIES IN THE SAMOYED

by Judy Bennett, AKC Judge

Unlike people, dogs exhibit most allergies through skin eruptions, even inhalant allergies. One of the first signs visible to the owner may be a wet spot in the coat where the Sam has been chewing and scratching to relieve the itch. Upon closer inspection, a red, irritated patch of skin may be noted. If left unattended, this irritated area will begin to "weep," and infection will begin to cover the surface of the skin. Combined with the dog's continuous attention to it, the area will soon be a flaming mass of oozing infected skin that will spread at an alarming rate.

Like many conditions, an ounce of prevention is worth a pound of cure. Once an animal is suspected of being allergic, he should be sensitivity tested by a qualified veterinary dermatologist to determine just what allergens are involved. A course of antigen injections may be prescribed and custom mixed to the individual. By far the most common allergen and the most stubborn to treat is an allergy to fleas. Compared with the expense of treating hot spots, not to mention the associated discomfort, allergy treatment is a bargain. It should be stressed that it may not always be a cure; however, it should lessen the severity of the dog's reaction.

If the problem is caught early, topical treatment can also be very effective. One type of product used very successfully in my kennel is a spray calamine lotion that contains an antihistamine with eucalyptus and menthol. The cooling effect of this spray helps relieve the burning, and the calamine controls the itching. Better yet, the dog also does not care for the chalky taste and gives the area a chance to dry and heal. It should be noted that veterinarians recommend cleansing of the area before any treatment. I have found this contrary to my ultimate goal, that of drying the area so that healing may begin. In this situation, coat need not be removed because the spray goes through the hair to coat the skin. If such an aerosol product cannot be found, a similar liquid product may be sprayed through any disposable pump spray bottle.

Breeders should be aware that although specific allergies are not inherited traits, the tendency to contract allergies is hereditary. Animals that are constantly exhibiting the described symptoms and are found to have sensitive skin should not be candidates for a breeding program. It is through the efforts of breeders like ourselves that the healthy future of the breed will be insured.

SUMMER CARE

Regarding special care of Samoyeds during the hot summer months, Dr. William Ivens, veterinarian and Samoyed breeder of the past, wrote:

> In my opinion it is not essential to change the diet to any extent; a good, well balanced diet should do in hot as well as cold weather. However, the addition of any of the sour milk products to the daily schedule is sometimes wise. Sour milk, buttermilk, or cottage cheese will do; the most effective is acidophilus milk, which has merely a greater concentration of the active organisms than the former have. Tomato juice, about one half cup per day, is also good. Merely mix it in with other foods. In the average dog, a diet of straight meat is sometimes conducive to moist eczema in hot weather. One might also use a variety of basic meats, such as lamb, or fish, in place of the more widely used beef or horse meat. With the occurrence of eczema, any dietary change may bring improvement.

WATER

Provide fresh water regularly. Ice cubes or blocks of ice can be added to a dog's drinking water.

If neonate puppies are in distress, fill plastic gallon milk jugs with iced cold water, and place them in the whelping box or puppy pen. Watch the puppies snuggle up to get cool.

Keep the coats groomed regularly.

Never clip a Samoyed! Clipping exposes the sensitive skin to the elements and can do great harm. Your Samoyed's coat acts as insulation against both hot and cold climates.

For skin treatments, home style: Use Bactine for moist eczema, cuts or most abrasions. Use vitamin E oil to help on "hot spots" or after hair is removed for surgical reasons and you are helping it to grow back.

HIP DYSPLASIA

The mysteries of hip dysplasia (HD) will not be solved in the foreseeable future, but it is hoped that DNA will be the key that unravels this problem. John Cargill and Susan Thorpe-Vargas, B.A., M.S., have written extensively about HD, and in a nutshell we may say here that their conclusions in part (up to February 1997) are as follows: "Genetics is the foremost causative factor of canine hip dysplasia. Without the genes necessary to transmit this degenerative disease, there is no disease."

Affected dogs may vary from practically normal to severely dysplastic.

Millions of words have been written on this subject with which we have dealt and watched for fifty years, but none are more succinct than the foregoing statement.

WHY IS HIP DYSPLASIA STILL WITH US?

After fifty frustrating years of reading yearly the results of research, estimating the billions spent by the dog Fancy on required X rays and the awareness of human egos "to protect their bloodlines," we submit here the answer to our question, "Why is hip dysplasia still with us?" as written by Susan Thorpe–Vargas, B.A., M.S.

> Unfortunately, hip dysplasia is a genetic disease that does not follow a simple Mendalian inheritance pattern. It is also a disease where nutritional and environmental factors can play a large part in whether or not the genes are "expressed," i.e., become physically apparent.
>
> But before we can understand the level of complexity involved, we should look at three genetic terms that seem to explain the inheritance and expression of hip dysplasia; these are *polygenic, incomplete penetrance,* and

epistasis. If at this point your eyes are starting to glaze over, forge ahead as these concepts are not all that difficult to comprehend. Polygenic simply means that more than one gene is involved. That is, the trait is passed on through several genes, each contributing its part as it is finally expressed physically in the animal. That is why you can breed a dysplasia-free dog to another and still produce dysplasia in their progeny. To add to the difficulty, some genes are not expressed completely. This is referred to as incomplete penetrance. Genes that display this phenomenon carry more information than is actually apparent in the animal, but can be fully expressed after they have been passed along to a new generation. To make matters worse these "semi" genes can be associated with a desirable trait that is being selectively bred for. Epistasis is the final term that might apply to the expression of hip dysplasia. This is a process where the presence of one gene can prevent another gene from being expressed. If these genes are close together on the chromosome they have a high probability of being co-inherited—they are "linked." However, somewhere down the line they might be physically separated and the hidden gene would finally be expressed.

It is also highly unlikely that a genetic test will be available for hip dysplasia in the near future. Besides its complex mode of inheritance, researchers must first link a physical trait to a particular set of genetic markers. One orthopedic surgeon, Dr. Barclay Slocum, D.V.M., feels that the angle of the dorsal acetabular rim is the determining link to hip dysplasia. Another researcher, Dr. Gail Smith of PennHip, feels that "passive hip laxity" is a useful predictor of the disease. Whether or not either of these clinicians is correct is beyond the scope of this paper. What is known and what is necessary, is breeder compliance. Not only must the animals being used as breeding stock be radiographed and eliminated if they show any signs of the disease, but all their siblings, their parents and any get, must be radiographed and the results tabulated and made available in some type of open registry. Without this extensive database any genetic research would be seriously impaired. The take home message to breeders should be, if you have the choice of choosing a dog where the radiographic status of the dog's parents, get and siblings are good or fair, choose that dog over one who has been assigned an excellent evaluation, but no other data on the rest of the pedigree is available.

In closing, in this imperfect world fraud and duplicity are always with us. Any genetic research that did not require some form of positive identification of the dogs included in the study would be null and void. Through our AKC delegate, we should urge the American Kennel Club to require positive and tamper-proof identification of all dogs as a prerequisite to registration.

MICROCHIPS

The newest means for pet owners to identify and prove ownership of specific animals is with a computerized tracking device, or microchip. The procedure is equal to a shot given by your veterinarian. An encoded microchip, the size of a grain of rice, is placed under the skin between the shoulder blades by means of an injection. The number of the "chip" is registered with whichever organization the dog is enrolled, such as AVID or Home Again, to maintain a registry for animal identification. The future use of microchip identification has endless possibilities, such as X rays, eye checks and AKC event records.

HEALTH MISCELLANY

In matters of health care, we believe one must depend mostly on one's veterinarian. Of course, there is much to be shared among all breeders. Paula Exline writes about health in the SCA Bulletin. Although hip dysplasia has been addressed earlier in this chapter, one fact that just about covers fifty years of X-raying and research is that HD is known to have both genetic and environmental causes. Environmental factors that affect HD are overexercise and overeating. The probable incidence of hip dysplasia is greatly reduced by breeding only from OFA-certified clear animals.

With progressive retinal atrophy (PRA) the same cautions exist as with HD in having a dog's eyes examined by a veterinarian certified by the Canine Eye Registry Foundation (CERF). The object is to avoid breeding to or from affected stock. To do so can result in blind offspring. Testing for PRA must be done yearly; there is no lifetime diagnosis.

So before buying, besides a general good health requirement, one should see the evidence of both clear hips and eyes.

It takes an objective and philosophical viewpoint to be a breeder, and we must take particular care to keep the hip dysplasia problem in proper perspective. One cannot breed for clear hips alone and throw away breed type, conformation and temperament. Nor are normal hip joints the only aspect of soundness to consider in a breeding program. There are certainly dogs whose hips are certified Excellent by OFA who are otherwise poor breed specimens and/or have temperament problems.

CARE OF THE ELDERLY DOG

by Rosemary Williamson, New Zealand

[*Authors' note:* While on a judging visit to New Zealand, we stopped for tea at George and Rosemary Williamson's Patterdale Farm in Auckland, and visited their spotless quarantine kennel. It was a highlight because we met their grand Border Terrier "Winston"—eighteen years and four months old. He was the "Head Man" of all terriers and quarantine boarders at the kennel—where both old and young experience such tender loving care. We asked Rosemary for these helpful observations because, as she says, "Whatever the breed, old age will form the same pattern."]

"Winston" was named for Winston Churchill. He looked so much like him, and he was as determined and as bold a character.

Winston entered the show ring at the age of ten years, and was greatly admired by many overseas judges. Even at sixteen years, his body was wonderfully preserved and firm, and he came home with many Best Veteran sashes.

I mention all this because old age can start as young as ten years old. The term *deterioration* is probably better. Fortunately, this is a slow process, and one becomes quite used to the situation and adjusted to having to really care for an old dog in the house. If you have really loved the dog in its young days, and it has done well for you and has given you years of pleasure, you will find that you will do all you can for it in its last few years, months or days. I must emphasize that patience and understanding is very necessary, especially with a dog like Winston [*Authors' note:* or any Sam] at his age.

Each month the VET suggests we review the situation to see if there has been any further deterioration. The main reason for this is that we must never have a dog that suffers from pain or is just thoroughly miserable.

Dogs in old age must be fed twice a day, a small meal in the morning and a small meal in the evening, instead of one large main meal. They love their food like all old folks!

Diet plays a large part in keeping the old dog healthy. Raw grated cabbage, raw grated carrot, raw meat with fat, bone broth gravy and kibble with wheat germ, and regular vitamin pills is a good meal for a dog of twelve weeks up to even eighteen years old.

Regular worming and grooming and flea spraying is essential. Regular visits into the garden for the aged dog are essential. It is rather like having a baby, as you have to think for them. In this way carpets will not be soiled.

The aged dog sleeps for many hours. Make sure the room is draught proof. If the windows are open, close the door and always have a wool rug to cover the dog with [*Authors' note:* Sams have their wool coats], while sleeping, for warmth. Immediately after they wake up, put them outside. A coat for the winter is well worth having to keep the back warm, as the aged dog feels the cold.

Quite often, the aged dog will go deaf or partially blind. As long as he can see enough to get around and hear enough to be called, he will be happy.

Naturally he will be much slower with everything; this is where patience on your part will be practiced!

All of a sudden he is more dependent on you and wants to follow you everywhere. This is where you have to learn to be conscious of a dog behind you when you turn around, otherwise you can do yourself harm by falling flat on your nose over him! Or you go into a bedroom and he has followed you into the room, and he will come out only when he is ready, after he has sniffed at this or that or the other thing! Unlike a young dog who does this and in seconds has beaten you out of the room, the old dog takes his time to do exactly the same thing! So you have to have patience and to realize he is doing just the same thing as the younger dog, but taking so much longer.

Touch plays a great part in old age. With Winston being a small dog, he is lifted down the steps into the garden but he manages to come up by himself. If you catch at them quickly or suddenly it will startle them if they are partially deaf. It is better to touch them gently first and then lift them up and gently place them on the ground, because generally their legs are not as strong and it puts them off balance.

It is amazing when a bitch is in heat how an aged dog can lose many years off his life and play the part of a virile young dog! Particularly with Winston. At his great age, he is first in the queue for the girls! So he thinks. Instead of walking every which way, his legs suddenly acquire extra strength and he has been known to run, at great speed, if he thinks that the bitch in heat is in the offing for him. I am sure that it is these sparks of interest that keep him going.

I have found that all the other dogs have a great respect for him. I know for sure that he is top dog and that all the others realize he is to be regarded as a very respected veteran and a very popular one, too.

Physiotherapy is a good thing for the aged dog with weak back legs. It is very helpful to have heat and massage. I am very fortunate to have a physiotherapist who will use his wonderful hands on dogs, cats and even cows. A slipped disc can be manipulated back by a physiotherapist, so therefore the dog doesn't have to suffer unnecessary pain.

Enjoy your veterans. They deserve it.

SAMOYED RESCUE OF SOUTHERN CALIFORNIA, INC.

In 1993 a small group of Samoyed owners and the members of the Samoyed Club of Orange County joined forces to establish Samoyed Rescue of Southern California, Inc. (SRSC). During its first three years of existence, SRSC was instrumental in placing more than 400 abandoned or unwanted Samoyeds. At the time of its conception, the members of SRSC had no idea how many animals would be helped or how much an organized rescue network was needed in southern California.

Running SRSC as a business has contributed to its overwhelming success. The organization is advertised in local pet stores, veterinary offices, *Mutt Matcher's* magazine and on local radio. SRSC also holds fund-raising events to enrich its financial resources. But most important, each new adoptive family is asked for a donation. SRSC's membership believes that emotional and financial stability are necessary to properly care for any animal. Every animal that physically comes into the rescue network is totally inoculated, groomed and altered.

The primary goals of SRSC are to find good homes for these rescue animals and to be sure that they do not return to rescue in the future. These goals are achieved by extensively interviewing each person who calls wanting to adopt a Samoyed. The callers are educated on what it takes to properly care for a Samoyed and are sometimes even guided away from adopting because they do not fit SRSC's idea of a good home.

SRSC has much to be proud of and urges other groups interested in rescue to get started. The good people of SRSC had no idea of the need until they began their admirable work.

Send donations or inquires to: Samoyed Rescue of Southern California, Inc., 916 Muirfield Road, Los Angeles, CA 90019; or call: (714) 966-6180.

AKC CANINE HEALTH FOUNDATION

R. J. Hritzo, M.D., is president of the AKC Canine Health Foundation and a past board member and presently is treasurer of the AKC. We proudly add that he and his family have bred Samoyeds for many years under the prefix North Starr. There are stories about both his dogs and his children in these pages. The Hritzo family has contributed mightily to the good of the breed.

Dr. Hritzo writes:

The Foundation was established about a year ago when the AKC Board of Directors placed one million dollars into an endowment to establish this not-for-profit entity. Our legal staff were able to successfully get us a 501 C3 status so that all contributions are tax deductible.

The mission of the Foundation is to develop significant resources for basic and applied health programs with emphasis on canine genetics to improve the quality of life for dogs and their owners.

chapter 13

The Well-Groomed Samoyed

by Mardee Ward-Fanning

With this breed, something that is lacking counts as a plus. Samoyeds have no doggy odor, it's true, but they must be groomed for health and beauty regularly. They do not need a bath to be clean. Dry baths are possible, using only brushing and a mixture of cornstarch and baby powder or commercial powdered preparations that are rubbed through the coat and brushed or blown out again. Some owners bathe their pet Samoyeds only several times a year for holidays or other special occasions. Show dogs are bathed more frequently to condition the coat and skin. A dog being shown regularly must be "kept up"; it could take months to correct a neglected or damaged coat.

The equipment needed is as follows: grooming table and grooming arm; a pin brush with long pins set in rubber; a shorter-bristled, "soft" slicker brush; a nylon brush; coarse- and fine-tooth metal combs; pet nail clippers or an electric nail grinder; scissors and thinning shears; and a "chalk" box. A high-powered blower is an invaluable tool; however, it is expensive ($150–$350) and may not be practical for the single-pet owner.

A daily grooming is ideal but isn't often achievable; therefore, once or twice a week is a more realistic goal. This may not mean you do a complete all-over brushing. It would be better to do one area thoroughly (brushing followed by combing from the skin out) than to "skim" the complete surface.

BRUSHING AND COMBING

The purpose of frequent brushing and combing is to maintain cleanliness and to remove the loose and dead hair; to prevent matting and knotting of the silkier portions of the hair, especially behind the ears; and to tone the skin and stimulate new hair growth.

The method: First, decide where you will begin. Divide the dog's coat into sections—the forequarters, the hindquarters, the sides, back, neck, stomach, head and tail. I find it much easier to have the dog trained to lie on

206

its side while being groomed. Then as you work and take periodic breaks, you can remember where you left off. I prefer to begin in the shorter hair on the legs or stomach and work into the longer hair. So with your left hand, part the coat as you move up the leg, briskly brushing down small sections from the skin out. Left-handed groomers do the reverse. The slicker brush and fine comb work best on the shorter hairs. With the longer hairs, the pin brush and coarse comb work better. Be sure to concentrate on the problem areas. The elbows and hocks need special attention as do the stomach and inside the legs. When *carefully* brushing around the sensitive parts of the male and female, use a soft pin brush or nylon hair brush. You may need an assistant when working in this area.

Particular attention should be paid to the heavy ruff under the neck. It helps to train your dog to hang his head over the table, enabling you to get at the thick hair from his chin down the neck and front. Be especially gentle on the tail. Most Samoyeds do not like this part and will try to turn to keep you from getting at it. The grooming arm comes in handy here, the noose around the neck keeps the dog from turning around. Grooming arms are made in several styles and are available from any dog show supply company. Using the pin brush or nylon brush, start at the base of the tail and brush out away from the tailbone. Establish a part and work up the tail, when you reach the end, go back to the base and start again. Repeat until you have gone around the tail completely. Never brush or comb the tail hairs straight down the tail bone as the hairs do not grow that way, and your dog will protest.

Finally, after he has been brushed and combed by sections, use the pin brush vigorously, brushing the body coat toward the head, the coat on the stomach down and the pants and tail hair out. Remember that brushing is always followed by combing. The high-powered blower/dryer is very effective here. Loose hair, dirt, stickers, fleas and anything not belonging on the dog is blown away. Be careful not to direct air flow in your dog's eyes, ears or any other sensitive region. Samoyed exhibitors who are most proficient in show ring preparation recommend a complete grooming before a bath.

THE BATH

Equipment needed: A shampoo for white or silver hair (often blue), Ivory soap or any other biodegradable soap; mineral oil to put in the eyes; cotton to plug the ears; towels and wash cloth; the forced-air or high-power warm air dryer (either for people or dogs); a bathtub or large stall shower; and a spray attachment with a sturdy fastener for the faucet. On a hot day you may bathe your Samoyed on a table in the yard, using the garden hose. Water can be cool to warm—not too cold or too hot!

There are two kinds of baths: a quick bath and a full, wet bath.

The quick bath is used when you want a clean-looking dog and his outer coat is dirty, but his skin is fairly clean. This method is often used on a show dog between full baths. The quick bath uses very little water, so, drying time is greatly reduced. First, in a small pan or bucket, mix warm water and a little soap. Dip a wash cloth in the soapy water, wring it out and rub it all over the dog, getting just the outer portion of the coat damp. This picks up the surface dirt without saturating the undercoat. Repeat until the dog has been completely wiped down.

Then, using a pan of clean warm water, rinse the dog in the same fashion as washing. Towel dry so the dog is just damp, not dripping wet. Work a mixture of cornstarch or baby powder and grooming powder (2:1, respectively) into the coat, with a small brush, i.e., a "veggie" brush, concentrating on the legs, stomach, ears, face and rear. Be careful not to get too much powder in the body coat because it is more difficult to get out of the longer hair. Continue rubbing with the mixture until the coat feels dry, then let the dog shake (outdoors for this part). Now you are ready to start brushing out the powder. A strong blow dryer is excellent at this stage because it helps separate the coat and blows the powder out while you wield the pin brush. When you are finished, your dog will sparkle and smell fresh; a quick bath takes one-third the time of a full bath.

The full wet bath is called for when you want that total and complete shine from the skin out. Prepare your dog for the bath after he has been brushed and combed before bath day. Put the cotton in his ears and a drop of mineral oil in each eye (to prevent soap irritation). Use a rubber mat to be sure the dog will have good footing in the tub or shower, and have the water lukewarm before starting.

Washing: Prepare the shampoo in a container with warm water. Most shampoo mixes 8:1. Completely wet your dog and begin soaping. Begin with the head and back and work your way down to the toes and the tail. Scrub, scrub, scrub, with your fingers, especially on the elbows, hocks, hips, feet and ears. Squeeze the coat in your hands in a kneading fashion rather than circular movements because this can tangle the coat. One sudsing should be sufficient unless he is really dirty. The secret to a clean Samoyed is in the rinsing.

Rinsing: Begin at the head and be careful not to get water down the ears. Squeeze the coat as the warm water runs over the hair as you work down the back to the shoulders, neck, chest, sides and legs. Always rinse the stomach, legs and tail last because the soapy water goes there last. No creme rinse is necessary because the Samoyed coat has a harsh texture of its own that allows it to stand up rather than lie down.

Drying: Use your hands to squeeze out excess water and slick down the coat on the body and legs. Take your Samoyed to where he can shake himself well. Next, towel dry with several towels, rubbing briskly back and forth. The dog will normally shake often; if he doesn't, blow in his face and say "Shake." Place him on the grooming table for blow drying, using cool to warm air. It takes from thirty-six to forty-eight hours to dry an adult Samoyed in full coat without a dryer, so if you must dry him naturally provide some

Ch. Polar Mist Cover Gyrl of Lazy S (Ch. Winterfrost's Gyrfalcon ex Ch. Polar Mist Champagne on Ice), owned by Nancy Hermle. At six months, this promising puppy has learned good manners on the grooming table.

Ch. Moonstar Big Sky of Hoof 'n Paw, bred by B. J. and Sakura Moses and owned by the Zimmermans, is much in need of an emergency cleanup.

Am., Can. Ch. Hyalite's Classical Jazz, TD, owned by Ron and Jolene Stolba, patiently endures a grooming session. *Doug Loneman*

clean, draft-free quarters, preferably in the house. The crate is indispensable at this time.

Conditioning a damaged coat: A coat can become damaged by sunlight, urine stains and neglect. Should you be called on to correct such damage, bathe the dog as described earlier, following the bath and rinse, a coat or hair conditioner (diluted with warm water) can be worked into the coat; let stand fifteen to twenty minutes, then rinse.

When thoroughly dry, comb as you did before the bath. It will be easier now. Before he steps out for his showing, whether for a family reunion or a dog show, polish with the following: Comb with the fine-tooth comb on the thickly furred head, face, ears and chin. Brush with pin or nylon brush up and out on the ruff, chest, shoulders and leg feathering; brush down and out on the belly fringes, thighs, pants and inside legs. Fluff the tail by holding the tip, and brush out from the base and working up to tips of the hairs.

TRIMMING

Samoyed fanciers in Europe, the UK, Australia and New Zealand all abhor trimming. They favor the profuse featherings around the hocks and feet. By contrast, many Americans and Canadians feel it is necessary to "clean up"

Here are the gratifying results of a big grooming job! Jim and Sharon Hurst with eight Orion champions from nine months to nine years.

the long hairs on the feet and hocks. If you choose to trim, aim as much as possible for a natural, uncut look.

Hocks and feet: Do not overtrim, just neaten these. Clip hair from the bottom of the foot even with the pads. *Do not* remove hair between the toes.

Whiskers: These are natural and useful to our beautifully headed breed. Whiskers are living sensors. In the past, several breeders chose to cut them for showing, however the SCA voted to keep the Standard unreformatted in 1993 and added only "Whiskers are not to be removed."

Dental care: Dogs over one year of age need monthly care on their teeth and gums. Natural bones large enough to be safely chewed help reduce tartar buildup and stimulate the gums. If your dog does not chew or "work a bone," you will need to brush and possibly scale your pet's teeth. Do not use human toothpaste on your dog's teeth. Before tackling dental care, seek your veterinarian's advice and training.

Cutting nails: Use nail clippers specifically made for dogs or use an electric grinder. Long nails will cause arched toes to become splayed and will spoil otherwise good feet. Long, unattended nails can also catch on objects and may be pulled out, causing great discomfort to your dog.

The body coat should *never* be scissored or clipped unless for medical reasons. The Samoyed is a natural breed, and his coat affords natural protection for his benefit. As mentioned earlier, the coat not only protects from extreme cold but also aids in insulating from the heat. A shaved Samoyed is susceptible to sunburn.

If you take your Samoyed to a grooming shop, make sure the staff know how a Sammy should be groomed and caution them not to overtrim if at all!

After all these instructions, we might add that nothing takes the place of consistency in care, good health and daily brushing. Excuse us while we groom a Samoyed.

Show Handling and Related Issues

by Mardee Ward-Fanning

Y ou can start training your Samoyed for the show ring as early as eight weeks old. However, since he must be at least three months old before participating in AKC-licensed sanctioned matches and at least six months before he can go to a point show, you'll have plenty of time to prepare yourself and your dog for that first outing. Use this time wisely to check out some of the following:

- Write the American Kennel Club, 5588 Centerview Drive, Raleigh, NC 27606-3390, for the free booklet *Rules Applying to Registration and Dog Shows.* Read it thoroughly at least once and then study particular sections. Keep it for reference. Amendments appear in the AKC's official magazine, *AKC Gazette.*
- Study the Samoyed Standard. This will enable you to better evaluate your dog. Learn not only about your dog's virtues, but also the faults, according to the Standard. Each dog does have faults. Knowing these will be of value to you in the show ring so you may avoid calling attention to them by poor handling.
- Attend sanctioned matches and dog shows as a spectator. Observe the handlers and ask questions. We repeat, ask questions!
- Inquire about local handling classes and attend them. These classes will give your dog exposure to noise, other dogs, strange surroundings and people. At the same time, you will learn the basic principles of show handling.
- Enter your dog in match shows for practice. Classes are the same as in point shows, but there is no "Winners class" as there is in a point show. Point shows are so named because judges award points to the Winners Dog and Winners Bitch that count toward their championships.

CONDITIONING

Both you and your Samoyed need to be in condition for the show ring. You two are a team and must practice together to present a picture of harmony. Since you must run when the dog gaits or trots, practice running with your dog so it looks smooth and natural. A well-timed cadence during gaiting is of utmost importance and requires both handler and dog to be in fit condition.

To achieve this team effort, hours, days and months are spent running or gaiting with your dog. Since dog shows are held in a variety of places and on different surfaces, you should practice accordingly—on the sidewalk, in the street, at the park, in a parking lot and inside a building if at all possible.

Conditioning implies that a dog exhibit good muscle tone, healthy coat and skin, and healthy teeth and gums—in essence, be a true picture of vitality.

TRAINING FOR THE SHOW RING

The initial training of a puppy is the same whether he is to be a family pet or an illustrious show dog. Five to ten minutes, two or three times a day is an ideal time allotment for working a young puppy on the leash. Train with a choke chain collar so the puppy doesn't learn to pull you around. Short jerks accompanied by a vocal command to "heel" will encourage good response. Work the dog on your left side with the leash in your left hand. You can teach young puppies to "bait," or alert for treats, in the kitchen or family room. Tell the puppy to "stand" and "wait" or "watch." Bait treats can be anything the puppy will alert to, such as kibble, cheese or crackers—whatever works.

The older dog—six months or more—has a longer attention span and should be worked fifteen to thirty minutes daily. Training for the show ring consists of posing with all four legs square ("show stance"); examination (being touched all over); and gaiting or trotting. Practice with the proper show equipment—a thin choke chain/nylon collar and a thin show lead about four feet long. Be firm, but make it *fun!* Coordinate your hand and voice commands, and, most of all, be consistent. The sequence you use to stack your dog in a show stance should be the same every time; for example, command the dog to "stand," then set the left front leg, then the right front leg, then the left rear and finally the right rear leg. With the leash in your left hand, bait or alert your dog with your right hand.

Once your dog or puppy is standing, have another person "examine" him so he gets used to having strangers' hands go over him, especially having his teeth looked at to see how the bite comes together. Males will need to allow their testicles to be touched because they'll be checked in the show ring by the judge. In developing a vocabulary with your dog, use clear, one-syllable words whenever possible. For example, "Stand," "Stay," "Wait," "Trot," "Good Boy," "Good Girl," "Bait" or "Cookie." Remember, when communicating with your dog, your tone of voice is of great importance. At the end of a training period, be sure to praise your dog both physically and verbally.

A FEW DOS AND DON'TS FOR DOG SHOWS

Here are some dos for showing your dog:

1. Before Samoyed judging, observe the judging of the breeds ahead of you by the judge you will be showing under. Note his or her ring procedure, and you will know what is expected of you and your dog when it is your dog's turn to be judged.
2. Before entering the ring, be sure your armband obtained from the ring steward is on your left arm so the number is clearly visible to the judge.
3. As you enter the ring, have your dog on your left side under control and looking alert. The first impression the judge gets of your exhibit is most important.
4. Remember, you and your dog are working as a unit to bring out the best in the dog. *All* attention is to be on the dog, not on you, the handler. You will detract from your dog if you bend over him or allow too long a lead to drape over him. Women should have long hair tied some way; *don't* let your hair hang in the dog's face when setting him up. By standing too closely to his side or allowing him to lean on you, you do not present him well. Hold the bait unobtrusively.
5. When gaiting—moving your dog at a trot—keep him at an arm's length on a loose lead.
6. Be sure to follow the judge's instructions. If you did not understand them or did not hear the judge, ask the judge to repeat or clarify.
7. Last but not least, if you must correct your dog's behavior in the ring, do so inconspicuously. Be firm and positive when correcting behavior. Keep one eye on your dog and one eye on the judge. The finer points of handling come with experience. However, it's possible that you may never quite get the hang of it—in which case you should hire a professional handler or seek the assistance of a capable exhibitor.

Dog showing is an active sport. If you are handling, dress appropriately. Here are some dos:

1. Men should wear a suit or slacks with a sports jacket.
2. Women may wear slacks; however, a nice A-line skirt with pockets (for bait) and blouse are dressier. Be careful not to wear too full a skirt or dress because it can interfere with the dog gaiting.
3. Be sure to wear comfortable running shoes. Heels, sandals or clogs are dangerous for showing dogs.
4. The colors of your clothes should complement your Sammy, so stay away from white or light-colored apparel and shoes.
5. The dog show goes on regardless of the weather. Plan your showing wardrobe to include rain jackets, coats and all-weather footgear. You must still be able to move and run.

Here are some don'ts for dressing for the ring:

1. Avoid wearing dangling jewelry that may distract your dog or get caught in his coat or lead.
2. Avoid having money or "jingly things" in your pockets because they are distracting to other exhibitors, to the judge and to your own dog.
3. Avoid wearing sunglasses in the ring. Eye contact with the judge and your dog will be lost. Both are very important.
4. Don't bait your dog just before the "bite" is examined. The judge doesn't want to see the dog chewing and swallowing before checking its teeth.

JUNIOR SHOWMANSHIP

Many children go along for the ride while their parents engage in the sport of dogs, whether it be conformation showing, obedience or sledding. Many children will have a natural desire to participate when they are ready.

Junior showmanship is divided into Novice and Open divisions, and these are further divided by age: 10–13 year olds and 13–17 year old. The beginning age group, Novice, is for handlers who have not yet won three firsts. The Open division is for kids who have won three first places finishes in either Novice division.

Among other things, Junior Showmanship is supposed to teach good sportsmanship. If manifested in a good light by the parents, it will be learned in that light by their children. If the reverse is true, it is unfortunate. This is the pattern of learning, though it may have its exceptions. Therefore, the adults in the dog game must teach the younger set the right way—to win and lose gracefully. This can be a challenge.

Junior handlers also learn the proper care of their dogs and how to communicate with them. Instead of getting into trouble because they have nothing to do, nothing to be superior to, nothing to love, they may be found grooming and training their "show dog."

Steve and Kathleen Kersten and their daughter, Erin Rose, are staunch supporters of dog activities as a family sport. Erin qualified for the prestigious Junior Showmanship finals at the Westminster show—8 Juniors chosen out of 118 entrants when Erin was only eight years old!

Erin was the SCA top Junior Handler for 1991 and 1992, as well as for the Greater Milwaukee Samoyed Club showing Ch. Samtara Striking Reflection, who is a multi BISS and multiple Group winner. In April 1996, Striker went BIS at the Packerland KC show under judge Donna Buxton and is co-owned by his co-breeder, Edward Trojan. Striker is by Ch. Risuko's Mister Moonlight and Mithril Cheers Samtara On. Several kids have begun their show handling experience in the conformation ring because they were not "old enough" to participate in Juniors.

Michelle Heth began at age ten and won well in 1989 with Ch. T-Snow Star's Orion, CD, and again in 1994, practically all grown up with Am., Can.

Mardee handled Ch. Tasha of Sacha's Knight to a good win at the Houston Specialty, and BB at Westminster, 1982. During the 1990s she started a bitch of her breeding, Ch. Hoof 'n Paw's A Rose Is a Rose, on the campaign trail, later sending her out with a young handler, Robert Chaffin, to beat the "records."

Ch. Samtara Striking Reflection with Junior Handler Erin Rose Kersten at Westminster 1992 with judge Eleanor Rotman. *John Ashbey*

Ch. Risuko's Debutante O'Trilogy. Mother Julie Beatty, writes, "Juniors are so special. They learn to care for and love these beautiful dogs at an early age. In addition, they also become aware of the importance of the Samoyed Standard and will become its guardians into the twenty-first century."

Don and Heidi Neiman's daughter Heidi, aka Scooter, was five years old when they acquired their first show dog, Toga. Scooter started practicing then for the show ring. She was eight when she was allowed to choose her own puppy to show. She trained and showed him exclusively, and he grew up to become Ch. Saratoga's Speed of Sound. Scooter was nine when she showed "Mach" at the 1991 SCA National to his Best in Sweepstakes. She finished him ten months later, scoring multiple BBs and Group placements. Five days after Mach finished, the team won BOS at the 1992 Washington State Specialty. In 1995, she and Mach won BOS at the Denver Samoyed Association Specialty.

Scooter handled Ch. Saratoga's Lost Aviatrix at the 1994 SCA National to RWB and Best Bred-by Exhibitor. She finished "Amelia" the following weekend. Subsequently, she started Amelia in Obedience, and together they earned Scooter's first CD title at the 1995 SCA National. Scooter has pointed most of the Neimans' dogs en route to their championships.

In the Junior ring, Scooter was SCA Best Junior Handler 1992–95. She was SCA Top Junior Handler in 1994 and 1995, qualified and showed at Westminster at age thirteen and qualified again the next year. Scooter has been Best Junior Handler at many All Breeds and Specialty shows. She ran her first dog sled race at thirteen and hopes to do it more often. Several of the Saratoga dogs actively work in harness both in sled racing and weight pulling. Scooter has her own bitch from Amelia by Kitt with which to start her own line.

One of the more prestigious competitions for Juniors is held at the Westminster KC show in New York City each February. The rules for entry are based on previous wins, and competition is very keen. Kathy Hritzo (Heimann), at age sixteen, won the Junior Showmanship competition handling her Samoyed at the 100th Anniversary Westminster in 1976.

PROFESSIONAL HANDLING ORGANIZATIONS

Not everyone can handle dogs in the show ring or has the time or inclination to do so. We are all individuals of different leanings and abilities. For these reasons, there will always be a need for the services of professional handlers.

The Professional Handlers Association (PHA) maintains high ethical standards, and its members are what they are titled—"professional" in this field. This is equally true of a more recently established group, the Dog Handlers' Guild (DHG). However, not all professional handlers are members of the PHA or the DHG. Names and addresses of handlers may be obtained from dog show superintendents, show catalogs or specialty magazines.

In selecting a handler, you will want to talk to each prospective candidate you are considering, to "size them up" for yourself, to see them handle dogs and to visit their kennels or facilities. Fine reputable handlers will welcome such an investigation as the sign of a caring client.

Michelle Heth was winning in Junior Showmanship by age ten. She was Best Junior at the Denver Samoyed Association's 1994 Specialty, handling Am., Can. Risuko's Debutante O'Trilogy. *Wayne Cott*

Junior Handler Heidi Nieman, shown here with Ch. Saratoga's Speed of Sound, has shown several dogs to their championships and also competed in the finals at Junior Showmanship finals at the Westminster KC. *Joe Rinehart*

CLUB MATCHES AND SHOWS

Some people are joiners and some are not. What you do depends on what kind of person you are fundamentally. Even if you've never liked social clubs or church groups particularly, you might try a dog club. All human relationships found in any group may be found there. You must deal with people if you are in a club. It is no place for a hermit! There are few hermits if any who go to dog shows or join clubs even if they do own a dog.

Would you believe that dog clubs are not just for dogs? Well, it is true, and those who say "This is a dog club, let's keep the people out" are unrealistic. Constitutions, which are the rules of the game, are read and debated by people, not their dogs, even though the club is formed because of the underlying common interest.

All activities relating to purebred dogs are supervised by the AKC. Know the AKC rules and regulations and always abide by them. A copy of the rules may be obtained by writing to the secretary of the AKC.

Parent Specialty clubs are formed for the breed on the national level. Parent clubs, such as SCA, work with the AKC for the protection of the breed, guarding the Standard and the activities influencing the breed. On the local scene, regional Specialty clubs are formed by area fanciers for holding shows, training classes, providing education, referrals, rescue and conducting social programs.

All-breed clubs are formed to hold AKC-sanctioned events, which include one or two dog shows a year, usually on the same weekend each year. At these shows breeders bring out the best examples of their breeding. It is also an opportunity for novice dog owners to attend their first show unless their Specialty club has been actively holding fun matches and sanctioned matches for their breed alone. Also, the all-breed club people put forth their best efforts to "put on a really big show." Many delightful social activities may be combined with competitive sport.

Samoyed people are beginning to become a part of this broader aspect of the dog game. Usually "Sammy people" stay within their own group, hardly casting an eye to any splendors of another breed not of their choice. While this may be considered meritorious and faithful, it is also a type of tunnel vision we are glad to see waning as more Sammy people begin to join all-breed clubs and look at breeds other than Samoyeds at a show or other dog event. We need not fear that Samoyed people will choose any other breed because of "exposure."

Do not hesitate to locate your local clubs formed for education about dogs in general and your breed in particular. There is as much of a hobby to be had in clubs and their work as there is in enjoying your Samoyed.

Matches are of several formats. Fun matches are completely informal and provide practice opportunities for the more formal sanctioned matches representing the next level.

Sanctioned matches are held to give puppies and young dogs training in a ring situation; owner-handlers practice in managing their dogs; club members practice in the various facets of putting on a dog show; and aspiring judges and stewards an opportunity to put their book learning into the living laboratory of actually judging dogs and dealing with people, learning everything from handling to good sportsmanship. Seek out such advertised events and attend them, first as a spectator and then as a participant.

The sport of dogs is composed of numerous parts, and no one will ever learn them all to perfection. But just think—you can try for a lifetime. Shows give you a destination for travel and something to do when you get there. Condition your Samoyed, love your Samoyed, train and show your Samoyed and take him or her to shows, and it can make a whole life for you and your family. The most wonderful people in the world have become our friends through "dog game" activities, which are all-inclusive.

LOCAL SPECIALTY CLUBS

Local Specialty clubs devoted to the care and improvement of the Samoyed are established in many parts of the United States and Canada. These clubs often provide family and dog-oriented activities such as pack hikes, fun matches and picnics with games in which the dogs participate. Activities include obstacle courses, Samoyed softball, weight pulls, fun sledding, training classes, meetings, agility courses and the presentation of annual awards.

This is the place to find other Samoyed Fans and meet the local breeders. Members of local Specialty clubs generally must adhere to a code of ethics. If a local breeder doesn't belong to the local club, it might be prudent to discuss why he or she doesn't participate before purchasing a puppy from them. Membership in these clubs usually requires that you own a Samoyed and have two members in good standing sponsor your application for membership.

Many local Samoyed clubs put on one Specialty show each year; some really active clubs put on two. A Specialty is a dog show devoted to only one breed, in this case the Samoyed. Specialty shows draw entries of the show dogs in the area and many from the surrounding states and sometimes even from Canada and Mexico. Exhibitors sometimes fly in with their dogs for the weekend, thus affording local Samoyed admirers and breeders the opportunity to see and evaluate celebrated dogs from distant areas.

Many clubs have newsletters that contain helpful articles on local events, training, feeding, breed history and general animal husbandry. The newsletters alone are worth the annual dues.

Club officers can change annually. To locate the regional Samoyed Specialty club in your area, write the AKC at 5580 Centerview Drive, Raleigh, NC 27606-3390 or visit its Web site, www.akc.org, for the name and phone number of the current club secretary.

Jim and Sharon Hurst successfully traveled the British Columbia 1995 circuit with four of their Orion champions in their luxurious motor home. This sumptuous transport is a long way from the old "Woody" station wagon that got the authors to the shows more than forty years ago!

This was the old "Woody" we used in 1954 for driving to shows and doing the circuits—precursor to the fancy rigs and motor homes so prevalent today. Shown here (from left), our "fifties" girl Vicki, Chatter (Ch. Starchak, CD) and his son Chande at an Oregon rest stop.

chapter 15

To Be or Not to Be Obedient

by Don and Dell Wells

Until as recently as twenty years ago, a Samoyed was considered virtually untrainable, as far as top competition was concerned. Even today, many of the best longtime trainers consider our beautiful "big white dogs" obedience casualties.

This became a challenge to me because I found the Samoyed to be above average in intelligence and affection and to possess a loyalty to their masters that would be difficult to surpass.

In my opinion, some training techniques used in the past were abusive and overly harsh, physically forcing an action without first letting the dog understand what was being asked of him. I then vowed never to use excessive force on either my own or my clients' dogs.

As trainer-handlers, we should first know and understand exactly what we want our dogs to do and then should devise a way to show them step-by-step what we want. A Samoyed, being an intelligent and willful animal, will not usually be forced into any action he does not understand. While he won't break down in spirit, he will actively resist. On the other hand, if he is shown true affection and understanding, and given praise for correct action, he will cooperate fully.

If you aim to obedience train a Samoyed, you must first earn (and I mean *earn*) his respect through daily—even hourly—contact, genuine care and affection, fairness in corrections and consistency in your actions and expectations.

Understanding and praise are what dog obedience is based on. Your dog wants with all his heart to please you. So show him how, then *praise, praise, praise* and watch him sparkle!

Obedience groundwork begins long before you physically take your Samoyed out to the training grounds or training class. Wise trainers will first spend considerable time observing their dogs to learn about their likes and

Ch. Snowline's Joli Shashan, CDX (Ch. Joli White Knight ex Ch. Lady Sasha of Kazan, CD), owned by Mary and Thomas Mayfield and bred by Nancy and Laurel Alexander, was the first winner (1969) of the annual trophy for the outstanding Obedience Samoyed, which was donated by the Juliet T. Goodrich Trust Fund and awarded by the SCA.

Am., Can. Ch. Nordika's Polar Barron, CD (Ch. Snowacres Nordika ex Ch. Princess Tovara of Snowacres), owned by Barbara and Dan Cole, was an achiever in conformation and Obedience. He was a Specialty and multiple Group winner.

dislikes and how they respond to differing tones of voice or to hand corrections. No one should know your dog better than you do. Observe how he reacts to various situations. Do you know which way he turns when retrieving a ball? Is he left-handed or right-handed? Does he panic easily or is he supercool? What makes him happy or sad? Only when you've studied your dog are you ready to start serious obedience training.

Many Samoyed owners as well as owners of other breeds are firm believers in basic obedience for all dogs, whether they are kept as pets or entered in competition. Only the degree of accuracy demanded needs to differ.

OTCH Barron's White Lightnin', owned by Barbara and Dan Cole, was the first Obedience Trial Champion Samoyed in AKC history and Top SCA Obedience Samoyed for 1979, 1980 and 1983 and a multiple High in Trial winner.

Look for an obedience class taught by a competent and humane trainer. Then you, as owner-master, will understand how to teach, and your dog, in turn, will learn to understand and please you.

You must be an assertive leader, and your dog must be a willing "pack member" for your efforts to result in a really good obedience Samoyed. This leadership must never be relinquished—even for a moment. I stress again that you do not need to use physical force to maintain this leadership. Once the status is established, your Samoyed will recognize it more than you will.

This leadership status should be established as early as possible and maintained throughout your dog's life. You will find this rewarding even if you only want to teach your dog good manners, so that you are both at ease in nearly every situation, and you can be proud of him.

It is quite easy to establish the leader-follower status with a puppy. However, as your dog reaches adolescence, he will challenge your "right" to be leader, as he would in the wild. This challenge can be quite mild in a shy or easygoing Samoyed and not become a problem. But with a dominant Samoyed, a physical challenge for authority may be made, and you—as master or pack leader—must not back away, or your authority will be lost.

Some other beginning suggestions: Before starting a training session, try to allow your dog a few minutes to relieve himself and to become accustomed to the training field. And always try to end your training sessions with a "Well done!" exercise so you both may stop on a happy note.

Early in practice training, it is good to choose a method to release your dog from strict attention to your commands, such as a hand clap or any signal that will let him know he may relax his concentration on you, a relaxation that lets him be a dog instead of your "shining star" until he is called to heel position again. In the beginning, your dog's attention span will be quite short, say ten to fifteen minutes, but as he learns, the sessions can be greatly extended. They should always be spaced with short rests so you and your dog can collect your collective wits.

Ch. Hoof 'n Paw's Drifting Snow, CDX, TT came to the Addamo household in 1986, at age three and a half to be obedience trained. "Smurf" earned her CD in three trials, finishing at the 1986 National Specialty with High Scoring Champion of Record. In 1987, Smurf with Gini, earned her CDX. She also passed the TT test and had the testers chuckling at her look of "you can't be serious" when the supposed threat came out of the bushes wildly waving a stick and wearing a white sheet with a dunce cap–like hat on. (Anyone who knows Smurf would never question her ability or, more important, her willingness to protect.) She was just too smart to be fooled. We had to say goodbye to Smurf in 1996 at fourteen and a half years. *Fox & Cook*

At the start of the first lesson, teach your dog to sit by your side in the heel position. One method to get him to sit is to pull up on the leash and push down on the hips, repeating the word "Sit." Once he sits, praise him lavishly. If he gets up during this praise period, correct immediately in a stern voice. Place him in a sit position, and praise him in a friendly, pleasant voice.

Pets and companion dogs are continually confused, especially when young and in the process of forming lifelong habits. Since a dog is basically a creature of habit, make every effort to avoid this confusion and maintain consistency. A prime example of unintentional confusion for your dog might be allowing him to get up on your furniture one time and then chastising him for doing it the next time. You must be the controlling party. Your dog may not be able to distinguish between the two different sets of circumstances. When he is a puppy, a dog can be molded into whatever you want him to be by using simple obedience techniques and an understanding of canine behavior. Decide what your dog will or will not be allowed to do, and then enforce the established rules.

Another example of training and consistency is "Area or Room Training." By correcting a dog whenever he enters a room that he is not allowed into and then praising lavishly when he leaves on your command, he will soon learn that room is "off-limits" and will not enter. After all, no one—not even your dog—will invite an unpleasant experience. An angry tone of voice, as contrasted with a happy one, will surely show your dog the difference between right and wrong.

This same procedure—using a friendly or stern voice to convey "right" or "wrong," respectively, to your dog—will work for any situation. It is not necessary to use a loud, screaming voice because a dog's hearing is better than ours and they respond to the tone of voice, not the volume.

Sometimes a dog will learn one exercise very quickly and be very slow learning another, depending on his particular experience. Each exercise, no matter how simple, will have to be repeated many times. So always be patient, correct as necessary and praise—even after you have physically moved him to the desired position. Remember, each small success deserves a large praise, which then leads to another success. Two or three correct actions *with praise,* and most dogs will never forget that exercise. You then reinforce his actions by repetition and praise, attaining greater accuracy as you continue day-to-day training.

I have trained Samoyeds (and other breeds) that have sorely tried my patience. It seems that at just about the time you feel your Samoyed is getting "solid" on a given exercise, he will find some new way to foul things up! That's our Sammys.

Let me cite an experience with one of our own Samoyeds, a fine performer who carried an average of 198.5 out of a possible 200. While training for the Novice recall (in which the dog comes and sits in front of the handler on

Shown here is a group of Elfenbein champions by Ch. Risuko's Joi of Snowonder ex Ch. Elfenbein Miss Sassafras, owned and bred by Jim and Elfie Shea. They are (from left) Limited Edition, CGC TDI; Lotus Esprit; Crown Victoria; Lincoln Continental and White Barracuda.

command), she decided it would be great fun to run right past me. This girl did recalls at an absolute dead run and often was going so fast that to even begin to stop in front of me (let alone, sit) was impossible. We worked on the exercise for some time, with my jumping out of the way, getting run into, or being by-passed completely. (However, I would never take her enthusiasm away from her because I want my dogs to be enthusiastic and fast.) Finally, we got the exercise done correctly, and she realized what I wanted from her. From then on, we had perfect recalls nearly every time. The point I want to stress here—never dampen your Samoyed's enthusiasm. Instead, make every effort to capitalize on it!

It is well to note here and now that a Samoyed may try your patience to the point where you lose your temper. This happens to experienced as well as to inexperienced trainers. When it happens to you—and it will—if you are really trying to work up a good dog-handler relationship, recognize the situation for what it is and stop, sit down, get your dog next to you and "talk" to him. If you have established a good understanding with your dog, he will "talk back"— and tell you by his actions that he is really sorry. When you both have relaxed and made friends again, resume your training. Losing your temper can be a problem. Recognize this, and don't hesitate to take the time to think it out or else find a different way to show your dog what you want him to do.

In closing, keep the following key points in mind:

1. *Praise, praise, praise!*
2. Take your Samoyed to a competent, humane trainer.
3. Visit the training classes without your Samoyed first.
4. Do not let anyone give harsh corrections to your Samoyed.
5. Never, ever attempt to train your Samoyed by withholding real affection or human contact.

Ch. Crizta's Cover Girl, CDX, TT, by Ch. Ice Way's Flash Cube ex Snoko's Nishi of Silveracres, was bred by Teena Deatherage-Schulz and is owned by Gini Addamo and Dany Canino. "Lace" was shown in conformation and obedience competition at the same time. She earned her CD in three trials when she was ten months old. The following year she earned her CDX. Lace went High in Trial (HIT) twice, the first time at the 1987 Los Angeles Specialty and the second time at the 1988 Northern California Samoyed Fanciers Specialty. For three years Lace consistently placed in the top five (she placed first twice under System I) of the *Samoyed Quarterly* Obedience ratings. At one show Lace was just landing on the return over the high jump with the dumbbell in her mouth when she was jumped (and literally flattened) by a wild, runaway Newfoundland. Being a true "working Sammy," Lace got up and finished the exercise. Lace celebrated her thirteenth birthday on March 25, 1997, and she's still going strong.

chapter 16

The Samoyed Club of America's Working Samoyed Program

by Pam Landers

The Samoyed served his original breeders in northern Siberia as an all-around helper, working as sled dog, reindeer drover, seal and polar bear hunter and companion. That versatility is an important asset, distinguishing the Samoyed from dogs bred for more specialized purposes. To honor and preserve that versatility, the Samoyed Club of America decreed that the organization should recognize and encourage members who worked with their Samoyeds as well as those who showed Samoyeds in conformation.

In 1991, in response to growing member interest, the SCA approved requirements that would allow a Samoyed owned by an SCA member to be awarded a series of working certificates in a variety of categories reflecting the dogs' capabilities. The awards are intended to encourage Samoyed owners to work with their dogs and to breed for those working dog abilities.

The Working Samoyed (WS) certificate can be earned by accumulating 1,000 points in any single category of work or a combination of categories. These categories are sledding (both racing and excursion), weight pulling, packing, skijoring, herding instinct and therapy. Agility, herding (except for herding instinct) and obedience were not included as categories because the AKC has programs open to Samoyeds that reward those abilities and for which the dogs can receive titles. The Working certificates were not intended to duplicate other awards.

A WS dog that earns 500 or more points is awarded a Working Samoyed Excellent (WSX) degree. An owner whose dog does special work, such as search and rescue, guide dog, hearing ear or service dog for the disabled, can submit a special application for points to the SCA's Working Samoyed Degree Committee on an individual basis. The Master Working Samoyed

The OWS Top Sled Team Award for 1994 was won by Kriskella Sams of Geoff and Brenda Abbott, breader-owner-drivers. The dogs shown are right lead dog, Kriskella Turns to Gold, WS; left lead dog, Kriskella top Billing; right wheel, Kriskella Fleks of Gold, WS; left wheel, Ch. Frostipaws Champagne Bud.

degree (WSXM) can be awarded to a Samoyed that has accumulated 5,000 points in a minimum of 4 categories (including special application) with a minimum of 200 points in each of the 4 categories.

Several Special Application requests have been awarded. The committee has honored two requests for complete degrees. These were for work as a service dog for a wheelchair-bound woman and as a public relations dog for the Dog Museum (ironically, the only dog allowed in the museum). Points have been awarded for dogs that took part in skijor racing, for members of two sled teams involved in the making of a movie for television, for a dog that was a costar in the making of a videotape on backpacking and dog packing and for a dog that was used to help clear trails of timber and rocks.

In the years that the Working Program has been in effect, dogs and owners have achieved 82 degrees; 42 WS, 37 WSX and 3 at the highest level of achievement, the Master Working Samoyed (WSXM). Interest in the degrees and in working with Samoyeds has been growing exponentially of late. At the 1994 SCA National, five working events were offered in addition to the conformation classes. This was a first for this number of events. More than 280 dogs competed in those Working events, in addition to the more than 480 entries in the conformation classes. Some Samoyed owners attended the Specialty specifically for the Working events.

The requirements for the Working certificates are not easy. The program is intended to be a true test of the dog's abilities and the degrees a source of pride for their owners. Even so, there should be some form of work in the variety of categories in which any Samoyed owner can participate, wherever that owner lives.

Ch. Tundra Winds Glacier Lily, WSX, a proven producer and lead bitch on Ken and Donna Dannen's all-Samoyed sled team. *Ken Dannen*

The Samoyed Club of America's board of governors agreed that the reasons for encouraging people to work with their dogs are many. They include the satisfaction the human member of the team receives from the growth and strengthening of the bond between team members, the health benefits for both human and dog, the knowledge to be gained about the true physical capabilities and endurance of the dog under stress and what can be learned about the mental abilities the dogs have inherited. One of the greatest benefits is the enrichment of a relationship that occurs when one learns to know one's partner's moods, behavior and reactions over long periods together and by sharing a wealth of experiences.

WORKING SAMOYED TITLE HOLDERS

We honor some early WS titlists:

Ch. Barron's Night Kap, CD (Barbara and Dan Cole)—Herding, therapy

Tundra Wind's Arctic Gentian (Kent and Donna Dannen)—Race sledding, packing, excursion sledding, herding

Tundra Wind's Polar Knight (Kent and Donna Dannen)—Race sledding, excursion sledding

Tundra Wind's Midknight Sun (Kent and Donna Dannen)—Race sledding, excursion sledding

Risuko's Teddy B. Cupps, CD (Vickie and James Cupps)—Therapy

Cotton Candy Kodi (Carol Kinne)—Packing

Am., Mex. Ch. Arno's White Arctic El Tigre, CD, TT, HIC, WD (Barbara and Jerry Mathe)—Therapy, herding instinct, weight pull

Ch. Sno-E's White Hot Mogul (Julie West)—Race sledding

Summit's Frisco Kanduit (Connie Rudd)—Race sledding, excursion sledding

Summit's Miss Muffit (Connie Rudd)—Race sledding, excursion sledding

Ch. Krystall's Misty Moonbeam, CD (Tom and Nancy Lisec)—Packing, herding instinct, therapy

Kriskella's Fleks of Gold (Brenda and Geoff Abbott)—Sled racing

Kriskella Turns to Gold (Brenda and Geoff Abbot)—Sled racing

WORKING SAMOYED EXCELLENT TITLE HOLDERS

To gain a WSX title, dog and handler must earn 1,500 points in any one or a combination of the recognized categories as listed previously.

Kamelot's Danish Shadow Von H'NP (Christie Smith)—Therapy, herding instinct

Thor, The Thunder Boy (Jeff and Babette Bott)—Weight pull

Woodland Spirit (Debbie and Darla Haynes and Nancy Johnson)—Weight pull, herding instinct

Misty's Long Journey Home (Babette S. Bott)—Weight pull

Nina's Silver Aleksi (Jim Becklund)—Weight pull

Ch. Saratoga's Sonic Boom (Lori McAllister)—Race sledding, excursion sledding, skijoring

Arctic Mist's Chinookwind, CD (Lori McAllister)—Race sledding, excursion sledding

Chinookwind's Trek T'Saratoga, CGC, DOB (Jeffrey L. Bott and Lori McAlister)—Weight pull

Ch. Sno-Kidin's Back in Time, CD (Carole Selleck)—Weight pull, therapy, herding instinct

Ch. Tundra Wind's Mtn. Thunder, CD (Connie Rudd)—Race sledding, excursion sledding, herding instinct

Summit's Keystone (Connie Rudd)—Race sledding, excursion sledding, herding instinct

December's Kodiak Chief, UD (Pam and Scott Barbe)—Therapy

Tarahill's Treasure Me Always (Joan Froling)—Special application: Service

Sno-Kidin's Spirit Walker O'Kesar, CGC (Deborah J. Spillar)—Weight pull

MASTER WORKING SAMOYED TITLES

To earn a WXSM title, dog and handler must earn at least 5,000 points in at least four of the recognized categories named previously, and at least 200 points must have been earned in each category.

Sheba the Thunder Girl (Jeffrey L. Bott)—Race sledding, excursion sledding, skijoring, weight pull

Ch. Wind River Talkeetna Karibou, CD (Kent and Donna Dannen)—Race sledding, excursion sledding, skijoring, packing, therapy

Ch. Tundra Wind's Glacier Lily (Kent and Donna Dannen)—Race sledding, excursion sledding, skijoring, packing

SLEDDING

by The Wards

Activities outside the show ring bring many pleasant moments in the company of like-minded colleagues, and the insight you can gain about your dogs makes what you do even more rewarding. The second Samoyed who owned us was named Ch. Starchak, CD. We called him Chatter because of the way he talked in the morning. While Chatter was successful in the show ring, it really was in other fields that we enjoyed him most. As a lead dog, he acquired the knack of judging the length of his team. Before making a turn, he seemed to look back and gauge the width needed to swing the team around a corner or tree. We actually believe that he did not like the sudden jerk and abrupt halt that came with wrapping the sled against a tree. Whatever his reason, it was amazing to watch him. This talent did not come to him at an early age but at about five years. Considering that he was in harness and competition at age twelve as a lead dog, there were many years of learning for us. Chatter's uncanny ability is, however, not unusual for lead dogs.

Some people maintain that dogs do not think but are creatures of habit. Consider this incident. During a mail run from Ashton, Idaho, to the West Yellowstone Ranger Station, a distance of sixty-four miles, Lloyd Van Sickle, famous dog driver, lost the trail in a blizzard. After many attempts to find the road in eight feet of snow, Lloyd told Rex, the lead dog of his all-Samoyed team, to "Go home." Several near disastrous turns and stops later, Rex took off through the forest. (These sudden stops really create tangles in the lines when one is driving a fifteen-dog hookup.) Rex began threading his way through the National Forest, leading the team with only a slight pause and cocking of his head now and then as if listening, and the team and Lloyd eventually reached Ashton. But they came into town from the south instead of the north as would be usual from Yellowstone. We went out with Lloyd several times to look at the path that Rex had followed into town, but it just didn't make much sense to us. Determined to find out what Rex knew that we didn't, we took him out on a leash and tried the same thing over again. Finally, when off the main traveled path and with repeated commands, "Go home," he finally cocked his head, listened and took off at a trot in the still deep snow. Thankfully (as we were running behind in deep snow), he stopped and cocked his head as if listening again. This time we listened. We heard the humming and crackling of tiny voices and realized that the noise was coming from the Forestry Telephone lines laid through the trees rather than on regular telephone poles. We were convinced that Rex associated the humming of the lines with people, and by following the sound of the telephone lines into town, we duplicated the "new" trail that he created that day.

This same Rex and his kennelmates were removed from the show bench of the Golden Gate KC in 1949 for a rescue mission. They were taken to the Donner Pass area of the High Sierras, where a plane had been forced down in a heavy snowstorm. Lloyd Van Sickle hooked two teams together to drag the small plane down to where a track-laying jeep could be attached to it and execute a rescue.

TRAINING A SLED DOG
by Robert H. Ward

To train your dog to harness, you first need a lead dog or "pilot." If you are to work only one dog, he needs to be a lead dog. When the goal is a complete team, you must have a good lead dog for safety and for your own physical comfort. An accomplished leader will eliminate much running in the snow by the driver to straighten harnesses. A well-trained leader requires fewer commands, and there is less confusion in crowded or noisy situations.

Start with a fifteen- to twenty-foot training lead, and permit the dog to walk out in front of you. Use either the training harness or the Siwash-type pulling harness. Do not use a choke chain, but do use a leather or solid non-slip type collar. You do not want to confuse sled training with show or obedience training formats.

Make the work pleasant because you want to develop a willing worker. Once your dog begins to start out on his own in front of you, encourage him with commands of "Hi, hi," or "All right, all right." The command "Mush" is largely fictitious. It is not a sharp enough command word. Mush probably started with the French word *Marche*, which was sufficiently guttural, but Mush isn't. Many drivers add their own variations to commands—a great aid if one later participates in sled races with other teams. If you use different words, your team won't respond to commands from other drivers.

Traditionally sled dogs have been trained by other sled dogs. Lead dogs have been trained by other lead dogs. Today that is not feasible for most owners. Because of the speed with which a dog moves, a bicycle is an excellent aid to the training of a lead dog. Command "Hi" and whistle to start. At the beginning, it is a good idea to give a command whenever the dog begins to do something because this will associate the action with the command. The one independent action that you must not permit is stopping. Always stop a dog or a team before they get tired and stop of their own will.

Assuming that you now have a dog that will lead while you are riding a bicycle, permit him to go ahead on the lead until he is pulling you. Maintain a steady pace by the use of the brake to create just enough pull to keep your tug line taut. Take advantage of every fork or turn in the road that your dog comes to, to begin the commands, "Gee" for right and "Haw" for left. Many times you will have to jerk the dog to the right or left while giving the commands. Always give praise for success even if you had to do all of the turning. This system of jerking for right and left becomes valuable if you can settle for one jerk for right or "Gee" and two jerks for left or "Haw." This, along with the whistling to start, will be a help with many dogs and the leader when they cannot hear your commands. Do not rush your dog by placing other dogs behind him as soon as he begins to obey commands. Work the dog for several weeks by himself, and then only add one or two dogs if he is strong enough to drag them around on command.

To add the "Turn-about," use the command "Gee" followed by another "Gee" when the dog has moved a few feet in the new direction. This creates a wide, swinging turn that is necessary to avoid injuring or running over the dogs in the team with the sled as it spins. Some drivers command "Gee, come here," or "Haw, come here," but this creates quite a sharp about turn and often trouble. An about turn at high speed or while the team is running is also dangerous.

You will find that your lead dog prefers to stand when you halt for a rest. This is a good habit to foster. Tell him "Stand stay." If your halt is a long one, the command "Down" is necessary, for later when you are working a team, runaway teams are avoided if the team is trained to "Down." Your lead dog must be particularly good at the "Stand stay," for you will expand this to the command, "Hold it," when you are harnessing the team. When you tell him to "Hold it," pull on the leader's tug line and make him stay in position.

The command to "Whoa" and the reining in are the same as those used to stop a horse. A series of short jerks to throw the dogs off balance becomes their signal when voice commands cannot be heard in the wind and snow.

Once you have trained a lead dog, he becomes the trainer for all successive leaders. Your point dogs that run behind the leaders most often learn the commands in one season's work. When a point dog shows promise of leading, merely lengthen the tug line until he is running alongside the leader. Gradual lengthening of the line will place the novice lead dog out in front. Many drivers have been successful with a double lead dog hookup.

Although most dogs may be trained for simple work as lead dogs, remember that a great one is rare. Sex is no determiner. A lead dog must be able to resist temptations of chasing other animals or of being distracted. He must be able to outrun the majority of the team. He must be trainable to commands. Above all, the lead dog must like to work and run.

Thus far we have been discussing the training of the lead dog, not really dog team driving. To drive a team you must know that, as in obedience work, the voice and manner of command is all-important. The following suggestions seem to help many drivers:

- Limit each command to one word and as few syllables as possible.
- Gather the team in readiness to start by calling the dogs' names sharply. Some drivers call "Hupp-hupp" or "Now-now." These must have a tone of eagerness or anticipation.
- Command "All right" or "Hi" to start the team forward.
- Reprimand an individual dog by calling his name sharply. Do not use a word that would reprimand the entire team.
- Stop the team with a long drawn out "Whoa."
- Animate your voice to each need. Remember that the dog responds to sounds and inflections rather than to specific words. (Try your dog with his name spoken gruffly, then kindly.)

Major Rodman, of West Yellowstone, Montana, drove a team of Malamutes using a whistle and never a voice command. The team was gathered with a long whistle with a rising inflection. The dogs started with a series of short, sharp whistles. A right turn was signaled with one long blast and a jerk on the gangline, a left turn with two distinct blasts and two jerks on the gangline. Increased speed or rallying were accomplished with short sharp blasts repeated with enthusiasm.

Your training has begun with the lead dog. Then one or two dogs have been added to your beginning team. From this point on you will find that most of *your* effort and direction will be in training new dogs to add to your existing team. The tandem hookup or double-line of two abreast with a single lead dog. This is the most satisfactory method of harnessing because there will be a shorter overall length of the team, and it will thus be easier to handle in wooded or mountainous areas or amid the crowds, parades and traffic of modern life.

Training equipment is basically a harness and various types of lines and collars. The most versatile harness is the Siwash-type because it may be used for training and working. There are many other types for racing, but they do not give the control needed for newly trained dogs. The Siwash harness may easily be made of webbing and sewn by hand or riveted. Approximately sixteen feet of webbing material is adequate for one dog.

Remember to fit an individual harness for each dog. Make all strain and pressure rest on the dog's shoulders, neck and chest. Never permit pressure on the throat or back. Allow the utmost freedom to both the forelegs and hindquarters. The use of the ring in the rear of the harness prevents tangles and the pulling sideways of the harness in action.

In training your new additions to the team, do not expect too much at first. Place your new dogs next to and behind an experienced dog if possible. Maintain a slow pace with new dogs in the team, and stop immediately if a new dog is dragged or thrown off his feet. A dog once frightened is very difficult to train. Do not punish the new dog in harness because he does not yet know what is expected. Beginners rarely pull their share of the load, so be content if they run along freely.

The question "How young may we start?" will vary from breed to breed and according to size within the breed. Generally, puppies are started from six to eight months. Do not expect them to pull at this stage. In fact, many drivers do not hook puppies in with a tug line, but just with a neck line. If possible, avoid placing puppies in the wheel position, just in front of the sled, because a wheel dog must be strong and solid. Simple maneuvers are best when puppies and new dogs are in the team. The presence of puppies on a team requires that you limit your length of training time to a few hours until the puppies are at least ten months old.

Although the dogs are important, the driver will create the happy team. By making the sled work fun and by not allowing bad habits to develop, one trainer will be more successful than another. Most tangles and injured dogs occur when a driver permits the sled to run up on the team because the main gangline then becomes slack, and even the best lead dog cannot maintain a straight team line. A good driver will move dogs around in a team because some prefer or work better in one spot than in another. The successful trainer does not punish a dog in the team—only when the offending dog is alone. Perhaps the one thing that distinguishes the good driver from the inept is that he drives his team from the rear without anyone leading them.

If your sled team training progresses beyond the pastime stage, you may be working by yourself in isolated areas. Under those circumstances a few words of caution are needed.

Great problems may occur during harnessing and unharnessing unless you have a consistent system that the dogs understand. A good method is to fasten the main gangline to the sled and stretch it out on the ground. Anchor your gee line to a post or stake in the ground. The gee line runs from the tug line ring to the driver, usually under the sled, and trails loosely. With the sled thus secured, a runaway team is prevented. Now the leader is hitched with the command "Stay" or "Hold it." This keeps the tug line taut and prevents the remaining dogs from becoming tangled. With all dogs harnessed, place the steadier dogs in the team first and command "Down" to each as they are hitched in place. Do not have your team hitched up too long before you intend to start because the dogs' natural eagerness to go will be lost.

In unharnessing a team, the sled must again be anchored from the rear by fastening the gee line to a post or a tree. The great driver Leonhard Seppala carried a metal rod that he drove through a hole in his brake lever deep into the snow to hold his team on every halt. Many drivers merely turn the sled on its side. Unharnessing usually begins with the swing and point dogs because the wheel dogs cannot be very easily entangled with others as they are fastened to the sled, and thus cannot go very far sideways or backward. This is also an excellent time to check foot pads for any injury and bodies for chaffing from the harness.

If it sounds like dogsledding is a wonderful hobby, be assured that it is. Consider, for example, Betty Sprunger who started with one Sam and with her sons ran the one Sam into a team. Her hobby for almost four decades has been "hitching up a bunch" (including Siberians) and running just for the hell of it. It started in Murphys, California, and continued after a move to Michigan. Betty writes, "We still have 30 dogs in the yard. . . . Nanook is 13 and still wants to run. Fawn is 12 and still flies around the exercise yard."

Betty also runs a 4-H Junior Mushers' group. They all went to Alaska to attend an international training camp, and she spoke at the Alaska Dog Mushers' Association's October 1995 symposium in Fairbanks. The group toured the kennels of Rick Swenson, Susan Butcher and Roxie Wright to see their sledding champions. This exciting tour included a visit to the University of Alaska. One of the girls planned right then to go to school there!

Betty is also one of the breed's dedicated "spinners" and enjoys Samoyed hair on the wheel as well as she does the dogs on the trail.

A Samoyed is truly a dog for all reasons.

WORKING SAMOYEDS

Walt and Judy Schirber of Warlord Kennels are ardent supporters of the Organization of the Working Samoyeds (OWS, to sledding Samoyed enthusiasts in the United States and around the world). Thirteen years ago, they moved to the western edge of the Adirondacks and remodeled a 200-year-old farmhouse and barn into perhaps the most ideal, efficient Samoyed kennel in the United States. Now they can train, condition, race and raise their Samoyeds in a natural environment, much as Msgr. Keegan did fifty years ago. The vanishing heritage of our breed is being revived.

Walt and Judy Schirber have been in the breed for twenty-eight years and have continuously worked their dogs in weight-pulling and sprint racing for twenty-five years. Their kennel probably has the longest sprint-racing record. Walt and his daughter, Christina, both run teams, Christina beginning at age four in the Pee-Wee Class with one dog. Walt puts on weight-pulls for both of the sled-dog clubs that they belong to. The Schirbers began in the conformation ring and went on to Obedience and then into racing.

The Schirbers' most memorable Samoyed, Bru, was one of Walt's leaders on his sprint-racing team. Bru was a flawless leader, seldom making a mistake, and together with his sister, Kvik, led an all-registered team of Samoyeds that dominated the Mid-Atlantic Sled Dog Racing Association's five-dog class within a five-state area from 1974 on into the early 1980s.

Their nine-month-old puppy bitch Molly is the granddaughter of Ch. Wolf River's Drumlin and the great, great granddaughter of Ch. Alpine Glo Nuvak Chin-Mana (Chin'a). Molly was obtained from Carole and Joe Rost because of the strong, working lines behind her and is running on Christina's four-dog team as this book goes to press.

PACKING

Dog packing is as old as sledge team driving. Many natives of the north use their dogs to carry belongings over terrain that is too rough for sledding. There is practically no place a pack dog cannot go with a load.

Loads by the natives generally average one-half the dog's weight. For weekend excursions to the mountains, the hiking clubs of the Samoyed owners limit the loads to one-third the dog's weight.

Training consists of learning to follow behind the hiker. A dog that has been taught to "Heel" is at a definite disadvantage on a narrow trail. The command here is "Back," and the dog is taken out on a lead and tapped gently on the nose until he remains in back. The "Down, "Stay" and "Come" commands are, of course, very necessary for the protection of the small packs that the dogs carry.

The pack consists of two pouches, one on each side of the dog, held on by a breast strap and a belly strap. A dog is a loose-skinned animal and thus cannot be packed on the same principle as a horse. The pack must be balanced and stabilized on his back. For serious and heavy work, a breeching strap is advisable to keep the pack from slipping forward.

When the pack is first used, it is usual to load it with bulky, light loads, such as straw, to accustom the dog to the art of missing trees and rocks with the projecting pack.

HUNTING WITH SAMOYEDS

Not everyone wishes to work their Samoyeds in harness and mush through the snow; something should be said for other activities Sammy fans can enjoy. There have been only two experiences known to us personally of using the Samoyed for hunting—one for ducks and the other for deer when it was legal to use dogs on a leash.

The Samoyed duck retriever was purchased by a lady who wanted a dog at home when her husband went hunting with his Labrador Retriever. These people lived near Fresno, California, a great area for waterfowl. The Samoyed was taken along first because there was no dog-sitter at home. He romped and played until a duck was brought down. In he plunged with the Labrador to get the duck, and the bird was carried downstream by the current. Jack, the Samoyed, didn't get that duck. For the second downed bird, this two-year-old Samoyed took one look at the duck floating downstream, ran ahead down river, jumped in and retrieved the duck. Quite a time was had by all to get that first duck away from him, but by midmorning Jack was bringing them in like a retriever. When Blackie, the Labrador, passed on, our duck-hunting friend used a Samoyed to retrieve for the next seven years.

WEIGHT PULLING

An unusual Samoyed bitch appeared on the weight-pulling contests scene in the 1980s. Ch. Alpine Glo Nuvak Chin-Mana owned by Carole Harrigan-Rost of Irwin, Pennsylvania. "Chin'a" pulled 1,138 pounds at Saranac Lake, New York, an all-time record for a Samoyed bitch. This by a bitch who weighed less than fifty pounds! Chin'a won the Organization for Working Samoyeds Club Award for weight pulling for 1981 and the Trailbreakers' Sled Dog Club Weight-Pull Dog of the Year 1981 Award. Trailbreakers is an Ohio-based club, with more than 100 members in 5 states. Chin'a was the first Samoyed to receive an award from this club.

Chin'a was bred to work as well as to look good. She was what mushers call a natural leader. Carole reports that many mushers expressed chagrin over the fact that she was a Samoyed. The Malamute people wanted her bigger; the Husky-cross people wanted her taller.

Chin'a and her owner began by studying Mel Fishback's book, *Training Lead Dogs My Way,* and then borrowed a few other dogs and began training in the autumn of 1979. In the winter of 1980 Chin'a ran lead on a three-dog team some of the time, but her really outstanding mark was made in weight pulling. Chin'a was undefeated in the Under 50-pound class in 1980 and placed first in a field of nine dogs in the 50–80 pound class against other breeds at one race.

Carole believes that the bitch's attitude was a great part of her ability. The steady training did it, too. They ran during the early autumn and in the early winter. Chin'a ran with the team on weekends, averaging about four to five miles per run. On weekdays, they ran as singles at the local high school track to emphasize building muscle tone and endurance rather than just high-level weight pulling. Carole used a child's plastic sled that can be used on a dry track or on snow. It is designed so that items such as an old tire or two can be added for weight. By jogging alongside the sled and dog, the trainer also becomes conditioned for the upcoming racing season.

Probably the hardest part in pulling is to have the dog understand the technique in "breaking the weight." Sled dogs, which have always had the

Ch. Alpine Glo Chin-Mana, owned and trained by Carole Harrigan Rost, was a weight-pulling bitch par excellence. Entered in the 50–80 pound class, "Chin'a" is pictured pulling 1,138 pounds at the Alpo International competition at Lake Saranac, New York, in the winter of 1980–81. *Jon Nedele*

sled follow easily behind, are often confused by the resistance. Starting with easier weights and building up will aid in keeping the dogs' attitude "up." Carole advises, "Always make certain that the dog finishes a pull. Even if he can't do it on his own, walk him through it to show him that it can be done. Remember that Sammies are quite intelligent and usually pace themselves. Do not ask the dog to do something he is not physically or mentally ready to do."

Following the racing and pulling season, Chin'a was bred and had eight healthy puppies and a very easy whelping. She was 20½ inches tall and weighed forty to fifty pounds. An excellent mover, which fit with her soundness and well-balanced physique, she was owner-handled to her championship.

Carole advises newcomers to use the proper equipment because her dog quickly learned the difference between a racing harness and a weight-pulling harness. Both harnesses came from Mel Fishback-Riley. Weight pull is a good area for many-, one- or two-dog Sammy owners. You don't need an entire team or a lot of equipment. Just be sure your dog is in good health and proper condition, and you can have many pleasurable winter weekends together.

ORGANIZATION FOR THE WORKING SAMOYED

by Donna Dannen, President, OWS

The Organization for the Working Samoyed (OWS) began as an idea by a few sled dog racing enthusiasts in the early 1970s. At that time, a few Samoyed teams competed in sled dog races. Then, as now, racing enthusiasts considered Samoyeds too stubborn or too playful and too slow to be competitive as sled dogs. However, a few people who loved the breed successfully trained Samoyeds to work with great resolve and joy. These people saw potential in the breed and founded OWS to encourage other Samoyed owners to work their dogs.

The purpose of OWS is the same today as when it was started: to be a vehicle to exchange information on training Samoyeds as good working dogs. A quarterly newsletter, *The Yapper*, originated by the late Mel Fishback-Riley, founder of OWS, discusses Samoyed training, conditioning, nutrition and health issues. Charter members Walt and Judy Schirber also contribute their experiences of working with the Samoyed as a sled dog. All OWS members can add to the printed body of knowledge about working Samoyeds by submitting letters and articles of their own. Regular columns cover the areas of work OWS recognizes. Other member-written articles appear about the great working Samoyeds of the past and present and their lineage.

OWS provides an annual award system to recognize outstanding Samoyeds competing against other breeds specializing in various performance events. The annual awards allow Samoyeds to compete with one another from around the country to see which among these all-purpose workers is faring best against dogs that specialize in particular types of work.

OWS recognizes performance events that best exemplify the indigenous uses and qualities of the Samoyed. Annual awards honor the Top Sled Dog Team, Most Improved Sled Dog Team, Top Weight Puller and Top Obedience Samoyed. Obedience is included because tractable Samoyeds should also make good workers. Two other popular areas of competition may go in annual award status: Top Skijoring Team and Top Herding Dog.

Over the years various breeders' lines repeatedly have produced top working Samoyeds. Their genes are in many of today's top OWS winners. Agnes Mason's White Way line is present in today's top working kennels, along with some gritty Northwest Coast-bred lines. The smaller, East Coast Samoyeds of English Kobe lineage have been used most notably by OWS members Wall and Judy Schirber in their successful Warlord Samoyeds sprint teams and by Jack Price in his Bubbling Oaks distance teams.

Donna Yocum's Tsuilikagta line was the beginning of several OWS working kennels on the East and West Coasts. Her dogs were used by Mike Cook and Carole Montgomery to produce exceptional sled dogs. Cook's Alpine Glo dogs were the start of Pennsylvania mushers and breeders such as Lenny Miller (Foxfire), Joe and Carole Rost (Nuvak) and Tom and Sharon Polovina (Willow Winds). These dogs also have been outstanding weight pullers.

Ch. Sunburst's Hot Flash, CD, CGC, WSX, HIC, TDI (Ch. Ice Way's Flash Cube ex Crizta's Christmas Package), owned by John and Kathy Regan and bred by Kathy Vincent and Teena Deatherage Schulz. Throughout her life, "Cherokee" has been actively involved in weight pulling, therapy and obedience work. At the 1993 SCA National Specialty, she was the top veteran weight puller.

Roger Landers skijoring at Bemidji, Minnesota, with (from left) Am., Can. Ch. Sylvan's Cascade, CD, WS (Cassie) and Sylvan's Flying Free (Flyer).

In the early 1980s Kay Hallberg's Wolf River line came to the forefront as a supreme working kennel of extraordinarily well-built Samoyeds. Kay was very single-minded in her wish to produce a line of solid sled dogs made up mostly of White Way–based bloodlines. She certainly succeeded with her mid-distance racing teams that competed in the John Beargrease distance race in Minnesota as well as in other tough Midwestern sled dog races. Her line is included within the gene pool of almost every currently successful OWS working line today. On the East Coast, Alan Katz (Kashartic) and Tony McDonald (Kodiak) have used Wolf River dogs in their lineups. In Colorado,

The Wolf River racing team doing what they like best. Twenty-five miles into a fifty-mile race, this all-champion team exhibits the stamina and endurance for which the Samoyed earned fame on Arctic and Antarctic expeditions. This team competed only in the toughest mid-distance races, always against mixed-breed competition. They won both the Samoyed Club of America Top Sled Dog Team Award and the Organization for the Working Samoyed Top Sled Dog Team Award. Most are also multiple Group placers in the show ring. They are (alphabetically) Ch. Wolf River's Dune (F), Ch. Wolf River's Eagle (M), Ch. Wolf River's Falcon (M), Ch. Wolf River's Hawk (M), Ch. Wolf River's Kestrel (F), Ch. Wolf River's Pebble (F), Ch. Wolf River's Siberian Taiga (M) and Ch. Wolf River's Terra (F). Six of these were sired by Ch. Wolf River's Star, and a seventh is a granddaughter. All were bred, owned and driven by Kay Hallberg of Wolf River.

Exemplifying the gentle nature for which the Samoyed is famous, this multiple all-breed and SCA Specialty BIS team of four Wolf River champion stud dogs is affectionately known as "The Birddogs and the Tiger." Bred, owned and handled by Kay Hallberg, this formidable foursome includes (from left) three littermates, Chs. Falcon, Eagle and Hawk (by Ch. Wolf River's Star ex Ch. Seamist's Raven of Wolf River) and their cousin, Siberian Taiga (Ch. Sparrow Hill's Taakowah ex Ch. Wolf River's Ruffian, CD). This crowd-pleasing team was never defeated in any competition. *Kim Booth*

Katie Carter's Elmfield line in combination with Wolf River are present in the working Samoyeds of Darlu Littledeer (Abakan), Heidi Nieman (Saratoga), Lorrie McAllister (Chinookwinds), Lana McClellan (Galadriel) and David Holley (Frostfire). Connie Rudd also has Wolf River bloodlines represented in her Summit Samoyeds, also made up of Trailblazer, Tundra Winds and Danica dogs.

A successful working kennel composed of a Silveracres and Blue Sky combination is Geoff and Brenda Abbott's Kriskella Samoyeds. Geoff is a tough competitor on the sprint-racing circuit in Colorado, first in the late 1970s and early 1980s, and now in the mid-1990s. His dogs exhibit a terrific enthusiasm that stands them well in sledding competition.

In OWS weight-pull standings, Debbie Spiller's Ch. T-Snow Star Kesar Spirit 'O Fame, CD, WSX, has been a top contender. He represents Silveracres and Risuko lines. Also outstanding in weight pull have been dogs of Wolf River lineage represented by Dan and Belva Posila's Saranac Samoyeds. Jeff Bott's exceptional weight puller, Chinookwind's Trek 'T Saratoga, WSX, has won high honors in OWS and in the International Weight Pull Association's international medal competitions. Trek goes back to Wolf River lines plus the legendary Ch. Valadamir of Elmfield, who was a top OWS weight puller in the 1970s.

Kent and Donna Dannen started in Colorado in weight pulling with their Abakan and Wind River—bred Ch. Wind River Talkeetna Karibou, CD, WSXM, which also goes back to Ch. Valadamir of Elmfield. He represents basically White Way breeding through several different lines as well as Idesta Green's dogs. The Greenstar Samoyeds helped the Greens eke out a pioneer existence in the Alaskan wilderness in the 1950s. The Dannens' sprint racing force came with the addition of lead dog Ch. Tundra Winds' Glacier Lily, WSXM (out of Snowflower and Alever lines) to Karibou's lead abilities. Their dogs won many OWS awards with Glacier and Karibou breeding at lead. Later additions of Mithril, Moonlighter, Hoof 'n Paw and Saratoga have kept the Dannens' Tundra Winds Samoyeds in the forefront of various working activities.

At this writing, the Organization for the Working Samoyed is entering the world of the Information Highway. In training for competition, questions need to be asked and answered immediately instead of waiting for a quarterly newsletter. As a result, OWS plans to go online to provide its computer-using members with the ability to get answers more quickly. *The Yapper* will remain the printed publication of the organization and will report much of the online dialogue. It is an exciting time for OWS as it seeks to expand its ability to educate and reward the owners of top-notch working Samoyeds.

Am., Can. Ch. Bykhal's Northern Exposure (Ch. Bykhal's In Your Dreams ex Bykhal's California Dream), informally called Roxie, is the foundation matron of Bonnie's Prell's True North Samoyeds.

Three Sylvan "working girls"(from left) Am., Can. Ch. Mithril's Free To Be Me, CDX, WS; Ch. Sylvan Parka of Tundra Winds, WSX; Am., Can. Ch. Sylvan's Cascade, CD, WS, enhance the Spectacular view 14,000 feet above Aspen, Colorado. *Donna Dannen*

Ch. Novaskaya Modesty Blaze of Ostyak, Novaskaya Moonlite Marauder, Ch. Novaskaya Silva Snowblaze, Ch. Icezones Moonlite Artemis, Silvasnows Novaskaya Cover Girl and Novaskaya English Rose make up Betty Moody's Novaskaya Samoyed Team. John Moody keeps them sharp in this off-season practice run.

There they go! Notice the rear gait of the dogs and the tree bar of the harness attached to the tug line making the gear comfortable for the dogs.

chapter 17

The Versatile Samoyed

THE SAMOYED AND DOG AGILITY

Does your Samoyed love to run? Does he love to jump? Do you have enough confidence in your Samoyed and yourself to let her run without a collar or leash? Can you work as a team with your Sam and have fun?

Then Agility just may be the activity for you and your dog! Agility is an exciting, visual sport.

Dog Agility combines elements from equestrian jumping events and obstacles derived from the military K9 Corps regimen. Dogs maneuver their way through a timed course designed to test their agility as they leap over hurdles, burst through tunnels, traverse a seesaw, scale an A-frame, weave through a line of poles and more.

Starting in Great Britain in the late 1970s, Dog Agility first appeared on the United States dog sports scene in 1985, based on Agility's international standards, through the efforts of the founders of the United States Dog Agility Association. The United States Dog Agility Association, Inc., coordinates the Pedigree Grand Prix of Dog Agility, a major national tournament supported by Pedigree brand dog foods.

Agility was recognized by the AKC in 1994. Three titles are available in AKC Agility Trials: Novice Agility (NA), Agility Excellent (AX) and Master Agility Excellent (MX).

The United States Dog Agility Association (USDAA) offers three titles. They are Agility Dog (AD), Advanced Agility Dog (AAD) and Master Agility Dog (MAD).

The North American Dog Agility Council (NADAC) also offers three titles. They are Novice (NAC), Open (OAC) and Elite (EAC).

There are also "games" with nonstandard titles available in USDAA and NADAC: Gamblers and Jumpers in NADAC and Gamblers, Pairs or Relay, Snooker and Jumpers in USDAA.

Am., Int. Ch. Samusz's Spectacular Bid, CD, owned and bred by Terry Bednarczyk literally "flies" over the high jump.

In NADAC five faults are allowed to qualify, either time or course faults (such as knocking over a bar). AKC Agility has a perfect score of 100 and a qualifying score of 85, which means minor deductions are made for faults if the dog has not disqualified herself. USDAA formats allow no time or course faults whatsoever.

The most important recommendations to make to anyone who wants to compete in Agility are (1) you must work as a team, (2) you must make it as much fun as possible (if you don't, you can be sure that your Sammy will get even with you in the ring), (3) keep your dog in good physical condition and (4) practice, practice, practice.

To compete in Agility a dog should be eighteen months old or older, not aggressive, in good health and under control. Obedience training is not required but is highly recommended. It is both a help and a hindrance. Obedience training helps to obtain a good degree of control but teaches your Sam

RoseAnn Baune's "Cookie" at ten years old is retired from Agility but still gets excited when she sees the course.

Barron's Blithe Spirit, UD, HT, NA, owned by Barbara and Don Cole, exits the closed tunnel.

Saw-Yeds Legend of a Star, CD, NA, TDI, owned by Dawn Sawdey, carefully executes the Teeter-Totter exercise in Agility.

to work at your left side and close to you. To compete in Agility, your dog needs to learn to work from both sides as well as away from you.

Up close, all the Agility equipment appears forbidding. Heights appear higher when you picture your dog up there, and a jumps looks much more imposing when you look around the course and see ten others just as high, some broader and some downright strange looking! There isn't much room for error on those planks, and how on earth can a dog be taught to weave so fast through those silly poles?

In getting you and your dog ready for the sport of Dog Agility, the following basic factors apply:

- Key words—*Jump, Tire, Teeter, Tunnel, Get in, Weave, Go out.*

- Basic obedience—*Come, Sit, Stay, Down, Here* (with me).

- Lots of praise—*Good boy/girl! That's the way! Let's go!*

- Bonding with your dog—This can be a good and positive way of showing teamwork.

ATTITUDE

Nothing is more important to education than a positive attitude. Here are three basic guidelines for developing the positive attitude you and your dog need to get the most from your mutual education and Agility in particular:

1. Attitude comes first, before the task is mastered. Like it or not, you are shaping attitude with the feelings you project.

2. Begin your dog's training with challenges easier than you think she needs, and progress only when your dog needs more challenge, not when you do. A positive attitude toward the first Agility obstacles helps assure a quick and early success. When you hit a snag later on, leave that lesson alone for a week or so while you go back to those delightful basics.

3. Choose your training time, enticements and challenges according to what will best strengthen your dog's educational foundation. Don't let someone else's timetable for progress dictate your own. Every dog learns unevenly and needs direction differently.

Agility is a sport meant for safe, competitive fun for the dogs and for the handlers. In all my experience, I haven't found anyone who didn't enjoy themselves in Agility.

Enjoy Agility with your dog, and you will find camaraderie, socialization for the dog and you—a huge confidence builder, humility and pride of accomplishment. What more can you ask for between you and your Sammy?

Ch. Elfenbein La Salle Coupe, owned and trained by RoseAnne Baune, is in the SCA Hall of Fame for her achievements in Agility. "Keila" holds an AKC Open title and a leg toward her Excellent title as well as a USDAA Starter's degree. She is shown in the top photo coming off the wall, "hitting the contact" (hopefully). In the bottom photo, Keila is shown in the midst of successfully negotiating the weave poles. Notice the handler's hands "telling" the dog what to do.

HERDING

by Barbara Cole

One of the many versatile activities Samoyed dogs did for their masters in the Arctic was to help move the reindeer herds. The nomadic Samoyede people kept small herds as a main food staple and as a source of protein.

The AKC approved Samoyeds to participate in AKC-sanctioned Herding Trials in 1993. Samoyeds were the first breed not in the Herding Group [*Authors' note:* They are "misplaced" in the Working Group] to be allowed to do so.

There are three types of courses offered in AKC Herding events, three types of livestock used (ducks, sheep and cattle) and six different titles that may be won.

The courses offered are Course A (used at the majority of trials), which is used as an all-around farm or ranch course. It is designed to demonstrate the versatility of the Herding dog, and consists of four obstacles and a handler's post in a 100 × 200-foot pen. The stock approved for Course A are ducks, sheep and cattle.

Course B is approved for ducks and sheep only. It is held in an open field of 300 × 75 feet or more and is a modified version of the International Sheepdog Society course.

Course C is designed to reflect a tending shepherd's day on a farm, and only sheep are used. It is a modified version of courses used in Europe, and the sheep must be moved down a road across a bridge and be allowed to graze restfully. In all classes, the dog has a ten-minute time limit to perform the required elements for each class. At the test level, the dog must pass under two different judges. At the trial level, the dog must pass and qualify under three different judges.

The Herding Test classes are the Herding Tested (HT) and Pre-Trial (PT). Dogs must be preexposed to stock before entering either of these classes. The Herding Test is a standardized gauge to measure a dog's basic training ability as a Herding dog. The Herding Test consists of five elements in which a dog must move the sheep in a controlled manner between posts, change direction and perform a down and a call off. It is scored in a pass-fail manner.

The Pre-Trial Test is designed to expose a dog to pre-trial conditions. The pre-trial dog must put the stock in motion, collect and control the stock, stop, move along a fence and put the stock in an exhaust pen. It is also graded on a pass-fail basis.

Herding Trial dogs must receive a qualifying score under three different judges to receive their title. Herding Trial titles are Herding Started (HS), Herding Intermediate (HI) and Herding Excellent (HX). Also available is the Herding Champion title (HCh.), which is the most advanced and only attainable after the HX is achieved.

In Herding Started (HS), the handler can move around the course and stay with the dog. The dog gathers the stock, takes them through a "Y" chute, a "Z" chute and a straight chute, performs a cross drive and pens the sheep.

In the Herding Intermediate (HI) class, the handler stands at a cone or marker and sends the dog on an outrun. The dog must bring the sheep in a directed pattern until a designated time when the stock have negotiated the start of the "Y" chute. Only then can the handler leave the spot and move about the course with the stock and dog. The elements are the same as the Herding Started class with a one-minute hold of the stock in the three-sided pen.

In Herding Excellent (HX) the handler stays in one spot the whole time except to move to the hold pen. The handler continues to direct the dog from the hold pen until the dog is ready for the final penning, at which time the handler moves to the exhaust pen. The elements are the same as the Herding Intermediate test.

The Herding Champion (HCh.) title can only be attempted after the dog has its Herding Excellent title. Fifteen points are required, and points are awarded according to the number of dogs entered. A maximum of five points can be awarded at any one trial, and one win must be a first-place win carrying championship points (one win of three points or better with seven to nine dogs competing in the class).

There are many different styles that Samoyeds exhibit while working the stock, each being unique to that dog. Some Sams work very tight on the stock, not being afraid to grip when necessary, while others exhibit a Huntaway style with a lot of barking to move the stock. Both are appropriate. Many Sams start off with only the chase instinct and try to single out one animal.

Ch. Winterway Omega Icy Naiad, PT, HCT, owned by Francis and Louis Thompson and bred by Audrey Lycan, takes it slow and easy around sheep.

When there are no reindeer to be had, "Clifford" will make do perfectly well with goats. Am., Int. Ch. Samusz's Spectacular Bid, CD, whom you met earlier in the Agility section, counts herding among his many talents. *Terry Bednarczyk*

Herding is a modification of the hunting instinct, so while not acceptable, this is not unusual to see. Good training will help encourage appropriate behavior, and Herding is a sport Sams seem to enjoy. There are many good books on how to train a Herding dog. A good recommendation is *Herding Dogs: Progressive Training* (New York: Howell Book House, 1994).

Although practice for trial competition takes access to livestock and large open areas, Herding is a popular, new and ever-growing sport for Samoyed owners.

TRACKING

Tracking trials were originally a requirement for the AKC Utility Dog title, becoming a separate event in 1947. Currently, there are three Tracking titles: Tracking Dog (TD), Tracking Dog Excellent (TDX) and the newest, Variable Surface Tracking (VST), added in September 1995. In addition to the VST title, a dog can also now earn a Champion Tracker, or CT. This championship title is given to a dog that has earned all three tracking titles. The CT will appear before the dog's registered name as a prefix.

Ginny Corcoran and "Robin" tracking in Colorado. Because the line she is using is made of parachute cord, Ginny wears gloves to protect her hands.

It must be admitted that Tracking is just not for everyone. Even though this activity can be great fun for the dog and his handler, it can be physically challenging and requires a real "stick to it" attitude. Tracking dogs are taught to recognize an individual's scent and literally trace the path the person has taken step-by-step. This is in contrast with dogs that are taught to "air or wind" scent. Law enforcement officials often find it advantageous to use an air-scenting dog and a tracking dog side by side during a search.

At the beginning of 1996, the Samoyed breed had a total of twenty-five AKC Tracking titled dogs. Two of these deserve special recognition because they also achieved the TDX, a difficult title to earn, with the average dog taking up to five tries to pass the TDX trial. Hazel and Ken Kukendahl's White Shadow UDTX was the first Samoyed to earn a TDX. She earned this title in 1981 at the age of thirteen years! Our breed's second TDX went to Am., Can. Ch. Dajmozek, Am., Can. UDTX. He received his title at age eleven!

Even though the Samoyed was never bred for tracking, the capability of the Samoyed to do so has been proven. Again we see our breed's amazing versatility!

The National Association of Dog Obedience Instructors may be helpful in locating a trainer near you. Write: NADOI, Gwen Coon, 22866 E Steel Road, St. Johns, MI 48879.

Spinning Samoyed Hair

by Carol Chittum

There is nothing lovelier or more unique than an article of clothing made from the combings of our beautiful Samoyeds. This chapter aims to give you some practical suggestions about this fascinating by-product of our distinctive breed.

CONTEMPORARY CONSIDERATIONS

It is not our thought here to provide an actual course in spinning. A glance at the Yellow Pages of most city telephone directories will yield the names of weaving and spinning supply stores where you may take classes. Such stores can also be gold mines of books on the subject or places to discover the names of qualified teachers. If you want to make good progress and become skillful, I urge you to take a class. It is possible to learn from a book, using Samoyed hair to start with (I did), but it was so painstaking that I finally listened to my good friend and experienced spinner, Gertrude Adams, and took a workshop. The difference was remarkable. Today there are so many more resources available that there is no need to experience such frustration. You can also obtain the names and locations of local guilds of spinners by writing to the Handweavers Guild of America, 65 LaSalle Road, West Hartford, CT 06107. Such guilds frequently offer workshops or demonstrations of the various aspects of spinning and using handspun fibers.

COLLECTING THE HAIR

Not every part of the undercoat is equally as lovely and usable, so I will discuss the elementary step in achieving the product you wish, whether a garment or some other article.

Since it is much more pleasant to spin clean hair and since spun yarn is easier to wash than loose hair, let's start with a clean dog. As soon as you see that first telltale loose tuft in the area of the lower stifles, bathe your dog.

Carol Chittum, the author of this chapter, spins Samoyed combings into yarn on a wheel of Norwegian manufacture while her Ch. Belaya Sergeant Pepper intently supervises. Carol has demonstrated the drop spindle technique of spinning on national television and teaches classes in all art forms of working with fleece.

Then, frequent attention with the slicker brush will yield clean, spinnable hair with no other preparation required.

The most desirable hair for garments comes from the sides and shoulders. Therefore, I always brush those areas first and put that hair in a separate brown paper bag, labeled and dated. Sort your hair as you groom because it is very tedious and consuming to do so later. Keep each quality of hair stored separately for ease in planning your projects. Back, ruff and pants

Church organist Tommie Lohmiller wears a shawl she made by spinning combings from her Samoyed, Holly. This elegant pattern is called "The Queen's Crown." Mrs. Lohmiller also made a similar shawl for Betty Moody of Novaskaya Samoyeds. The Lohmillers live in Wyoming, where Tommie also raises Angora bunnies, from which she spins the Angora, sometimes combining it with the Samoyed hair for yarn that combines the best qualities of strength and softness.

coat often yield too much guard hair to be pleasant (unless you are fond of hair shirts!), but this coarser mixture may be spun into a textured, usable yarn. Leg hair below the elbow and stifle and tail hair are not worth saving as spinning material but can be useful as pillow or quilt stuffing. It also goes without saying that matted or damaged coat should be discarded.

DESIGNING YOUR YARN

In order for any yarn to be sound (i.e., to hold together), the individual fibers must wrap one and a half times around the diameter of the finished yarn. This is necessary to avoid weakness, especially important in garments where friction is a factor, as in elbows of sweaters or fingers of mittens. Thus, due to the short length of the Samoyed fiber (not usually more than one and a half inches), it is necessary to spin it into a moderately fine yarn if you want it to wear well and not shed excessively. A bulkier yarn should be achieved by plying two or more singles together rather than spinning a heavy single.

Interesting, beautiful yarns can also be created by a blending of Sam hair with other fibers. A blend with wool yields a soft but much stronger yarn. Blending is done in the carding process, and fibers should be nearly the same length. (Longer fibers, such as wool, will need to be cut.) I have successfully blended Samoyed hair with wool, alpaca, llama, mohair, cashmere and angora. For a composite yarn, I suggest using 40 percent or less of the other fiber so as not to overpower the downy quality of the Samoyed hair. The lovely, heathery tones produced by the admixture of any of these other animal fibers can be surprisingly pleasant.

Ch. Sitka's Mardi Gras (Ch. Winterway's Rain Man ex Ch. Sitkin's Uptown Girl), bred by Allison Baker and handled by Su Catlin for owners Dr. and Mrs. Timothy Grubb. "Casper" amassed some 250 BB wins in his successful career—125 group placements, 27 firsts, five-time all-breed BIS winner and #1 male Samoyed 1996.

Samoyed hair can, of course, be dyed. I suggest using those dyes specifically formulated for protein fibers. Due to the molecular structure of the hair, it is difficult to achieve bright, high-intensity colors. Most dyes seem to yield more pastel shades. It is interesting to dye a wool-Sammy blend because the wool takes up the color more intensely and the resulting yarn will take on a heather tone.

It is essential to remember the Samoyed's subpolar origins when designing yarn for a garment. Keep in mind that the hair is very warm in spite of its feathery lightness. Many spinners spend hours making sweaters that could only be worn in mid-January in Minnesota because they are not aware of this fact. This is another excellent reason for using a finer two-ply in a more open or lacy pattern, unless the finished garment will be worn in a very cold climate. Consider making shawls, scarves or hats from your Samoyed hair because they can be useful and appreciated nearly anywhere.

MISCELLANY

Be sure to keep hair from your different dogs labeled and separate because there are many shades of white, ecru, cream and even pale beige Samoyed undercoats. This is important if you want the result of your project to be one color. Hair stored in brown paper bags will stay fresher longer. Plastic does not breathe, and hair stored for a long time in plastic bags tends to take on an "old wet dog" odor.

Spin the hair, regardless of diameter, with a fair amount of twist, and your yarn will shed less. If you want a softer finish, you can achieve this by

Ch. Hoof 'n Paw's Prairie Dawg or "Varmi" (Am., Can Hoof 'n Paw's Knight Shadow ex Clark's Tekoa of Caribou), owned by Bob and Dolly Ward was Best Brood Bitch at the 1993 National. This happy group includes (left to right) Kathy Carr with her Ch. Hoof 'n Paw's Knight in Flight, Best Puppy at the 1992 National; Robert Page, Arctic breeds judge; Mardee Ward-Fanning with Varmi; and Gerald Sevigny with Ch. Hoof 'n Paw's Gladys Knight. Varmi is now Dolly's therapy dog companion. *Lindemaier*

lightly tapping the finished garment with a slicker brush. This will raise a napped finish similar to brushed mohair.

Refrain from offering to spin your friends' and relatives' dog hair unless you know in what condition the dog is kept and unless you can give them the sorting instructions beforehand. It is very time-consuming and frustrating to sort years of combings into usable lots.

Always wash your spun yarn after spinning and again after completing the project. Samoyed hair gets a grayish, dingy look from handling, both from the spinning and the subsequent processes. Your finished project should be the same sparkly white as a freshly bathed Samoyed. Treat your Samoyed yarn and articles as you would any fine woolen. Avoid very hot water, detergents and agitating in washing.

Learn, experiment, innovate and create with this beautiful fiber! There is no satisfaction quite like the one you will derive from seeing your Sam's hair transformed into a unique, usable article of apparel. It makes all the other time and work expended on your dog's care seem so much more worth it.

chapter 19

A Short History of the Samoyed in Canada

by Dr. Bob Gaskin

For this condensed version of the history of the Samoyed in Canada, the time span covered is divided into four periods. The first three cover twenty-five years and the fourth covers twenty-two.

PERIOD 1: 1900–25

It is believed the first unregistered Samoyeds were brought into Canada via the Bering Strait. Credit for this was given to Leonhard Seppala, the famous Norwegian-born sled dog driver. It is believed to have occurred during the early 1900s.

Examination of the Canadian Kennel Club Stud Book, vol. 17, reveals the results of a dog show held in Victoria, B.C., in 1913. There were three Samoyeds exhibited and listed: Pompey II, owned by Mrs. McConnell and placed first—Open Winner; Zulu was second place, owned by Mrs. G. Wood; and third place was Muggins, owned by Mrs. Roper. The owners were all from Victoria City, B.C. This is the earliest written record of Samoyeds being exhibited in Canada.

Dog shows were few and far between in Canada in the early 1900s. For example, in 1903 there were only four bench shows held in all of Canada. However, ten years later in 1914, just before World War I, the number of dog shows had grown to twenty-five, and by 1924 thirty-nine shows were being held. There was a slow but steady growth both in the number of dog clubs and in the number of shows put on by these clubs.

It was also during this time that the first mention of a "suggested" breed Standard for the Samoyed was put forth. An article published in the September 1912 issue of the *CKC Gazette* mentions a proposed Standard submitted through the "kindness of Mr. James Eley, Secretary of the Samoyede Club of

England. Any one on this side (of the Atlantic) interested in the Samoyede and requiring further information would be advised to contact Mr. Eley." Another forty years would pass before a breed Standard was approved by the CKC.

No Samoyeds were registered with the Canadian Kennel Club between 1900 and 1925.

PERIOD 2: 1925-50

The first year that Samoyeds were registered with the CKC was 1925. There were four Samoyeds registered, and they were all imported from the United States. Two of the dogs were owned by Mr. Frank W. Ward (no relation to authors) and had the English line of Farningham in their pedigrees. Over this twenty-five year period, there were some United States and English imports. English lines imported into Canada included Kobe, Farningham, Kara Sea, Snowland and Crownie.

There were no Samoyeds registered in 1926, 1928 and 1933. A review of the CKC records show only 392 Samoyeds registered for the twenty-five year period. There were imports from England and the United States; one, in 1927, was Jack Frost of Farningham. R. Anson Cartwright of Toronto, Ontario, was the first of several owners of this dog. The last owner was George Davis of Gormley, Ontario, whose kennel name was Kindon. To him and to a few other breeders goes most of the credit for keeping the breed alive in Canada during World War II.

Another landmark during this period was the first Best in Show awarded to a Samoyed in Canada in 1940. It went to Ch. Spark of Altai, out of Koraleva of Altai, imported by Dr. C. Seldon Benzanson of Samoyland Kennels in Nova Scotia.

Also during this period a Canadian-bred dog, Prince Autataki (Omar ex Princess Olga), owned by W. Copley, was the very first Samoyed to attain a New Zealand championship awarded—this in 1929.

The number of dog shows held annually continued to increase, and by 1944 CKC recorded a total of forty-four conformation shows, thirteen Field Trials and five Obedience Trials. However, Samoyeds were only exhibited in about five of those forty-four dog shows. The records indicate that Samoyeds were yet to enter the Obedience ring.

In summary, the Samoyed in Canada at this time was inching up slowly in popularity, and the number of dedicated breeders was also increasing and staying with Samoyeds over a long period.

Canadian Breeders and Exhibitors

George P. Davis, Kindon; Dr. C. Bezanson, Samoyland; Pat Howden, Bonllyn; Mrs. Gordon Purves, Kanda; I. M. Clendenning, Lesclen; Mrs. P. Thomson, Treasure Valley; Blair Wilson, Blairdale; Betty Dickson, Ziska;

Barbara Clarke, Kandor; Romaine Jones, Igloo; Mr. and Mrs. F. Freeman, Sno-Glo; Mr. and Mrs. G. MacDonald, Bri-Pen; Ian Miller, Saminto; Mrs. A. Shepard, Shep's Valley.

PERIOD 3: 1950-55

The first half of the 1950s witnessed an explosion of growth for the Samoyed. This growth was reflected in the numbers registered; for example, in the ten-year period,1960–70, more than 6,000 Samoyeds were registered in Canada. Naturally, this growth indicated a dramatic increase in the number of breeders. The increased number of owners and owner-breeders naturally led to the establishment of Samoyed Specialty clubs in Canada.

The first national Samoyed club was founded in 1957 and was called the Samoyed Fancier's of Canada. This club lasted only one year.

The Canadian Samoyed Club, Inc., was also founded in 1957 and for the next fifteen years carried on with many activities. The club held a number of Specialty shows, the first being held in the club's second year of operation. The club issued a newsletter and kept in touch with Sammy activities in the UK and United States through what are now called foreign liaison officers. The correspondent for the United States was Mrs. Doris McLaughlin of Silveracres Samoyeds. The 1961 Specialty BB was the English import Ch. Snowland's Ziska Buck, owned by Betty Dickson. The club submitted the first breed Standard to the CKC in 1959.

Only one national club, the Samoyed Association of Canada, founded in 1966, continues to operate today. It is one of the few national breed clubs to maintain a registry of HD-certified clear Samoyeds. The Hip Dysplasia Program was started in the late 1960s. The award-winning SAC bulletin, *Sammy News,* is published quarterly. The club has a "Registry of Merit Canada" Program to recognize those that have produced ten or more Canadian conformation and/or Obedience-titled offspring. For bitches, the figure is five or more. The membership totals about 100 from across Canada and elsewhere. The SAC has held a number of Specialty shows since 1975.

The SAC recognizes the CKC Top Dog award system and has a Top Stud Dog and Top Brood Bitch award program. This gives recognition to those Samoyeds being exhibited regularly throughout the calendar year. Here are the winners of the Top Dog award from 1950 through 1975:

1956—Ch. Ziska's Nansen

1957—Ch. Snow Cloud of Cedarwood

1958—Ch. Snowland Ziska Buck

1959—Ch. Frosty Ledge's Nigannmush

1960—Ch. Zandelda's Chip Off Twig

1961—Ch. Kapegah's Okanok of Nichi

1962—Ch. Snowland Ziska Buck

1963—Ch. Run-dell's Rose

1964—Ch. Mister Silver Showman of Totem

1965—Ch. Mister Silver Showman of Totem

1966—Ch. Kombo's Silver Ruff

1967—Ch. Fer-views Hi-star

1968—Ch. Fer-views Hi-star

1969—Ch. Nike Kingsley Silver

1970—Ch. Lulhaven's Snomist Ensign

1971—Ch. Lulhaven's Snomist Ensign

1972—Ch. Samko Klanlov

1973—Ch. Frostymorns Big Blizzard

1974—Ch. North Star's King's Ransom

1975—Ch. Kristik's Satan Sultan

In summary, this twenty-five year period was one of explosive growth for the Samoyed in Canada. This was followed by a leveling off to the degree that the breed had a well-established foundation of breeder-owners to take it into the next twenty-five year period.

PERIOD 4: 1975-97

In Canada the Samoyed is shown in the conformation ring in Group III—the Working Group. During the 1980s the Working Group, the largest Variety Group, was divided and Working breeds traditionally used to manage live-stock formed a new classification called the Herding Group—Group I. For a time a move was being considered to put the Samoyed in this new Group. Eventually, the CKC decided against this proposal, so today the Samoyed continues to be included in the Working Group.

The 1959 breed Standard was reviewed when the CKC lifted the ban on changes in 1991. The SAC, through its members, were invited to make sug-gested changes to the Standard over the next twelve months. The proposed changes were submitted to the CKC in 1992 and approved in that September to become effective January 1, 1993. The major revisions were in the catego-ries of height (now the same as the United States and eleven other countries), a more specific description of the forequarters, body and hindquarters and the elimination of hind dewclaws as a disqualification.

Ch. Bobmardon's Splendid Survivor, Can., Am. CD (Am., Can. Ch. Orenopac's Chaena, Am., Can. CD, TT), owned by Connie and Bob Gaskin demonstrates Flyball at the 1990 French National all-breed championship show, held in Paris. In May 1988 "Aziza" became the first Samoyed in North America to earn a Flyball title. Flyball is a fast and exciting sport for handlers, dogs and spectators. A flyball team consists of four dogs and their handlers, a box loader and a spare dog or two. In Flyball each dog on the team goes over a series of four short jumps set ten feet apart, steps on a pedal that releases a tennis ball and returns with the ball over all four jumps, where the next dog eagerly awaits his turn in a relay race of sorts against the clock.

Here are the recipients of the CKC's Top Dog Award for Samoyeds from 1975 to 1996:

1976—Ch. Jasam's Viktor

1977—Ch. Kristik's Nukiluk Chinook

1978—Ch. Samovar's True Grit

1979—Ch. Snow Fantasy Main Man

1960—Ch. Jasam's Viktor

1981—Ch. Brydawn's Winter Chinook

1982—Ch. Jasam's Viktor

1983—Ch. Orenopac's Chaena, Can., Am. CD

1984—Ch. Beretta of Kara

1985—Ch. Karon's Hasta Be Shasta

1986—Ch. Karon's Hasta Be Shasta

1987—Ch. Summerhill's Blame It On Rio

1988—Ch. Summerhill's Blame It On Rio

1989—Ch. Takenak's May King Mischief

1990—Ch. Summerhill's Saigon

1991—Ch. Snowghost's Go Better With Coke

1992—Ch. Snowghost's Go Better With Coke

1993—Ch. Takenak's Make My Day

1994—Ch. Bobmardon Quasar O'er Ladakha

1995—Ch. Samovar's Chinook Winds

1996—Ch. Bobmardon Quasar O'er Ladakha

For those breeders and/or owners who worked their Samoyeds in the Obedience ring, top awards were also made yearly. Earlier, the Samoyed as a breed was not considered to have high aptitude for Obedience competition. However, with the help of breeder-judge-author Betty McHugh of Napachee Kennels and others, that attitude has changed. The second Samoyed to earn a UD title in Canada was Ch., OTCh. Napachee's Snowdrifter. The top winning Obedience Samoyed for 1983, 1984, 1985, 1986 and 1988 was Ch., OTCh. Shebaska's Malyenki, Am. CDX, TT, HIC, bred by Frank and Helga Gruber and owned by Judy Wasserfall and Dave Cann.

The 1993 top Obedience Samoyed, Ch. Sunstar's Boginskaya, CDX, owned by Sharon and Gary Bottomley, was by Connie and Bob Gaskin's Can., Am. Ch. Orenopac's Chaena, Can., Am. CD, ROMC, one of Canada's top Samoyeds. Chaena is also the grandsire of Ch. Bobmardon Quasar O'er Ladakha, owned by Barbara Van Loon, 1994's Top Dog award for conformation.

Since 1975 other "working events" have owners of Samoyeds participating in ever increasing numbers. Events such as "Weight pulling," "Pack hiking," "Therapy dog programs," "Agility Trials," "Herding instinct testing" and "Flyball tournaments" among others. The first Samoyed to earn a Flyball title in North America was Ch. Bobmardon's Splendid Survivor, Can., Am. CD, FbD in 1988. Once again, the aforementioned Chaena was the sire of this dog.

In concluding this abbreviated history of the breed in Canada, special recognition must be given to those breeders who have been active in the breed twenty-five years or more. Some have ceased operations, and others are still raising and exhibiting their Samoyeds and are likely to do so into the twenty-first century.

Veteran Breeders (active twenty-five years or more) are as follows:

B. Selock—Al-Araf

G. Nagus—Alexann

C. and B. Gaskin—Bobmardon

E. Currie—Brialin

J. and K. Wilson—Cusona

F. Mcleod—Deshelda

I. Aitchison—Glokon

J. and S. Post—Jasam

B. and P. Stonahm—Khingham

M. Lowe—Lodale

R. Orr-Milligan—Katimavik

W. and B. McHugh—Nepachee

P. Row—Resama

P. Cummins—Sancha

F. and H. Gruber—Shebaska

J and A. Goyetee—Sundari

J. Benson—Shakapaw

K. Mclain—Summerhill

B. and S. Marshall—Triarctica

THE FUTURE

Space does not permit the listing of all the Samoyed breeders in Canada for the past seventy-five years. However, because of their past efforts and those of today's breeders, the Samoyed is now well established in Canada. Breeding lines are well established in many kennels, and breeding stock from Canada now finds its way into the United States and Europe. With the advanced technology of canine reproduction, the first registered litter in Australia using frozen semen (1992) was from a Canadian sire, Ch. Orenopac's Chaena. It is always risky to speculate, but could the future witness the formation of the North American Samoyed Association? Because there is no doubt our Samoyeds do not recognize man-made geographical boundaries.

Can., Am. Ch. Takenak's Make My Day, a multiple BIS and BISS winner, owned by Drs. Jocelyn and Homik. Cally earned an Award of Merit at the 1992 SCA National from author Dolly Ward and BISS at Canadian National held with Credit Valley, December 1994, in Toronto, Canada.

Can., Am. Ch. Vanderbilt's Secretariat, TT, CGC, TDE, a six-time BIS winner, is owned and bred by Blair and Judi Elford, Milbrook, Ontario, Canada.

From the Newfoundland provincial report from *Dogs in Canada,* December 1995, we learn more about Judi and Blair Elford than they tell us in their own letter. Their Samoyeds, Tek and Fizzz (yes three *z*'s), are featured on the cover of this popular magazine, posed on the rocks of a Newfoundland Bay with the icy blue water and sky accenting their beauty. The Elfords agree that their location is *not the hub* of dog activities, and they need to track south or east for shows. They sought people who had historic knowledge and a visionary approach to the breed that went beyond their own bloodlines! They hail Helga Gruber of Shebaska, Ontario, and Kay Hallberg of Wolf River in Wisconsin.

It was from the first combination of these two bloodlines that the Elfords produced their biggest winners to date, which are multiple BIS Can., Am. Ch. Vanderbilt's Secretariat, CGC, TDI, and his sister, Can., Am. Ch Vanderbilt's Neon Nightengale, TT, ROMC.

Judi believes their most exciting producer has been Ch. Wolf River's High As A Kite. At this writing, they anticipate more "Biscuit Bombshells" as she produced the aforementioned "cover dogs." Fizzz won futurities and sweepstakes both sides of the border. Although the Elfords have had Samoyeds for eighteen years, they list 1988 as the year they began in earnest, subsequently breeding or owning twenty-seven champions, eight homebred BIS winners and several obedience title holders.

Takenak Samoyeds is the permanently registered kennel name for Dr. Leslie Jocelyn and Dr. Lawrence Homik of St. Germain, Manitoba.

"My dad 'rescued' our first Sammy in 1970," recounts Leslie. "When she died in 1981, my parents purchased a puppy who was later to become our foundation bitch, Can. Ch. Katimavik's Wasisso Kenak, CDX (Kenah), a multi High In Trial dog.

Takenak Samoyeds began in earnest in 1985 when Lawrence and I finished medical school and moved into a house. I had met John and Kathy Ronald at the GMSF Specialty in 1984 and bred Kenah to their "Dickens" (Am. Ch. Karon's Limited Edition), a Pepper son. From this first breeding, we kept multiple BIS and BISS Am., Can. Ch. Takenak's May King Mischief, #1 Samoyed in Canada in 1989 and his sister Am., Can. Ch. Takenak's Jani. Jani, herself a Group and Specialty BOS and Brood Bitch winner, was bred twice to produce six puppies, three American champions and three Canadian champions. From her first litter to Marian and David Bentons Am., Can. Ch. Romsey's Lord of the Rings (Frodo) we kept two BIS littermates, multiple BIS and BISS Am., Can. Ch. Takenak's Make My Day (Cally) and his sister BIS Am., Can. Ch. Takenak's Ms Charity Bear (Charity). Cally is the winner of nine Canadian BIS, four BISS, and was BISS at Canada's largest show, Credit Valley KC in 1994 under Dolly Ward and took group first under judge Bob Ward. Cally, always shown by Lawrence, is the top owner-handled Samoyed in Canadian history and the only Samoyed to win the Samoyed Association of Canada National Specialty three times (1993, Joyce Moulton; 1994, Dolly Ward; 1995, Lee Wacenske). He was the #1 Samoyed in Canada in 1993 and SCA National Specialty Award of Merit winner in 1992 and 1994.

Cally's sister Charity, always shown by Leslie, is also a BIS winner and was BW from the BBE at the 1991 SCA National Specialty under Tommy Mayfield. She was also a SCA National Specialty Award of Merit winner in 1992 and 1993 and was BOS to Cally's Canadian National Specialty win in 1993.

From Jani's second breeding to Am., Can. Ch. Samkitas Speak of the Devil (Boomer) owned by Coralie Ingram and Lee Wacenske, we kept Am., Can. Ch. Takenak's Mad About You (Maddie) the 1993 SCA National Specialty WB from BBE under Bob Page and 1994 GMSF BW from BBE under Dorothy Hutchinson.

Maddie was bred to Cally in 1994 to produce Can. Ch. Takenak's What's Up Doc (Bugsy) who at seven months of age, finished her

Can., Am. Ch. Bobmarden Quasar O'BR Lakakha winning Group first at the 1994 Credit Valley show under judge Donald Booxbaum, handled by Mr. Ross. "Erik's" owner, Barbara Van Loon (second from left), and breeder, Connie Gaskin, join in the presentation. He was #11 Working Dog in Canada in 1994. *Alex Smith*

Canadian championship with Group placements over specials, multiple Best Puppy in Show awards and an Invitational Tournament win.

Lawrence and I have taken great pride in our dogs accomplishments and are particularly proud of the BBE/Top Owner handled awards.

Connie Gaskin bought her first Samoyed in 1964 and three years later registered Bobmardon Kennels with the CKC. Five years later she married her husband, Bob, who is a veterinarian, and their long association with Samoyeds was underway. Owners of the #1 Samoyed in Canada in 1983, Can., Am. Ch. Orenopac's Chaena, Can., Am. CD, ROMC, and breeders of the #1 Samoyed in 1994, Can., Am. Ch. Bobmardon Quasar O'er Ladakha, a "Chaena" grandson. Over the years they have exhibited their Samoyeds in Specialties in Canada and in the United States and have been out of the ribbons only twice out of eighteen times. Quality not quantity has been our kennel's breeding plan.

CURRENT OFFICIAL CANADIAN SAMOYED STANDARD

General Appearance—The Samoyed, being essentially a working dog, should present a picture of beauty, alertness and strength, with agility, dignity, and grace. As his work lies in the cold climate, his coat should be heavy and weather resistant, and of good quality rather than quantity. The male carries more of a "ruff" than the female. He should not be long in the back as a weak back would make him practically useless for his legitimate work, but at the same time a close-coupled body would also place him at a great disadvantage as a draught dog. Breeders should aim for the happy medium, a body not long but muscular, allowing liberty, with a deep chest and well-sprung ribs, strong arched neck, straight front and especially strong loins. Males should be masculine in appearance and deportment without unwarranted aggressiveness; bitches feminine without weakness of structure or apparent softness of temperament. Bitches may be slightly longer in back than males. They should both give the appearance of being capable of great endurance but be free from coarseness. Because of the depth of chest required, the legs should be moderately long. A very short-legged dog is to be depreciated. Hindquarters should be particularly well developed, stifles well bent and any suggestion of unsound stifles or Cowhocks severely penalized. General appearance should include movement and general conformation indicating balance and good substance.

Temperament—Alert and intelligent and should show animation. Friendly, but conservative.

Size—Dogs, 21–23½ in. (51–60 cm) at the shoulder; bitches, 19–21 in. (43–51 cm); weight in proportion to size.

Coat and Colour—The body should be well covered with a thick, close, soft and short undercoat, which harsh hair growing through it, forming the outer coat, which should stand straight away from the body and be quite free from curl. The legs should have good feathering. Colour pure white, cream, biscuit, or white and biscuit.

Head—Powerful and wedge-shaped with a broad, flat *skull, muzzle* of medium length, a tapering foreface, not too sharply defined. The stop should not be too abrupt—nevertheless well defined. *Nose* and eye rims black for preference, but may be brown. Lips black, flews should not drop predominantly at corners of the mouth. Strong jaws with level teeth *Eyes* dark, set well apart and deep with alert intelligent expression. *Ears* should not be too long but rounded at the tips, set well apart and well covered inside with hair. Hair short and smooth before the ears.

Forequarters—Forelegs straight and muscular. Good bone.

Body—Back medium in length, broad and very muscular. Bitches may be slightly longer in back than males. Chest broad and deep. Ribs well sprung, giving plenty of heart and lung room.

Hindquarters—Very muscular, stifles well let down. Feet long, flattish and slightly spread out. Soles well padded with hair.

Tail—Long and profuse, carried over the back when alert, sometimes dropped when at rest. A judge should see the tail over the back once when judging.

Gait—A Samoyed should gait with a good, well-balanced movement. He should move with an easy, agile stride that is well timed. The gait should be free with a good reach in the forequarters and a sound, driving power in the hindquarters.

Faults—Unprovoked aggressiveness. Over and under allowed height. In or out at the elbow. Cowhocks or straight stifles. Double hook in the tail. Choppy or stilted gait.

Disqualifications—*Blue eyes. Any colour other than pure white, cream, biscuit, or white and biscuit.*

The *Dogs In Canada* cover for December 1995 featured this evocative portrait of Vanderbilt High Tek of O'Elmcrest (Tek), left, and Can. Ch. Vanderbilt's Break the Seal (Fizzz), right, with owners Judi and Blair Elford near their home in Newfoundland. The Elfords are especially proud of their deep biscuit Fizzz, an all-breed BIS winner. *Barrett*

chapter 20

The Global Samoyed

THE BRITISH SCENE

For all its size, the dog world is really very small in view of Diane Chenault's contribution to the second edition of this book (*The New Complete Samoyed*, published in 1985) in which she recounted visiting her friends Alan and Anne Brownlee and their daughter Serena, in Edinburgh, Scotland. Serena is now a veterinarian, has married and has made important contributions to the UK Samoyed Association's updated Yearbook. That fantastic book is edited by Geoff Grounds and has a foreword by Angela Danvers-Smith, another "daughter" of an earlier generation of Samoyed people. We refer, of course, to Eileen Danvers of the renowned Fairvilla Samoyeds.

So it is a second generation, supported by some of "the past," that moves forward for its beautiful, chosen breed.

Regretfully, it is impossible to present all the worthy kennels and Samoyed people in every country, but we can present an overview of the Samoyed around the world.

Diane Chenault, of Orlando, Florida, visited Edinburgh, Scotland, in August 1981 and narrates her impression of the English and Scottish dogs she met and the shows she visited:

> I stayed with my friends in Edinburgh, Alan and Anne Brownlee and their daughter Serena, who shows their dogs. They have acquired two bitches from Mrs. Eileen Danvers (Fairvilla Kennels) as well as much advice and guidance from her.
>
> The night before the show was set aside for grooming as the dogs had already been bathed. The only grooming was combing and brushing, for no whiskers or feet are ever trimmed over here. Grooming tables and crates are not commonly used here, in fact, equipment like ours is not available. [*Editor's note:* Since 1981, when these notes were written, British fanciers have availed themselves of many modern items of equipment and amenities of contemporary grooming and showing.]

Eng. Ch. Grenadier of Crensa, "Scotty," owned by J. H. James, won the first of his forty-four C.C.s at fifteen months, establishing a breed record until Ch. Hurkur Jingles surpassed that formidable total with forty-six "tickets."

At the show-ground I saw another difference: no motor homes, and very few vans. It was my first benched show. There was an entry of fifty Samoyeds for Mr. J. H. James to judge. He is the owner of the famous Ch. Grenadier of Crensa.

The dogs were beautiful, much more beautiful than I had expected from the pictures I had seen of English dogs. The bitches were breathtaking. I had always preferred the males until I saw the English and Scottish bitches. The difference in coat was particularly outstanding. Apparently they do not bring them out unless they are dripping in coat. Most of the coats are longer than ours, and just a lot more of it.

Another thing you notice right off is the absence of professional handlers. The presentation of the dogs is very casual. In fact, no one uses bait, yet many of the dogs would stand motionless for some time, alertly looking at their owners. I only saw one girl stack her dog. I don't know why they have so many classes for dogs to enter, but they do, and every one seems to enter more than one class with the same dog. The judge never changed the order of the dogs he had already judged. When new dogs would come in, he would judge them and then place them among the dogs already judged. From a spectator's and picture taker's viewpoint this was good, because the dogs were in the ring a long time and it gave you a chance to study them.

Eng. Ch. Hurkur Jingles, at about fifteen months, shows the delightful expression so essential in the Samoyed. Owned by James Dougal in Scotland, he held the record for the breed with forty-six C.C.s until his son, Ch. Zamoyski Lucky Star of Ostyak, established a new record for the breed in the UK.

I saw two dogs that day in Scotland that made quite an impression on me. One is Fairvilla Snowivan of Nenetsky. He was the most beautiful Sam I have ever seen. He was three years old, and stood about twenty-two inches tall. The Fairvilla dogs are known for their gorgeous heads and coats. He was far and away the best showman of the day. The judge didn't like him as well as I, for he was Reserve Challenge that day. Mr. James put a bitch BB. Three Challenge Certificates are needed for dog to become a champion and Ivan has only two at this time. All champions are shown in the Open Class so a dog must usually beat champions to win the Challenge Certificate.

The other dog I liked was Ch. Grenadier of Crensa, called "Scotty." The best word to describe him is breathtaking. He was so special, it brought tears to my eyes just to see how great a dog he really is. I had asked the Brownlees if Mr. James, the judge, would bring Scotty for me to see. After the judging Mrs. James brought him to the judging area. She had him on a long lead and he came bounding into the crowd. He was 11 years old, but could have been any age. He was like a spirited puppy, but with great dignity. He was larger than many of the other dogs I saw that day, heavier boned and more masculine looking. He was just outstanding!

As I was watching Scotty, I was reminded of a Samoyed I saw several times on the Florida Circuit—Ch. North Starr's King Ransom. I do not know how many people have seen both dogs, but to me they were very much alike. I thought Ransom was outstanding with the same spirit and dignity. They are also the same age with similar show careers.

Betty Moody of Novaskaya fame is that rare breeder who maintains contact on both sides of the "pond." Her first dog was purchased from Eileen

Eng. Ch. Zamoyski Lucky Casanova at Roybridge (Ch. Pykra Spring Bear at Roybridge ex Ch. Zamoyski Lucky Melissa), owned by Mrs. B. Enticott (Scotland) and bred by Mrs. Hamilton. "Topper" assured himself a permanent place in breed history when he prevailed in an entry of 4,982 dogs to win the Working Group at the 1997 Crufts show (the world's largest) in Birmingham, England. He was handled to this spectacular win by Donna Fleming. *Carol Ann Johnson*

Danvers in 1970 as a pet. Her first show bitch was Fairvilla Francesca, and from her everything Novaskaya has is descended. Her second show girl was Ch. Morgana Tisha Lafay of Novaskaya who produced Ch. Novaskaya Chandra Lafay and BIS winner Novaskaya Chanina Lafay in her first litter. For eleven years Mr. and Mrs. Moody bred and showed in England before returning to the United States in 1981.

Betty Moody has judged in England since 1972, gaining championship judging status in 1980. She judged an entry of more than 200 Samoyeds at Crufts in 1996. Novaskaya bred some 47 champions worldwide, including 11 in the UK. Others are in the United States, Canada, New Zealand, Australia, Spain, Italy, Sweden, South Africa, Norway and Ireland. Novaskaya was lucky to be able to use some of the finest stud dogs in England on its bitches. Dogs like Ch. Whitewisp Lunar Module, Ch. Grenadier of Crensa, Ch. Golway Mr. Chan, Ch. Fairvilla Emperor and Whitewisp Odin all contributed to the family's success. Of all the Novaskaya breedings, Betty believes the best stud dogs were Ch. Novaskaya Imry Lafay and his sire, Ch. Novaskaya Silva King, Novaskaya Tsar Lafay and Novaskaya Silva Starsun which produced champions in eight countries including England, America and Canada. The latest dog to gain his title in England is Ch. Novaskaya Xmas Star Lafay in December 1995. His younger full sister was BISS at the British Samoyed Club championship show in October 1995 and Top Samoyed on the British Samoyed Club rating in 1995, both by Ch. Novaskaya Imry Lafay. In the United States in December 1995, Sandy and Gary Pfifer finished their bitch, out of Irish., Am., Can. Ch. Novaskaya Modesty Blaze of Ostyak.

Mr. and Mrs. J. H. James, Top Acre, Selston, Notts, England, sent us this letter of their impressions of dogs they have seen in England:

When I first saw Fairvilla Istvan of Airebis who later became an English, American, and Canadian champion as a young puppy in 1967, I thought him to be quite outstanding. We eventually mated him to a young bitch of ours, Venus of Crensa. Venus produced seven puppies, all males.

We repeated the mating to get a bitch, and would you believe it—this time Venus had six puppies, all male! They were all sold, although I kept a very handsome puppy back until last. The purchaser did not show up so I decided to keep him. This was, of course, Grenadier of Crensa, or "Scotty" as he is called.

He was quite a shy puppy and it was a long time before he settled. He finally enjoyed showing. He gained his Junior Warrant whilst still a puppy. He won his first Challenge Certificate at nineteen months, and was a champion at twenty-two months. This was a very unusual feat for those days. He was a Working Group winner twice and Reserve three times. He has been BIS at the Northern Samoyed Society twice in succession.

Scotty won forty-three C.C.s and thirty-three BBs. This was a Samoyed breed record to be broken later in the 1990s by Ch. Zamoyski Lucky Star of Ostyak with fifty-two C.C.s an all-time record. [His picture appears in the White Water Dogs section.]

Ch. Grenadier of Crensa is a sire of champions in England, South Africa and the United States, and at 12½ years, has sired a litter to one of our bitches. He is a wonderful companion in the home.

Mrs. Eileen Danvers of Leicestershire, England, has been active and successful in the breed for over forty years. Her breeding and bloodlines have contributed to the success of Novaskaya (Moody) and the Ponts' Samoyeds through Ch. Fairvilla Katrina, and of Kiskas (Mitchell), Karaholmc (Stamp) and Crensa (James) through Eng., Can., Am. Ch. Fairvilla Istvan of Airebis. It should be noted that Ch. Fairvilla Katrina was BB at Crufts three times. Mr. and Mrs. Geoff Grounds of Whitewisp have also combined the old English Kobe lines with Fairvilla breeding.

The Mitchells founded Kiskas in the early 1960s, and their linebreeding to Arctic and Snowland followed their motto: "It's not the gale but the set of the sail that steers the ship to progress."

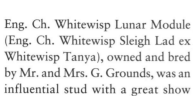

Eng. Ch. Whitewisp Lunar Module (Eng. Ch. Whitewisp Sleigh Lad ex Whitewisp Tanya), owned and bred by Mr. and Mrs. G. Grounds, was an influential stud with a great show record. *Pearce*

As judges, Gerald and Kath Mitchell have awarded C.C.s since 1975 in England and at Championship shows in Holland, America, and Spain. Gerald was a Kennel Club member, but Kiska has been silent recently.

One of the daughters of Ch. Orion (owned by the Mitchells), Lisa of Crownie, owned by Joyce and Tom Stamp, produced a litter by Cavalier of Crensa (full litter brother to Ch. Grenadier of Crensa). The Mitchells purchased a male puppy from this litter that they were enticed to sell to the authors in 1972. He became Ch. Kiskas Karaholme Cherokee, who was the SCA's Top Stud Dog in 1980. It is interesting to note that Cherokee was born in 1970 and True Grit (owned by the Mitchells) in 1976. They have almost identical breeding, their sires are litter brothers and their dams half-sisters by Orion.

The Stamps (Karaholme) have been in Samoyeds since 1968. In critiques, Karaholme Samoyeds are described as excellent movers and of the essential type, with good heads and excellent temperament!

Karaholme Sara won the Dog of The Year Award at the Scunthorpe Canine Association in December 1981.

Joyce and Tom Stamp write: "In being owned by Samoyeds, we have met some lovely people who became friends. The world of dogs is also a human world with all that entails. One of my favourite quotations, 'Beauty is Truth, and Truth is Beauty, that is all you know and all you need to know,' epitomizes the Samoyed breed."

Mrs. Muriel Hopkin was their doyen of the Samoyed world. The Stamps' dogs are linebred to her Kim Of Crownie. Mrs. Hopkin's knowledge and hard work was the foundation of their stock. Karaholme is a small kennel aiming at breeding good Samoyeds with soundness, type, movement and balance. Tom states, "We are very proud to have bred Ch. Kiskas Karaholme Cherokee in the first litter with Lisa."

In Scotland, James Dougall, Hurkur Samoyeds, sent these notes:

Ch. Hurkur Jingles was born on Christmas day thus his name. He had a will and character of his own; a handful in the nicest possible way. The best part of the day was the evening when he would wait until Jim (Hamilton) decided to watch television whereupon he promptly planted himself on Jim's lap for the rest of the evening.

Jingles was a great winner in the show ring with an arrogant *I'm here* quality about him. During his show career he won forty-six C.C.s from forty-three different judges, BIS at the Samoyed Association Specialty over 232 Samoyeds; BIS at Southern Counties over approximately 11,000 dogs; BIS at Birmingham over approximately 13,000 dogs were among his numerous wins. He was #1 Samoyed in the UK from 1981 to 1985.

Sadly, Ch. Hurkur Jingles died of gastric torsion the day after winning BB at Crufts for the second time as the 1980s ended. Ch. Hurkur Jingles was the sire of several champions, including: Zamoyski Lucky Star of Ostyak (1995 breed record holder); Zamoyski Lucky Claudia, Zamoyski Lucky Mascot and Can. Ch. Hurkur Hentler and Zamoyski Challenge. Ch. Heroine of Hurkur (Ch. Hurkur Hero ex Zamoyski Lucky Pendant) was a litter sister to Ch. Zamoyski Lucky Star of Ostyak, who was eleven years old in 1995.

Ch. Hurkur Harvester was Best of Breed at Crufts 1990. Ch. Zamoyski Lucky Claudia (Ch. Hurkur Jingles ex Ch. Fairvilla Imperial Sophia) was one of the all-time favorites of James Dougall.

Ch. Lucky Dexter of Zamoyski (Ch. Zamoyski Challenge ex Ch. Fairvilla Imperial Claire) boasts fourteen C.C.s and proved to be an excellent stud.

Most recently, James Dougall was on "cloud nine" over owning a two-year-old bitch, Hathe of Hurkur, who is linebred back to Jingles/Nicholas ex Lucky Dexter of Zamoyski.

Ch. Hurkur Harvester (Ch. Hurkur Jingles ex Ch. Fairvilla Imperial Sophia) at age two years. Harvester was BB at Crufts 1990 for owner James Dougall.

Ch. Zamoyski Lucky Claudia, a favorite of owner James Dougall.

Another American fancier, June Smith, writes:

Without a doubt, the best Samoyed I ever saw was Eng. Ch. Hurkur Jingles. I suppose this is so because physically he was closest in appearance to Ch. Americ of Kobe, my ideal Samoyed, but really it goes beyond that. It was Jingles himself that was so special.

Granville Pyne has written a famous essay on Ch. Kara Sea and how fifty years later he is as clear in his mind's eye as though it were yesterday. In this essay he states that Kara Sea was quite simply "other worldly." If one looks at pictures of Kara Sea one may see just a dog until one looks into his eyes! What wonderful eyes they are! No words are necessary, understanding is immediate.

Jingles was like that too, "otherworldly" and yet wholly of this world. He was not without faults; a lighter eye than preferred, but he inspired awe and no one who saw him would take their eyes from him. He was simply mesmerizing!

Amazingly, Ch. Hurkur's Jingles produced offspring that were almost his equal. His progeny are the foundation of several kennels, and his legacy of beautiful heads, coats and, most important, wonderful Samoyed temperament will be seen for many years to come in Sams in the United Kingdom.

Derek and Thelma Pont began their Samont Kennel when they bought their first dog Brnewin Andreyv, a son of Fairvilla Istvan Of Airebis, in 1969. Their next purchase was Ch. Fairvilla Katrina, which was also by Istvan out of Ch. Fairvilla Michelle and bred by Eileen Danvers. Katrina did a great deal of winning and went Reserve BIS at the Leeds Championship show—a rare event at that time.

Their present winning dogs are Ch. Samont Vanya of Aeylish, owned by Kerry Main, BB at Crufts 1995, and Ch. Karazoe Snow Kazam of Samont, bred by Mr. and Mrs. John Sharpe. Kaz won the Dog C.C. and BOS at Crufts

Irish, Am., Can. Ch. Novaskaya Blaze of Ostyak (Ch. Zamoyski Lucky Star of Ostyak cx Ch. Fairvilla Silver Jewel), owned by Betty Moody.

1995, was the top Samoyed in 1992 and has fourteen C.C.s. The Ponts have bred four English champions up to the time of this writing.

Beryl Grounds first had a Samoyed called Haakon of Asgard in 1931. With husband Geoff, their Whitewisp kennel was founded making important contributions to the Samoyed. The most famous of their dogs was Ch. Whitewisp Lunar Module who was not campaigned extensively but was BB at Crufts and was among those considered in the Working group. He also had a Crufts BOS and sired ten English champions (the record is twelve) and others overseas. These include Eng., Am., Can., Int. Ch. Whitewisp Snow Crystal, owned by Betty Moody, and Danish, Int. Ch. Whitewisp Salavador, which helped restart the breed in Denmark. He also sired Ch. Samovar Will O the Wisp, BB at Crufts for three consecutive years.

Geoff Grounds served as editor of the 1995 *Samoyed Association Book*. It contains a host of wonderful articles by many dedicated, knowledgeable people, including "The Breed Standard Explained by Beryl Grounds," "Life-long Care by Dr. Serena Sykes," "Pedigrees, Treatments and Therapies," "Memories of Kobe, Arctic and Snowland," "The Breed Abroad Standards and Services" and much more. Angela Danvers-Smith, president, wrote an important foreword. The book has a charming "pixieish" quality along with all its important information. Perhaps it shows the exact difference between the American show scene with its emphasis on winning compared with the "enjoy it all as you go" point of view typical of the British dog Fancy.

The new Samoyed Association book includes something wonderful to delight every Samoyed fan, and we recommend it as an indispensable addition to your library. Together with our book, you have the nucleus of an excellent reference shelf on our favorite breed. You can order *The Samoyed*, published by The Samoyed Association, from The Kennel Club 1–5, Clarges

Street, Piccadilly, London, W1Y 8AB. It is in its fifth edition, is 416 pages, and costs $35.00.

What is proved by both our books is that the keepers and protectors of the Samoyed have done a good job, and Samoyeds remain essentially the same the world over.

THE KENNEL CLUB STANDARD FOR THE SAMOYED (1995)

GENERAL APPEARANCE—Most striking. Medium and well balanced. Strong active and graceful, free from coarseness but capable of great endurance.

CHARACTERISTICS—Intelligent, alert full of action. "Smiling expression."

TEMPERAMENT—Displays affection toward all mankind. Unprovoked nervousness or aggression highly undesirable.

HEAD AND SKULL—Head powerful, wedge shaped, with broad flat skull, muzzle medium length, tapering foreface not too sharply defined. Lips black. Hair short and smooth before ears. Nose black for preference, but may be brown or flesh-coloured.

EYES—Almond shaped, set slanted, medium to dark brown, set well apart with alert, intelligent expression. Eye rims unbroken black. Light or black eyes undesirable.

EARS—Thick, not too long, slightly rounded at tips, set well apart, and well covered inside with hair. Fully erect in adults.

MOUTH—Jaws strong with a perfect, regular, and complete sissors bite, i.e., upper teeth closely overlapping the lower teeth and set square to the jaws.

NECK—Strong not too short, and proudly arched.

FOREQUARTERS—Shoulders well laid, legs straight and muscular with good bone and not too short.

BODY—Back medium in length, broad and very muscular with exceptionally strong loin. Chest deep but not too broad, well sprung ribs, giving plenty of heart and lung room.

HINDQUARTERS—Very muscular, stifles well angulated, viewed from the rear, legs straight and parallel with well let down hocks. Cow hocks or straight stifles highly undesirable.

FEET—Long, flattish, slightly spread and well feathered. Soles well cushioned with hair. Round cat feet highly undesirable.

TAIL—Long, profusely coated, carried over the back and to side when alert, sometimes dropped when at rest.

GAIT/MOVEMENT—Moves freely with strong agile drive, showing power and elegance.

COAT—Body should be well covered with thick, close, soft and short undercoat, with harsh but not wiry hair growing through it, forming weather resistant outer coat, which should stand away from the body and be free from curl.

COLOUR—Pure white, white and biscuit, cream, outer coat silver tipped.

SIZE—Dogs: 51–56 cms (20—22 inches) at shoulder. Bitches: 46–51 cms (18–20 inches) at shoulder. Weight in proportion to size.

FAULTS—Any departure from the foregoing points should be considered a fault and the seriousness with which the fault should be regarded should be in exact proportion to its degree.

NOTE—Male animals should have two apparently normal testicles fully descended into the scrotum.

BRITISH SAMOYED CLUBS' JOINT CODE OF ETHICS

This code has been agreed on by the four Samoyed clubs in Great Britain as acceptable guidelines to all who wish to own or breed Samoyeds.

BREED STANDARD—All breeding stock should follow closely the official Kennel Club Standard in all aspects with particular attention being paid to temperament of the dogs to meet the first characteristic of "displaying affection toward all mankind." Dogs which manifestly depart from the Breed Standard are not suitable for breeding.

BREEDING PURPOSES—All breeding should include the objective of improving the overall standard of Samoyeds. Equal weight should be given to type, temperament, health and soundness. Nervous or aggressive dogs are not satisfactory as pets or breeding stock.

REGISTRATION—All dogs used for breeding should be registered with the Kennel Club and full details of their pedigrees should be known.

PLANNING OF LITTERS—No one should breed a litter unless he or she has the right facilities for dam and litter and the time to devote proper care and attention to rearing the puppies and the well-being of the dam. There should be some demand for puppies before the bitches are mated.

BREEDING AGE—Bitches should not be mated before 15–18 months of age and not before the second season, and no later than the fifth year for the first time.

WELFARE OF THE BITCH—No bitch should be mated at every season. Bitches should not have litters on consecutive seasons. No bitch should have more than 3 or 4 litters and a bitch should not be bred from beyond her 8th birthday.

STUD DOGS—Only entire dogs should be used at stud and not before 12 months of age. Members who own stud dogs should be aware of the need to improve the breed and enhance the reputation of the sires. They should refuse stud services to inferior specimens of the breed and to owners who have neither the time nor the facilities to rear litters.

PUPPY SALES—Prospective buyers of puppies should be screened for suitability and abiliy to provide long-term homes. They should be advised of the characteristics and problems of the breed. These include the need for grooming, exercise and or family contact.

PUPPY INFORMATION—No puppy should leave the breeder before 7 weeks of age. Each purchaser of a Samoyed puppy should be provided at the time of sale with an accurate pedigree, a Kennel Club transfer form and registration certificates. He/she should also receive a diet sheet and information about training, worming, and inoculation. Advice should be given about suitable books and membership of a Breed Club.

PUPPY VARIATIONS—No puppy which has any physical defect or shows a clear departure from the Standard should be sold without the buyer being made fully aware of the defect or departure from the Standard. Breeders should replace any puppy which develops a defect to such a degree that on the advice of two independent veterinary surgeons the puppy has to be put down, or they should refund the purchase price. The breeder is to be properly notified before any such action is taken. It is advisable for breeders to take out insurance coverage on any puppy they breed for the first 6 weeks in its new home.

UNWELCOME SALES—No Samoyeds should knowingly be sold to laboratories, pet shops or dealers in dogs, or to persons known to sell puppies to any of the above. Owners of stud dogs should not provide stud services for such persons. No puppy should be sold or offered as a prize in any raffle or competition. No puppies should be sold to countries where they are not protected from anti-cruelty laws and where there are known social and ownership problems with dogs.

AFTER SALES—It should be impressed on buyers that they should contact the breeder in the event of problems with the puppies. Breeders should make every effort to assist in these circumstances. Breeders should be prepared to make adequate arrangements for re-housing if it becomes necessary. They should cooperate with the breed rescue organizations to the best of their ability,

HEREDITARY DEFECTS—Breeders should not knowingly breed from any stock which has hereditary diseases. It is advised that all breeding stock be x-rayed for hip dysplasia by a qualified veterinary surgeon. It is advised that all x-ray plates should be submitted to the BVA (British Veterinary Association)* for hip scoring even if the hips are poor so that a true picture of HD can be assessed.

ADVERTISING—Advertisements for stock should always be honest, factual and without exaggeration or distortion.

CONDUCT—Officers and committees of the four breed clubs are always ready to help with members' problems wherever possible. Members should conduct themselves at all times to reflect credit on the ownership of dogs. Members should not allow their dogs to roam and cause a nuisance to other people. They should accept responsibility of cleaning up after their dogs in public places.

---

*The counterpart in America is the Orthopedic Foundation for Animals (OFA).

The four breed clubs in the UK are:

1. The Samoyed Association—founded 1920.
2. The British Samoyed Club—founded 1932.
3. The Northern Samoyed Society—founded 1962.
4. The Samoyed Breeders and Owners League—founded 1980.

There is a Breed Liaison council that operates under the aegis of the Kennel Club, which has two representatives of each club serving on it. The above-named Clubs have elected Beryl Grounds as the breed representative to the Kennel Club. She has filled this post for many years and continues to act in that capacity. Her husband, Geoff, is editor of the fifth edition of *The Samoyed,* published in 1995 by The Samoyed Association (the first edition was 1971). Geoff Grounds's address is TIMBERLEE, 137 High Street, Riseley, Bedford MK44 1DR, England.

DENMARK

From Denmark we know that Kaissa Petrowa was Kirsten Jorgensen's foundation bitch. Kirsten then went to Birgit Hillerby of the Explorer Kennel in Sweden and later to the Wards in the United States to purchase a compatible stud. Mardee Ward-Fanning sent Sir Jonah of Banff, a grandson of Ice Way's Ice Breaker.

Jonah's top winning son, Int., Dk. Ch. Kaissa's First Son of Jonah, has produced well in Europe. Another Sir Jonah son is the well-known French Ch. Copra de Etoille de Neighes d'Or, bred and owned by Mme. Sylvette Fritch in France. Currently being exhibited is Kaissa's Balalaika Boy JR, a Jonah son out of Arnukska. He is the first Samoyed Obedience Champion in Denmark and shows Whitewisp Lunar Module through linebreeding of Int., Dk. Ch. Whitewisp Salvador.

A Jonah daughter, Int., Dk. Ch. von der Diamantenschlucht is now twelve years old. In 1995, she was Veteran of the Year, and her son Walter has been following in her winning footsteps. Another of Jonah's grandson's named Kaissa's Charley Chaplin is doing well in Italy for Roberto Benedetti, and a daughter of Ischka Star named Kaissa's Diana Ross is one of Giancarlo Mazzukato's foundation bitches in Italy.

In Finland, Tuula Hamalainen, of Kennel Humoresque, has imported semen from Kaissa's First Son of Jonah. Members of the resulting litter, including Humoresque Son of a Clown and Humoresque I'm a Clown Too, have enjoyed successful show careers.

Int., Danish Ch. Bjelki v.d. Diamantenschlucht (Int. Danish Ch. Sir Jonah of Banff ex Kalinka), owned by K. Jorgensen and H. Buus in Denmark and bred by Herr Klein in Germany.

Int., Danish Ch. Sammie's Kaissa Petrowa (Int., Danish Ch. Whitewisp Salvador ex Int., Danish Ch. Ishka of Kamassin), bred by Mrs. K. Stelkhahn, was the foundation bitch for Kirsten Jorgensen's Kaissa Kennel in Denmark.

Currently, two Jonah granddaughters are winning: Kaissa's Spring Jasmine and her sister, Kaissa's Spring Joey, the European winner in Courtrai, Belgium, November 1995. They are owned by Tina and Frits Thomsen in Denmark. A Jonah grandson was the 1995 Amsterdam winner, Kaissa's Mister Hot Igloo for owner, Mrs. Anca Molenaar in Holland.

Kirsten Jorgensen in Denmark had for some years Bubbling Oak's Fast Break who is now back in the United States. Bubbling Oak's U.S. Ambassador and Bubbling Oak's Vanilla Shake also made their presence felt in competition. Kaissa still owns Polar Mist Mr. Margeaux, nine years old and still going strong as a stable stud dog.

The newest imports at this writing are Borge's young American-bred male, Whitecliff Karu Joint Venture, already a Danish champion, and Vanderbilt Miss Marple and Vanderbilt White Oak, from Canada, who carry the line from Wolf River.

From Werner Degenhardt, in Brazil, Birgit Hillerby and Kirsten Jorgensen imported Jushka's Graf of Bjelkiers, a son of Ch. Hoof 'n Paw's In the Buff

Danish Ch. Kaissa's Wake Up Walter and a seven-week-old puppy with owner Kirsten Jorgensen. This attractive group was photographed immediately following Walter's good win in Verona, Italy, in 1990.

and Penasco's Bjelkier's Knight, which goes back to Hoof 'n Paw's Northern Knight.

In 1993 Kirsten Jorgensen linebred from JR and a daughter of Ch. Kaissa's Beaujolais Primeur, which produced Kaissa's Coco of Junior and the male Kaissa's Bounty of Junior, both quality Samoyeds with excellent hips and clear eyes.

THE NETHERLANDS

A. A. Paauwe writes from the Netherlands:

> For years I have been a Samoyed fancier. At this moment I am the owner of two Samoyed dogs, both champions. The older one is Ch. Samoya's Hanson, a son of the well-known Ch. Lucky Star of Ostyak, the breed record holder in England. His mother is from the well-known Snowcryst kennels.
>
> The Samoya kennel (founded in 1924) traces its roots mainly to English stock (Snowcryst and Lealsam), but includes crossings to Ch. Sir Jonah of Banff. A daughter of Sir Jonah and Ch. Samoya's Hannah is Dutch, Belg., Lux. and Int. Ch. Samoya's Kendu a top winning bitch in Holland.

There are no Samoyed specialty clubs, as we know them, in Germany, Belgium or Switzerland. The Sams there, together with all other Nordic breeds, are combined into one club, but they are all shown across neighboring borders in each others' countries. The Scandinavian countries cannot participate in this interchange of shows because of quarantine regulations.

Contact by Samoyed fanciers from the Netherlands with the British clubs is quite good even though showing is not possible due to quarantine regulations, but many Dutch owners are also members of the British clubs and vice versa.

AUSTRALIA

Peggy and Lloyd Winger of Syanaria Samoyeds began in 1980 when they added a Samoyed to their family of Border Collies that Penny had been training in obedience and for Agility Trials. Lloyd had always wanted a Samoyed as a pet, but when the Wingers went looking, the breeder convinced them that it would be nice to have a dog that could hold its own in dog show competition as well as be a pleasant pet. They agreed.

The show prospect they chose, Ch. Novaskaya Imry Lafay, became an instant winner as a puppy. In the course of his career, he won fifteen C.C.s and was BIS at the Samoyed Breeders and Owners League championship show. He was also first in the Non-Sporting Group at the South Wales championship show. In 1989, Imry won the C.C. and BB at Crufts, and in 1991, at age eleven, he returned to Crufts to win the C.C. and BOS. In 1995, Imry won the Stud Dog Award with five champions: Ch. Arianhrod Medi Arawn, Ch. Whitewisp Sylvia Rebel of Novaskaya, Ch. Syanaria Silver Emperor, Ch. Novaskaya Xmas Star Lafay and Ch. Sorcerer's Apprentice.

Imry's daughter, Novaskaya Tisha Lafay was BIS at the British Samoyed Ass'n. championship show in 1995. The Wingers now have an Imry grandson, Novaskaya Kharavitch Lafay, in whom they have great hopes.

Julie Oates registered her Elgianto prefix in 1964. At present she has twelve Samoyeds and one Shiba Inu. Her current standard bearer and one of Australia's top winning Samoyeds, Ch. Elgianto Heza Star (grandson of Ch. Elgianto Maska), won the Gold Cup for BIS at the Samoyed Club of Victoria 1995 championship show. He is also #1 Samoyed in Victoria, #1 dog in the Utility Group in Victoria and the only Samoyed to be a finalist in the Victorian Top Show Dog of the Year competition. His kennelmate, Ch. Elgianto Royal Showoff, by English imported Novaskaya Royal Blaze, was #2 Samoyed in Victoria for 1995.

Novaskaya Royal Blaze is co-owned by Julie Oates and Mrs. Mary Fairley. He has been selectively mated to bitches strongly bred on the venerable Kobe line. This approach has produced BISS Ch. Zamora Royal Krystalmint, Ch. Zamora Royal Krystalcharm, Ch. Zamora Royal Krystalmiss, Ch. Elgianto Royal Showoff, Ch. Elgianto Royal Sensation, BISS, and Ch. Tobalsk Royal Secret.

Silvasam Samoyeds, owned by Valerie and Paul Jackson, was established in 1973. The Jacksons describe their kennel as small but select with an

Aust. Ch. Kalina Imperial King, a big winner and excellent producer owned by Miss Glenda Hustwaite, was Australia's top Samoyed for three years.

Ch. Silvasam Road to Fame, owned by Mr. and Mrs. Paul Jackson, was an all-breed BIS winner before reaching nine months of age.

Ch. Samoya's Hanson, a son of Eng. Ch. Lucky Star of Ostyak, owned by A. A. Paauwe, the Netherlands.

outstanding show record. Their original stock was based on England's famous Kobe Kennels. The Jacksons have bred thirty-four champions, owning and showing ten others; eight became Australian and New Zealand champions. In recent years they have imported six dogs from New Zealand to enhance their breeding program. Val is an all-breed judge with demands on her services around the world, including the United States.

Eleanor Maitland from Australia and Glenys Grey are in partnership in the prefix Kimchatka in New Zealand, and it is also registered in Australia since the Maitlands moved over to Australia about 1988. David and Dianne Brown are partners with Eleanor Maitland and correspond via the Internet with many Samoyed fanciers in the United States so they keep abreast of the "news." Mrs. Maitland is approved for all breeds in Australia and judges extensively. She still keeps in touch with Brenda Romero (ex Blewitt) who now resides in California. They still have NZ Ch. Novaskaya Silva Sabya (Imp. UK), which the authors saw in quarantine at the Williams Quarantine Kennels in Aukland, NZ. Silva Saba only had three litters from which she produced twelve champions and five BIS winners. She said "Bob was 'Spot on' in his predictions" at that time. Bob Ward selected puppies as quality dogs.

Zamora Samoyeds in Ballarat, Victoria, Australia, was founded in 1969 by Miss Glenda Hustwaite. She began with Ch. Kalina Imperial King, a son of the import, Eng., Aust. Ch. Imperial Rebel of Kobe. King bore the stamp of his famous Kobe forebears and was Top Samoyed of Victoria for three consecutive years. In 1972, he won the coveted Gold Cup for BISS. He also produced well, and many Zamora ladies likewise contributed well. A BIS-winning King grandson won in Adelaide in 1989 and 1990 and Sydney in 1989.

In 1991, the valuable inheritance of Novaskaya Royal Blaze was included in Zamora breeding. A litter from Blaze and Zamora Hilton's Huckster produced Ch. Zamora Royal Krystalmint. She was Best Exhibit in Show at the Samoyed club of Victoria (SCV) Golden Anniversary Show under Christin Lang, Spitz specialist from Norway, in 1994. Kystalmint has produced an all-breeds BIS son, Ch. Kaizen Mistafire, for her owners, Ken and Vicki Ullman of Canberra.

Although breeding only infrequently in its twenty-six-year history, Zamora has often won the coveted "Most Successful Breeder Award"—in 1978, 1984, 1986, 1987 and at the Melbourne Royal in 1988 and 1982. Most recently, Krystalmint was the dam of nine puppies by Elgianto Heza Star, giving Miss Hustwaite good reason to look forward to future successes.

There were undoubtedly Samoyeds in Australia earlier than the 1930s because Antarctic Buck was known in 1909, but the earliest Sam that was fully documented and accepted for the pedigree book was Ch. Yukon Queen, whelped February 2, 1929, and imported from Miss Leonard in England by L. Maike. She was by Snow Elf ex Snowvit. Yukon Queen was the dam of the first Australian-born title holder, Ch. Blackeyed Susan. However, at the

Ch. Vashka Stormcloud, a top producing bitch owned by Eli Maitland.

Ch. Novaskaya Imry Lafay, owned by Mr. and Mrs. Lloyd Winger, has won fifteen C.C.s and a BISS and was BB at Crufts.

NZ Grand Ch., Aust. Ch. Kamchatka The Godfather, owned by Eli Maitland.

Ch. Tobolsk Royal Secret, BISS Samoyed Club of A.C.T. 1995, owned by Julie Oates.

1927 Royal Agricultural Society of New South Wales annual show, the results include in All Other Varieties Not Specified, under forty-five pounds—first in Open Dog, Prince Zero, whelped November 1925, by Zero ex Snowqueen (Samoyede), owned by Mrs. S. Hart.

Interestingly, Mr. and Mrs. Willis report that the largest show entries are at the breed club shows, not the Royal shows because the breed club shows have a full seven-class entry and are held on weekends. The Royal Agricultural shows are held on weekdays in conjunction with all types of exhibitions. Only four classes are offered in each sex: puppy, junior, intermediate and open, and they are open only for champions and dogs under three years of age. Thus entries at the Royal Shows average approximately 60–80 Samoyeds, whereas the club championship shows average 100–110 Samoyeds.

To acquire an Australian championship, a dog needs to earn 100 points. Points are obtained as follows:

Five points are awarded for each Challenge Certificate, plus 1 point for each dog/bitch defeated. (For example, if there were 5 dogs and 7 bitches in competition, the Dog Challenge would be worth 10 points, and the Bitch Challenge 12 points.)

A Best in Group is worth 5 points plus 1 point for each dog/bitch defeated in the Group, up to a maximum 25 points for each show.

Ch. Elgianto Heza Star, all-breed BIS and BISS winner, owned by Julie Oates, was the only Samoyed to make it to the Finals of Victoria's Top Show Dog competition for 1995.

A Best in Show win earns no points unless the Group win carried fewer than 25 points, in which case the dog's count is supplemented up to 25 points (taking into account the dogs beaten in other Groups).

Dogs are bred and judged by the English Standard, and this Standard cannot be changed or altered except by permission or instruction of the English Kennel Club.

AUSTRALIAN STANDARD FOR THE SAMOYED

CHARACTERISTICS—The Samoyed is intelligent, alert, full of action but above all displaying affection towards all mankind.

GENERAL APPEARANCE—The Samoyed, being essentially a working dog should be strong and active and graceful, and as his work lies in cold climates his coat should be heavy and weather-resisting. He should not be too long in back, as a weak back would make him practically useless for his legitimate work; but at the same time a cobby body, such as a Chow's would also place him at a great disadvantage as a draught dog. Breeders should aim for the happy medium, viz., a body not long, but muscular, allowing liberty, with a deep chest and well sprung ribs, strong neck proudly arched, straight front and exceptionally strong loins. Both dogs and bitches should give the appearance of being capable of great endurance but should be free from coarseness. A full grown dog should stand abut 52 cm (21 inches) at the shoulder. On account of the depth of chest required the legs should be moderately long, a very short legged dog is to be deprecated. Hindquarters should be particularly well developed, stifles well angulated and any suggestion of unsound stifles or cowhocks severely penalised.

HEAD AND SKULL—Head powerful and wedge-shaped with a broad, flat skull, muzzle of medium length, a tapering foreface not too sharply defined. Lips black. Hair short and smooth before the ears. Nose black for preference, but may be brown or flesh-coloured. Strong jaws.

EYES—Almond shaped, medium to dark brown in colour, set well apart with alert and intelligent expression. Eyerims should be black and unbroken.

EARS—Thick, not too long and slightly rounded at the tips, set well apart and well covered inside with hair. The ears should be fully erect in the grown dog.

MOUTH—Upper teeth should just overlap the underteeth in a scissor bite.

NECK—Proudly arched.

FOREQUARTERS—Legs straight and muscular with good bone.

BODY—Back medium in length, broad and very muscular. Chest broad and deep ribs well sprung, giving plenty of heart and lung room.

HINDQUARTERS—Very muscular, stifles well angulated, cow hocks or straight stifles very objectionable.

FEET—Long, flattish and slightly spread out. Soles well cushioned with hair.

GAIT—Should move freely with a strong agile drive showing power and elegance.

TAIL—Long and profuse, carried over the back when alert; sometimes dropped when at rest.

COAT—The body should be well covered with a thick, close, soft and short undercoat, with harsh hair growing through it, forming the outer coat, which should stand straight away from the body and be free from curl.

COLOUR—Pure white; white and biscuit; cream.

WEIGHT AND SIZE—Dogs 51 cm (20 ins) to 56 cm (22 ins) at the shoulder. Bitches 46 cm (18 ins) to 51 cm (20 ins) at the shoulder. Weight in proportion to size.

FAULTS—Big ears with little feathering. Drop ears. Narrow width between ears. Long foreface. Blue or very light eyes. A bull neck. A long body. A soft coat; a wavy coat; absence of undercoat. Slack tail carriage; should be carried well over the back, though it may drop when the dog is at rest. Absence of feathering. Round, cat-like feet. Black or black spots. Severe unprovoked aggressiveness. Any sign of unsound movement.

NEW ZEALAND

Mrs. Val Freer of Nikara Kennels, New Zealand, purchased her first Samoyed from Mrs. Danvers in 1977. Her name was Ch. Kamelia of Fairvilla, and Mrs. Freer was extremely lucky to have such a quality bitch as her foundation. This foundation bitch won twelve C.C.s in all and gave Mrs. Freer "the bug" to have more. Ch Krishe Khloe o Nikara (Nikara Kristal ex Golway Areus) was her most successful show dog—top puppy in the breed and the winner

Eng. Ch. Krishe Khloe of Nikara, owned by Mrs. Val Freer of the renowned Nikara Samoyeds, holds seventeen C.C.s.

Ch. Kalisa Christmas Knight (Aust. Ch. Samway's Summer Knight ex Ch. Kalisa The Angel), owned by Lyn and Gary Carleton and bred by Elizabeth Clausen.

Eng. Ch. Kamelia of Fairvilla has won twelve C.C.s and six Reserve CCs for owner Mrs. Val Freer.

of seventeen C.C.s overall in between producing three litters. Of her four champions, one went to Finland, Ch. Nikara Lord Leon of Zoox.

Over eighteen years, Nikara has bred thirteen litters. The aim has been to improve with good construction and movement, coats of correct texture, and, of course, good temperament. Nikara has had quite a successful time and, of course, the "knocks" that any successfull breeder learns to live with. At the end of the day, Val Freer loves them whether they win or lose.

The latest edition, Taronakits Kustom Maid for Nikara, gained a C.C. at ten months, has had numerous Best Puppy in Show wins and recently gained her Junior Warrant.

Elizabeth Clausen began Kalisa in 1985 with the purchase of her first bitch, Zaminka Sun Siouxsie in 1985.

To date Kalisa's most successful dogs are Ch. Kalisa Christmas Knight and Ch. Kalisa the Sun Stunner, both all-breed BIS and Specialty winners.

Ch. Kalisa the Angel joined this distinguished company by winning Reserve BIS all breeds, following in the footsteps of her granddam Ch. Novaskaya Silva Sabya, an all-breeds BIS and Specialty winner.

Elizabeth Clausen's goal is to produce Samoyeds that are lovely to look at, and easy to live with and have the capacity to work.

The history of the breed in New Zealand can best be traced through the imports, starting with the introduction of dogs from the Antarctic expeditions at the turn of the century. Captain Scott was known to have presented five Samoyeds to the Wellington Zoo, and imports from England and Denmark were later added to the group. The zoo bred its last litter in 1941, and its Samoyeds were then sold to the public, leading to an influx of breeding stock to establish the breed further. Other dogs were believed to be smuggled into New Zealand by any means possible.

The first Samoyeds that were registered with the N.Z. Kennel Club were in 1903. The N.Z. Kennel Club adopted the Standard of the breed from the Kennel Club (England), and it remains the official document. The first Samoyed to gain a championship title was Mrs. W. Richard's Ch. Doctor. The first Samoyed bitch to gain the championship title was Mr. Brain's Ch. White Princess of the Yukon. In New Zealand, the Samoyed is classified in the Non-Sporting Group.

Samoyeds are of a high standard in this country, and there is no doubt that the importation of Australian and English breeding stock on a regular basis has contributed to the caliber and success of contemporary specimens.

Note that due to the rabies quarantine in the United Kingdom, animals are in quarantine for one year before they are released to their new owners. The cost of transportation is usually more than the purchase price of the dog.

Ch. Kalisa The Sun Stunner (NZ Grand Ch., Aust. Ch. Kimchatka The Godfather ex Taminka Sun Siouxsie), a 1995 all-breeds BIS and BISS winner, owned and bred by Elizabeth Clausen (Kalisa Samoyeds).

BRAZIL

The revival of the Samoyed breed in Brazil was brought about by Werner Degenhardt, Bjelkier Kennels of Sao Paulo, Brazil.

In 1984 the Degenhardts took their bitch, Jenisej's Rebecca of Bjelkiers to be bred to Am., Mex. The Ch. Hoof 'n Paw's White Knight. From this breeding, they raised a litter of two. The male, Rebecca's Orion of Bjelkiers, stayed with them. The bitch, Rebecca's Olinda of Bjelkiers, was sold to Marie-Louise and Borge Lakjer in Espergaerde, Denmark.

Another Bjelkiers export, The Samoyed Blue, by Sabarkas Kurgan of Silvertip out of Jenisej's Zahrina of Bjelkiers, went to Mrs. Renata Fossati, Corno Bianca Kennels in Durfo, near Milan, Italy.

Brazil has adopted the American Standard. Werner Degenhardt reports the difference in Best in Show in Brazil. "From all the Group winners a Best in Show is chosen; then the dog that was Second in that Group comes in as a replacement to compete for Reserve; now a 2nd Best in Show is chosen; again the second to that dog returns as a replacement to compete for 3rd Best in Show and this continues until 4th place Best in Show is selected."

Brazil is a member of the Federacion Cynologique Internationale (FCI), and CACIBs (Certificate for Aptitude for Championship of International Beauty) are awarded only at International shows under FCI rules. To become a champion in Brazil, a dog must win five and a bitch must win four CACIBs under different judges. The judge may award one certificate for each twenty-five dogs in the ring—one certificate for the best dog and one for the best bitch. For the completion of a championship, a dog must win at least one Best of Breed.

To become a Grand Brazilian champion, a dog must win sixty points and a bitch forty points. No more than five points may be awarded in either sex at any show. At least three Bests of Breed must be won under three different judges.

SPAIN

Carmen Navarro, of Madrid, Spain writes of her kennels:

> Villaodon has dedicated the past ten years to the selective breeding of Samoyeds. Our first bitch was White Ball (Swordale and Fairvilla breeding) from which we have created our own line. Another Spanish Kennel, Garcibravo, imported Ch. El-Al's Elegant Prince Charly who carried lines from Ch. Kondako's Dancing Bear. After studying those two pedigrees, we put him to White Ball.

Our dreams resulted in Span., Gibr., And. Ch. Blanco Lobo de Villaodon, a multiple Specialty winner and Span., Port., Int. Ch. Bogart de Villaodon, four times BIS in international shows and 1993 BISS winner of Purina's Absolute Best Dog of Spain, the one and only Samoyed to win this award.

From Bogart and Span. Ch. Skardu's Xamanta (mainly of Novaskaya breeding) comes another of our most important bitches, Span., Int. Risa-Polar de Villaodon. In 1993, we imported, two-year-old Polar Mist Arctic Dreams, and a female puppy, Grengawls Silhouett O'Polar Mist (Ch. Hoof 'n Paw's Knight Shadow ex Polar Mist White Feather), from Oregon. So our third

Spanish, Int. Ch. Oso-Blanco de Villaodon, the top Samoyed in Spain for 1995, owned by Carmen Navarro Guisado.

Colombian, Peruvian Ch. Zares Kandu de Las Nieves (Col., Am., Ven., Puerto Rican, Ecuad. Ch. Kipperic Flashback ex Taistoy de Tierra de Fuego) owned by Patricio Nino Roca, was Group fourth at Club Canino de Valle 1995 in Cali, Colombia, under judge Robert Ward, handler Henry Garcia.

Spanish, Port., Int. Ch. Bogart De Villaodon, owned by Carmen Navarro Guisado, Madrid, Spain, is a multiple all-breed BIS and BISS winner.

generation has two decisive bitches, Span. Ch. De Villaodon Snow Fantasy and Span. Ch. De Villaodon Symphony White, twice BB and BOS in the 1995 National Specialty.

Symphony White, linebred back to her grandfather Bogart, has produced fully satisfactory results (including a number of BIS winners). In 1996 we imported eight-year-old Fr., Int. Belg., Ital., World Ch. Karazoe Snow-Fox and bred him to USA New Girl (a daughter of Ch. Bogart).

Bogart has established himself as a successful producer for Villaodon. Many of his offspring have been exported to France, Portugal, Mexico, Brazil, Columbia and Argentina, thereby spreading the gene pool of the Samoyed ever wider.

Authors' Thoughts— Denouement

ROUND IS WRONG

Having watched and judged Nordic breeds for many years, it has occurred to us that "round is wrong." This generalized statement applies to all Northern breeds, including wolves and coyotes.

If the eye rims are round, it's wrong.

If the head is round, it's wrong.

If the muzzle is round, it's wrong.

If the ears are round, it's wrong.

If the chest is round, it's wrong.

If the feet are round, it's wrong.

And, specific to Samoyeds, if the coat is "round," it's wrong.

Samoyeds are athletes—they *work* to please, they *work* to survive. Like their cousins, Siberians and Malamutes, they are angular in structure. So we leave you with this thought . . . *If it's round, it's wrong.*